KAZAKHSTAN

Syr Darya

Lake Balkash

KYRGYZSTAN

○ Samarkand

Zeravshan

TAJIKISTAN

● Dushanbe

Mullali ○

Vakhsh

Yakhsu

Sherabad

Sapalli ○

● Kulob

Surhan

Panj

Pamirs

● Qurgonteppa

○ Shortugai

Dashli sites

Hindu Kush

alkh ●

● Mazar-i Sharif

● Kunduz

○ Fullol

BACTRIA

● Baghlan

Kunduz

AFGHANISTAN

Kabul ○

ARCHAEOLOGICAL SITES OF THE OXUS

○ Archaeological sites   — Rivers

● Cities and towns

Scale (km)

0   50   100   150   200

N

TREASURES FROM

THE OXUS

'Treasures from the Oxus *offers a comprehensive coverage of the region and its unique content, which includes previously unpublished artefacts of great importance. Although many of these objects are in private collections or have been acquired by museums from antique dealers, Professor Vidale has the requisite expertise, due to his long experience in the field, to identify the ones that have archaeological relevance. The author is one of the most highly accomplished among those scholars who have an intimate understanding of the materials, as well as wide experience in the surrounding regions; and this knowledge gives him a very balanced perspective in his discussions. This book, in short, is a major contribution to our knowledge of a region that is once again becoming an important crossroads linking cultures throughout Asia. Massimo Vidale is an excellent writer and one of the most prolific archaeologists that I know. I highly recommend his book, and am looking forward to being able to use it in my teaching for years to come.'*

—**Jonathan Mark Kenoyer**, Professor of Anthropology,
University of Wisconsin-Madison

'*Dr Vidale's academic reach stretches from South Asia and across the Iranian plateau to include Central and Western Asia. His publications play an important role in my thinking about a raft of issues, and also in the courses that I teach to undergraduate and graduate students. Dr Vidale has published extensively on the archaeology of each of these regions, and his research consistently incorporates a careful balance between clever ideas and insights, on the one hand, and first rate archaeological investigation on the other. In many ways his background and approach make him the ideal person to write this interesting and innovative volume on the Oxus civilization, which I recommend with enthusiasm.*'

—**Cameron Petrie**, Senior Lecturer in South Asian and Iranian Archaeology,
University of Cambridge

TREASURES FROM
THE OXUS

THE ART AND CIVILIZATION
OF CENTRAL ASIA

Massimo Vidale

with photographs by Valerio Ricciardi

I.B. TAURIS
LONDON · NEW YORK

Foreword

By Sandro Salvatori

The archaeology of southern Central Asia – that still mysterious region extending from the Kopet Dagh foothills to the Murghab delta in southern Turkmenistan; from southern Uzbekistan and Tajikistan to northern Afghanistan; and along the banks of the Amu Darya, the famous Oxus of classical sources – came to the attention of western scholars only as recently as 1972, when *Central Asia: Turkmenia before the Achaemenids,* by Vadim M. Masson and Viktor I. Sarianidi, was published in London. Then in 1981 another game-changing book appeared, written by Philip L. Kohl: namely, *The Bronze Age Civilization of Central Asia: Recent Soviet Discoveries*; and again, a few years later, Kohl published a further groundbreaking work, this time a comprehensive account of archaeological research conducted on Central Asia from the Palaeolithic to the Iron Age. Seminal books such as these, while fascinating in themselves, can often be signs too of major cultural shifts. Just at the point when the Soviet Union was on the verge of dissolution and disintegration, a new era was about to begin in our knowledge and understanding of the archaeology of the region.

In northern Afghanistan, Viktor I. Sarianidi – innovative co-author of the first book mentioned above – had worked, alongside other professional archaeologists, at late Bronze Age sites like Dashli 1 and 3;[1] but he and his colleagues had done so while illegitimate and illegal excavations at middle Bronze Age cemeteries were being conducted in the same area at the same time. Stupendous finds and copious quantities of precious ancient artefacts (the majority originating from plundered graves) soon began to find their way onto the Kabul market. Books, scholarly papers and articles thus started to reveal the wonders of a hitherto unknown civilization: that of ancient Bactria, traditional homeland of the prophet Zarathushtra: the supposed founder of Zoroastrianism.

The final withdrawal of the Red Army from Afghanistan enabled Sarianidi to return to Turkmenistan, where he began large-scale excavations of Bronze Age sites in the Murghab delta.[2] He was not alone in his endeavours. Soon after the fall of the Berlin Wall, and the burgeoning independence of the Central Asian republics, European and American archaeologists were likewise digging and exploring sites in the Murghab delta[3] as well as in the foothills at Ulug Depe,[4] in Turkmenistan; in Uzbekistan at Djarkutan,[5] Bustan VI[6] and Tilla Bulak;[7] and in Tajikistan at Gelot,[8] Makonimor[9] and other sites.[10] Despite this strong foreign presence, most of the Bronze Age sites in Turkmenistan and Northern Afghanistan were nevertheless excavated by Soviet and – following the eventual collapse of the Soviet Union – Russian archaeologists who now disconcertingly found themselves, after Turkmenistan's declaration of independence, to be strangers in a strange land; or, to be more exact, to be working and operating within a country that no longer belonged to them, either politically or strategically.

This new period of Sarianidi's archaeological activity in southern Turkmenistan turned out to be pivotal in bringing to light the civilization of southern Central Asia, in linking Bactria to Margiana and in bringing fresh insights to the region's complex relationships, both political and commercial, with the major polities of the Middle East during the second half of the third millennium BC. Unfortunately, his fast and large-scale excavations were carried out to the detriment of the vital stratigraphic method (an archaeological idea closely related to geology, where sedimentation is thought to take place in relation to certain uniform principles); and he consequently left unsolved many questions about the rise of first Bronze Age cities in the Murghab delta as well as their collapse at the dawn of the second millennium.[11] Notwithstanding this deficiency,

Sarianidi's systematic excavations at the largest Bronze Age mound of the Murghab delta, Gonur 1 North (carried out from 1990 onwards[12]) sensationally unearthed the ruins of the most important ancient capital of the regions of southern Central Asia dating from the mid-third to the middle of the second millennium BC. For this, if not for any diligent stratigraphical insights or for their careful and sensitive application, we have much to be grateful for to Sarianidi.

Following the discovery of the huge middle Bronze Age cemetery of Gonur 1 North in the ancient delta of the Murghab river[13] and the subsequent excavation of around 5,000 graves, 95 per cent of which had been looted in antiquity,[14] it now became clear that the artefacts that had flooded the antiquaries market in Kabul were linked to those newly found in this area.[15] They included many of the mysterious composite statuettes of 'Bactrian princesses', now scattered across several museums or otherwise in the hands of private collectors. As regrettably few specimens had and have been uncovered in regular, legitimate excavations, it has been difficult and challenging (until now) to evaluate their differences, or understand how and why they changed and developed over time.

This comprehensive and beautifully illustrated book changes all that. Based as it is on a detailed analytical and technical description of these remarkable Bronze Age artefacts, Massimo Vidale offers clues as to their stylistic evolution across the span of several centuries. The same approach is applied to all the fascinating objects illustrated here, culminating in the close study of two exceptional decorated silver vessels. The resulting narrative succeeds in revealing and highlighting some crucial symbols of the ruling elites of the Oxus Civilization.

Professor Vidale's book furthermore presents a new and surely more meaningful interpretation of another series of stone composite statuettes of uncertain provenance (not one of the fourteen specimens so far described comes from controlled excavations). Most probably belonging to the same period, and to the wider Oxus Civilization (as indeed other scholars have suggested), these small sculptures are known as 'scarred men' or better by the French term, balafrés. Their intriguing and recurring features certainly point to very precise beliefs, rituals and lost myths deeply rooted in the ancient cultures of southern Eurasia.

Vidale's new book might seem, on the face of it, to amount to little more than a presentation of new southern Central Asian material derived from a series of private collections. Such an idea, though, would be entirely misleading because the book is very much more than that. In fact, it represents an outstanding and highly plausible attempt to construct a meaningful sequential narrative for the Oxus Civilization through a series of very distinctive artefacts and their structural relationships with the larger international world of the third millennium BC: from Mesopotamia to Iran, and from the Indus valley to the Persian Gulf. Ultimately, this outstanding book points to entirely new lines of research for exploring the complexity of this lost Civilization, which was virtually unknown until just a few decades ago, and which succeeded in large part in constructing a remarkably unified political entity across the southern part of Central Asia during the second half of the third millennium BC. It should remain a benchmark in the field for many years to come.

Sandro Salvatori is one of the excavators of the great Bronze Age city of Gonur, in Turkmenistan, and an internationally acknowledged expert on the art and archaeology of southern Central Asia. He is currently co-directing excavations in Sudan, under the aegis of the Centro Studi Sudanesi e Sub-Sahariani (ONLUS) based in Treviso, with the financial support of the Italian Ministry of Foreign Affairs.

p. viii. An aerial picure of the core of the Palace of Gonur North, showing the square towers along its sides

left. Some heads of 'Bactrian princesses' found in the excavations at Gonur

opposite. Silver pedestalled goblet (see p. 66)

A leopard's head, insert of faience or possibly fired steatite from royal grave 3210 at Gonur Depe, Turkmenistan

Introduction

The physical geography of Afghanistan, together with its valuable natural resources, has undoubtedly helped to shape its history. While the control and exploitation of its resources at different periods helps to explain some of the sources of wealth and power in Afghanistan, its geographical position where many routes cross at the hearth of Asia explains another critical feature of its history ... Control of Afghanistan has provided both a route to the fertile lands of the south-east and a means of protecting this valuable route. Afghanistan is easy to enter or to cross, but much more difficult to hold, let alone unite, because of this very geography.

– St John Simpson[16]

This book is an attempt to update and summarize, in a language accessible to a non-specialized audience and with the help of a substantial repertory of Bactrian-Margianan artworks, our current understanding of the ancient cultures of the Oxus river basin (extant during the third millennium BC). This sophisticated Bronze Age civilization extended from the plains of Bactria in northern Afghanistan to the endorheic basins of southern Turkmenistan, and also to the north-eastern corner of the Iranian Plateau (see map in endpapers).

The plundering of the Bronze Age graves of Afghanistan and nearby countries almost certainly started in the early 1960s, as witnessed at the time by the arrival on the antiques markets of the first composite statuettes.[17] Moreover, following the Soviet invasion of Afghanistan in 1979 and its aftermath the already weak and unsatisfactory state regulation of the protection of cultural heritage in the eastern regions of Central Asia had altogether ceased to function. Hundreds, if not thousands, of sites belonging to astonishingly rich and creative civilizations have been devastated by commercial excavation, and many of their treasures, buried in the graves of their elites, have been looted. Farmers were paid $50 for masterpieces sold for thousands of dollars, or more, at auction. The objects themselves progressively ended up in western and eastern collections, both public (including major museums in Europe and the United States as well as Asian institutions) and in countless private properties. Only a few Bronze Age settlements in the region had been scientifically explored by Russian archaeologists before the invasion. The truth is that despite large-scale regular (but often unsatisfactory) excavations carried out in the last 35 years in southern Turkmenistan, an enormous amount of scientific evidence lies 'reburied' on the inaccessible shelves of private collectors, its value compromised in any case by the uncertainty surrounding its provenance.

My research into this unfolding archaeological drama has taken me to two very different locales: both the dilapidated and

Composite statuette of a falcon made of gold and of white faience (or possibly fired steatite) from royal grave 3220 at Gonur Depe, Turkmenistan

A flower made of gold, faience or possibly fired steatite and copper, emerging from a grave of Gonur Depe, Turkmenistan

Admittedly, the majority of the objects presented here have travelled a long way from the place of their discovery, information that is now lost beyond recall. Pottier's artefacts had been found in Kabul's bazaar, while those presented in this book have crossed most of Central Asia, and sometimes other continents too, from auction to collection and back again, before (finally?) ending up as private possessions: in its own way a form of reburial. Many are recent acquisitions; others (and some of the most important ones) have been travelling around for more than half a century. Their attribution to the ancient centres of power of Bactria and Margiana is due not only to current scholarship, summarized in the pages of this book, but also to my own choices and interpretation. This similarly applies to the exclusion from this record of pieces that were most likely deemed to be fakes.

At present, even the recent publications sponsored by major historical museums have chosen to illustrate the Oxus pieces that they have acquired on the market alongside others that belonged to private collections.[19] Anyone who has tried to follow the vagaries of some of these objects from auction to auction will have realised that, currently, there are probably hundreds of 'Bactrian princesses' floating around on an unregulated antiques market.[20] Some are clearly ugly reproductions, a few others are true masterpieces; many have been constantly moved around and altered, and in some instances their heads and limbs have been removed, lost, exchanged and substituted. There is always the risk of accepting a recent forgery as an original. As a result, it is often very difficult, now, to give archaeological and historical meaning to the strong stylistic differences that could distinguish these images into groups. In particular, the arbitrary association of bodies to heads in assembled sculptures widely exhibited on the web has blurred the significance of these variations.

I was therefore fortunate to have the chance to examine a substantial number of 'princesses' concurrently, in the private collections surveyed, and thus was able to determine, at least in part, the original pertinence of the composite parts of the sculptures. And so – in spite of the limited archaeological information coming from excavations in the Bronze Age sites of Margiana – we can now outline a preliminary hypothesis of the stylistic evolution of these surprisingly sophisticated images across a span of five or six centuries, something that has never been attempted before, and which we hope will prove useful to scholars and students of archaeology, as well as engaging to a wider readership interested in ancient societies and cultures and in the prehistory of Central Asia.

ruined graveyards of south-eastern Iran, where I have attempted to salvage as much information as possible from the chaos of the pits and rubble; and also to the more comfortable setting of western collections, where the ravaged archaeological sites are but distant memories. This publication makes abundant use of artefacts and of artworks, many of which are previously unpublished, and which have been surveyed and documented thanks to the courtesy of, and permission given by, their present owners. Is such use, given the recent history and dispersal of these artefacts, justified? In reply I will quote what a colleague said in 1984 about a similar situation:

Cet ensemble est bien évidemment un échantillonage non raisonné dû au hasard des fouilles clandestines; il paraît cependant concevable d'admettre que le lot étudié ici est représentatif de la culture bactrienne au même titre qu'un matériel scientifiquement mis au jour, soumis également, quoiqu'on fasse, au lois de la chance. [This collection is obviously an assortment put together at random as a result of chance clandestine excavations; however, it would seem conceivable to admit that the selection of objects under consideration here is every bit as representative of Bactrian culture as if it had been unearthed scientifically, and equally subject to the laws of chance.][18]

I

The rise of a system of power

The Amu Darya, the classical Oxus, forms in its middle course one of the major waterways of Central Asia. Historically, its course was regarded as the 'natural' frontier between the northern provinces of the Iranian empires (c.500 BC–500 AD) and the outer Turanian world. At 2650 km in length, and with an annual flow of more than 70 km³, the Amu Darya is the greatest river of Central Asia, navigable for most of its course. From the Pamir Mountains, with different local names, it crosses the Hindu Kush range to form the modern political boundary between Afghanistan and Tajikistan. Further on, it divides Afghanistan from Uzbekistan and, subsequently, from Turkmenistan. Around 40 per cent of the surface water of its tributaries is found in the northern plains of Afghanistan, the core of historical Bactria.

As the Amu Darya, it flows on, crossing the deserts of Turkmenistan from south-east to north-west, dividing Turkmenistan from Uzbekistan. At the end, it branches into several minor courses, forming the great delta that used to feed the Aral Sea, before it was catastrophically drained southwards for the purpose of cotton monoculture by the imperialist interests of the former USSR.

The Persian kings had different names for the satrapies (administrative regions) of their north-eastern frontier: the western side – Kerman and its wide deserts – was called Carmania (in the ancient Greek transcription), Aria was used for northern Afghanistan, while Arachosia was the name of the southern slopes of the Hindu Kush valleys and the torrid plains of the Dasht-i Margo desert, in the nowadays bitterly contested Helmand province. Further eastward, Seistan, the ancient Drangiana (old Persian *Zranka*), is the last inner basin of the Turanian macro-region before the ranges that rise to form the Iranian Plateau.

The name of Bactria (old Persian *Baxtris*) is encountered for the first time in the epoch-defining rock inscription of Darius at Behistun in Kermanshah (Iran). It is also the name given by the classical sources to the twelfth satrapy, a wide stretch of foothills, steppes and agricultural floodplains between the eastern slopes of the Hindu Kush and the left bank of the Oxus.

Beyond the opposite bank, as far as the course of the second endorheic river of Central Asia, the Jaxartes (today's Sir Darya), extended Sogdiana, an enormous open land, sparsely inhabited and mainly desert, that was perennially exposed to the fast, destructive attacks of the Scythians and other nomadic peoples that roamed from north and east. Balkh, the capital of Bactria

1. A view of the Kopet Dag piedmont

2. An Iron age depe along the piedmont, formed on the ruins of a fortified settlement

in the middle course of the Oxus, the nearby centre of Mazar-i Sharif, and Merv, the historical capital of the endorheic delta of the Murghab River (Margiana, ancient *Margush*), were the historical poles of a belt of civilized life that first appeared more than 5,000 years ago, to survive through a cycle of almost paroxysmal swings of centralization, collapse and devolution until the present age.

All these exotic names, and the images of their defeated chiefs, certainly made a great impact on the royal monuments of Persepolis, but to what extent, and for how long, these outer regions were actually in the firm grasp of the 'King of Kings' and paid him tribute are major questions. As a rule, in fact, the archaeological evidence of direct Achaemenid presence and domination is still quite flimsy, just as it is on the eastern-most stretches of the empire, the plains of Sindh. On the other hand, the famous, or infamous, events of the revolt of the usurper Gautama (the 'Smerdis' of the Greek sources) and the rise to power of Darius, who was a native of Bactria from a peripheral branch of the Achaemenian family tree – a piece of history celebrated by the victorious king in the detailed records of Behistun – explain how crucial the impact of the north-eastern regions of the plateau could be to the core of the Iranian systems of power.

The Oxus is characterized by two main periods of overflow, in spring and summer, that regularly deposit on the banks thick layers of fertile silt over the fine loess (aeolian sediment) of the local rock formations. This constant supply of fresh water and silt, together with that provided by the minor tributaries and endorheic courses of Afghanistan's northern plains, was the base of the rich agricultural economy of the Oxus Civilization.

Since the Neolithic period, and more consistently since 5000 BC, the people of the plains have dug small-scale canals and temporary earthworks to divert the water of the Oxus and the minor courses towards distant fields. According to Andrianov these temporary constructions needed continuous maintenance and required wide-scale reconstruction after each seasonal flood,[21] but the task was made easier by the ample supply of the local fine loess that, being almost permeable, performs very well in different types of hydraulic works. Artificial irrigation, even if on a small and medium scale, was a crucial component of agricultural intensification and the early processes of urbanization in Bactria and Margiana.[22]

Moreover, the seasonal mud and fresh water gave life to a thick riparian forest 1–3 km wide, coexisting with the agricultural landscapes and inhabited by wild boar and birds, shadowed by poplars, tamarisks and willows. In some places during the flood seasons the Oxus grew to up to 1.6 km wide, taking the form of an enormous, temporary lake that flooded the woods and reached the edge of the steppes, where wild asses, wolves, big cats, foxes, vultures and other raptors could be encountered. South and east of the Oxus plains, the lower slopes of the Kopet Dagh (Figures 1 and 2) and of the Pamir–Hindu Kush hosted woods of pistachio with juniper trees; other trees found there included almonds, plane, maples and hazel. These woods were the realms of majestic markhors (*Capra falconeri*), ibexes and urials; they were populated too by bears, leopards, wildcats, foxes, hyenas and many different species of birds of prey. These landscapes, visualized as the stage for adventurous games of the wealthy elites of the plain and their big dogs, inspired some of the precious artefacts of the Oxus Civilization that appear in this book.

Besides the huge, perhaps unique, agricultural potential of the river's basin, the Kopet Dagh foothills offered valuable minerals like cinnabar, quartz, agates and marbles, while iron, salt copper, lead, silver, sulphur, gypsum and steatite were available in the valleys surrounding the Bactrian plains.[23] Along the courses of the Amu Darya and its main tributaries, ancient traders could transport and distribute raisins and pistachios, dried fruit, nuts, furs, wood, copper, gold, lapis lazuli from the inner valleys, turquoise and possibly tin from the north-eastern borderlands of Sogdiana. Indeed, among the mineral wealth presently included within the political boundaries of Afghanistan, Simpson enumerates gold-bearing sands from the tributary valleys of the Oxus, silver from the north-eastern regions, abundant and widespread copper outcrops, tin (cassiterite) deposits found from Seistan to Herat, and from Badakhshan to Kandahar; lead and arsenic mines near Balkh, lapis lazuli, rock crystal and garnets, and minor sources of turquoise.[24]

It is also possible that spices, drugs and valuable textiles including silk[25] could come from further east, while transhumant pastoralists ceaselessly moved their herds from the grasslands of the plains to the nearby high pastures, tying in the interests of the agriculturalists with those of the peripheral communities.

Traditionally, indeed, nomadic herdsmen seasonally migrate to the plains, bringing mixed flocks of sheep and goats, and exchanging their meat, dairy and wool for cereals, vegetables and fruit. Further afield, north-west of the Oxus plains, on the endless steppes that spread from the Caspian to the shores of the Black Sea, there thrived other nomadic or semi-nomadic cultures that had started domesticating horses since the mid-fifth millennium BC. The Bactrian (two-humped) camel that had been domesticated by similar marginal communities to the east, but, at least by the last centuries of the third millennium BC, it had been already recognized, together with the bow and archery, as one of the prominent symbols of the local elites (Figure 3).[26] Did the precious objects decorated with images of camels represent the kinship or ancestry of the chiefs that lived in the intricate palaces of the middle-to-late Bronze Age, or were they gifts and signs of alliance with nomadic pastoralists which, at present, are still unreadable to archaeologists? Currently, these questions, with many others, remain unanswered. The flowering of the Oxus Civilization was shaped by the cooperation and conflictual integration of peoples, tribes and nations with different economic interests, specialized in the exploitation of resources from faraway ecosystems, and was probably steeped in diverse and no doubt conflicting ideologies. Six thousand years ago, in hydraulically favoured zones, the areas with best access to water, intensive agriculture suddenly offered the chance for economic stability and demographic growth, while the interlacing of new resources and technologies opened new, unexpected economic perspectives; but

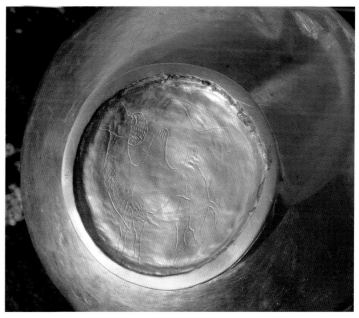

3. A bactrian camel incised on the bottom of a gold vessel found in royal grave 3220, Gonur Depe, Turkmenistan

local societies soon coalesced and almost crystallized in unique early urban forms, where the quite costly social investments involved must have made settled life endemically fragile.

What is certain is that, along their southern and south-eastern frontiers, they were linked to their neighbours by 'intraregional, highland-lowland relationships complemented by interregional, east to west movement of people and trade goods'.[27] At the same time, the limited agricultural and demographic potential of the highland plains of the north-eastern Iranian Plateau formed a natural buffer zone between the proto-historic cultures of southern Central Asia and the plateau itself, until this cultural boundary was suddenly and rapidly breached, in the late third millennium BC, during a climactic period for power and authority in the northern city-states. The same period witnessed, in north-eastern Iran, a growth of political centralization, with the construction of massive pyramid-like monuments (at Tureng Tepe in the Gorgan plain), and the appearance of elite graves, some of which were furnished with weapons. Miniature stone columns and other symbolic objects in alabaster at Tureng Tepe, Shah Tepe and Tepe Hissar, specific types of seals, hoards with silver and gold artefacts, objects carved in chlorite and pottery at Tepe Chalow near Sankhast show how 'wealthy and influential immigrants from Margiana likely migrated into northeastern Iran around 2000 BC, where they seem to have integrated into local communities in ways that we do not yet understand'.[28]

At the same time, the spread of similar collections of grave goods to Kerman, Baluchistan, Jazmurian, the southern coast of the Gulf and Fars (Susa) shows the depth of this cultural and probably political expansion of the Oxus people towards the south, where they came face to face with another great early urban civilization that was flourishing on the banks of the Halil Rud (the sites of Jiroft). This is surely an important page of the early history of southern Eurasia that still needs to be written.

II

Unbroken evolution

The realization that there was a fundamentally coherent, continuous evolution of societies in Central Asia from the Neolithic to Bronze Age urbanization and its devolution took a long time. To the west, starting from the 1960s, Russian archaeologists discovered that a flourishing early urban civilization had developed along the foothills of the Kopet Dagh, in southern Turkmenistan (c.6000–2000 BC), beyond the edge of the Iranian Plateau. Here, small-scale irrigation had first started in the late Neolithic (as revealed by grains of domesticated einkorn, emmer wheat and six-row barley). In the fourth millennium BC, agriculture prospered on ground periodically refreshed by seasonal, small-scale floods, supporting the lively village communities of the Early and Middle Chalcolithic period. Further on, between the left bank of the Amu Darya and the foothills, the endorheic deltas of two other rivers, the Murghab (ancient Margiana) and the Tedjen, hosted rich archaeological complexes dating from c. 4000 to the late third millennium BC. In the Tedjen river delta, at Geoksyur, a network of canals drew water from the main deltaic branches and associated reservoirs and discharged it near the settlements, allowing the irrigation of crop fields.

Later, in the 1970s, Soviet-Afghan expeditions discovered a highly developed Bronze Age culture in northern Afghanistan (ancient Bactria), between Daulatabad and Mazar-i Sharif. A chain of fortified sites stood along the beds of small rivers, inside the deltaic plains in the areas bordering the desert, where the seasonal wadis could be easily used for irrigation, by means of small canals.

In the decades since the beginning of the Afghan conflict and the epochal defeat of the Red Army (1978–89), local tribes in northern Afghanistan, and presumably in Turkmenistan, extensively plundered many rich protohistoric cemeteries.[29] Pottier reported a constant, large-scale flow of plundered antiquities towards the Kabul market between 1978 and 1980.[30] Many finds that ended up in private collections were distinguished by astonishing levels of beauty and technical sophistication.[31]

Finally, after the dissolution of the Soviet Union (1989), Russian academics started a new season of extensive archaeological excavations in Margiana, uncovering (with little or no stratigraphic control) large parts of the early urban and palatial contexts of Gonur and other sites dating to the late third millennium BC. Viktor Sarianidi, the most famous pioneer, and western archaeologists who followed him in putting this civilization into a historical perspective, have frequently referred to it by the acronym BMAC (Bactrian Margiana Archaeological Complex).[32] To start with, this label was perhaps justified by the fragmentary archaeological data that emerged from research in localized areas, but at present the term 'Oxus Civilization' proposed by H.-P. Francfort is

perhaps to be preferred, both reflecting a new, more comprehensive understanding of the whole process, and because of the analogy with other contemporary early urban civilizations. The term also accounts for the fundamental cultural unity of the Oxus lands in the second half of the third millennium BC. In the words of Sarianidi and Dubova:

---

numerous discoveries of archaeologists in the southern regions of modern Uzbekistan, Tajikistan, as well as in north Afghanistan, are so similar to the items found in Margiana, that the cultural unity of Bactria and Margiana in the Bronze age is unquestioned.[33]

Current research, furthermore, is expanding the extent of this civilization South towards Khorasan, the north-eastern corner of the Iranian Plateau.

Table 1 shows in a highly simplified manner the general chronology and developmental framework that is currently used by archaeologists to describe the continuous social evolution of this part of the Eurasian continent.[34] It does not encompass the Mesolithic beginnings, identified by Soviet archaeologists in the 1960s and 70s (c. tenth–sixth millennium BC or earlier) in the terminal branches of the local endorheic deltas, generally located north of the present flood areas. From the early Chalcolithic period to the early second millennium BC most cultural phases are named after the sequence of occupation layers excavated by Soviet scholars at the site of Namazga Depe, one of the most important early urban capitals of the southern Turkmenian foothills during the Regionalization and Integration Eras. This latter (phases Namazga IV and V) encompasses the replacement of the Bronze Age cities of the early and mid third millennium BC by large palace-centred fortified compounds surrounded by secondary urban clusters in the late third millennium. In this time span, the societies of southern Central Asia experienced a period of fast cultural integration, economic growth and intensification of international exchanges and communication.

Soon after 2000 BC, the 'Localization Era' saw the apparent crisis and abandonment of the largest early urban settlements, decreasing standards of socio-economic organization, the loss of important forms of cultural unity and the resurgence of local cultures. The rise of conditions of warfare and decreasing security is emphasized by the increased number of weapons in the graves, and the shrinking of settlements into small fortified castle-like constructions.[35]

Previously considered a secondary, collateral effect of the Neolithic revolution in the Near East, the late Neolithic culture of Djeitun (in the Kopet Dagh foothills) of the seventh millennium BC, is now considered an independent adaptation that laid the foundations of the Oxus phenomenon, even if some of the domesticated cereals that fed the earliest known villages may have been borrowed from the agriculturalists of the Iranian Plateau.[36] The Djeitun culture of southern Turkmenistan is the earliest evidence of sedentary, agricultural life in southern Central Asia, and was already advanced in terms of the development of a food-producing economy. Djeitun farmers of the Early Food-Producing Era used ground and surface water (from wells, along the marginal swamps of the Tedjen delta, but also irrigation canals and rivers) to grow wheat and barley. Cereals were both part of human nutrition and fodder for animals. In addition, dung was added to bricks fabricated in spring or summer.

The settlement was a cluster of single-room square cells, with well-built fireplaces at the centre of a wall and accessory partitions in clay or brick; rows of low parallel walls indicate bases for collective granaries (in open spaces outside the dwellings). Houses were reconstructed on their foundations for generations. In the late sixth millennium BC, special 'clan houses' have been identified, so named because they had walls thicker than normal dwellings, and sometimes the inner walls were painted with animal scenes. Also, they had longer life spans and were prominently placed, being isolated in one way or another from the other buildings.

Earlier sites may perhaps be found in the Kopet Dagh mountains, but none are known at present. The communities of the Kopet Dagh, following the beginning of farming and sedentary life, gradually evolved into incipient hierarchical social organizations. Architecture became more complex, with larger houses of up to three rooms or more, separated by irregular, narrow alleys. 'Clan houses' were still used, distinguished from the other buildings by their size, traditional ground-plan and longevity in the same spot. Copper metallurgy had a slow beginning, with the appearance of a few broken stems of pins and needles at sites like Monjukli Depe, around 5000 BC.

On the opposite side of the Kopet Dagh range, at the Iranian site of Zagheh, archaeologists excavated another 'clan house' provided with inner benches and embellished with wall paintings and skulls of ibexes, presumably hanging from the walls (c.5200–4700 BC). Around this exceptional building, there was a cluster of rich graves, whose occupants wore an impressive array of beads in various materials: thick shell from the Persian Gulf or from the coasts of the Indian Ocean, deep-red carnelian,

Table 1. General simplified chronology and developmental stages of the Oxus Civilization

Dates BC	Phases	Eras
7200–4600	Djetun Neolithic along the Kopet Dag	Early Food-Producing Era
4600–4000	Kopet Dag, Anau IA, pre-Chalcolithic	Regionalisation Era
4000–3500	Kopet Dag, Namazga I, Ilgynly Depe, early Chalcolithic	
3500–3200	Kopet Dag, Ilgynly Depe, Namazga II, middle Chalcolithic	Late Regionalisation Era
3200–2800	Kopet Dag, Altyn Depe, Namazga III, late Chalcolithic	
2800–2400	Kopet Dag, Altyn Depe, Namazga IV, early urban phases	
2400–2000	Kopet Dag, Altyn Depe Namazga V, full urban phases	Integration Era
2400–2000	Margiana, Kelleli phase, first palatial compounds	
2400–1900	Margiana, Gonur north palace and city, and others	
1900–1600	Margiana, Gonur south, *temenos* and fort, Djarkutan	Localisation Era
1800–1500?	Bactria, Margiana, late palatial compounds, Namazga VI	
1800–1500?	Khorassan, Iranian Plateau, fortified settlements?	
1500–1300	Final Bronze age, Takhirbay 3 phase	

turquoise and haematite, showing the importance of an intensive long-distance trade for elite display. At the same time, many of the beads of Zagheh are made of fired steatite and steatite paste, made with cheaper local stones but transformed artificially like those crafted at the same time in the Indus valley. Buildings like this, south and north of the Kopet Dagh, could have hosted important life-cycle ceremonies, and their exclusive management by elite groups might well explain their prestigious funerals.

By the fourth millennium BC, north of the Kopet Dagh, there flourished increasingly sophisticated villages belonging to at least three different regional cultural areas (as defined by individual pottery styles). The label 'Regionalization Era' (see Table 1) is explained by such cultural fragmentation. In the second half of the same millennium (Namazga II period), Chalcolithic villages farmed their land by means of artificial irrigation, rapidly developed an advanced metallurgy (copper, lead, silver and gold), intensively processed a wide variety of semiprecious stones and built a new type of possibly ritual building. These 'clan houses' were decorated with lavish wall paintings, coloured benches and highly symbolic artefacts. As these houses had, along the walls, rows of jars sunk into the floor, and piles of burnt pebbles nearby, steam seems to have been produced by putting red-hot pebbles in water. This is how people still wash themselves in Central Asia; hammams of this type were perhaps used for ritual cleansing, communicating and socializing at peer, rather than hierarchical, level.[37]

During this same period, settlements became differentiated into larger centres on the one hand and small rural villages on the other. Indeed, only seven sites, 50–70 km distant from one another and between 10 and 20 ha in size, could have counted 5–10,000 inhabitants. Ilgynly Depe, in spite of its limited size, hosted important crafts and ritual facilities. The other sites were rural villages occupied only by a few households or farms. After flourishing in the Tedjen delta, the populated Middle Chalcolithic settlements died out for some reason, but agriculture and settled life continued in the nearby watered areas.

During the third millennium BC, the central site of the foothills of Altyn Depe reached its maximum size of c.25 ha (perhaps amounting to 7–10,000 inhabitants), while Namazga Depe, about 100 km to the north-west, might have been much larger (at least 52 ha, a number suggesting some 17–20,000 individuals). In the Namazga III phase (c.3200–2800 BC) a distinctive ware, painted with solid geometric patterns, was in use. This was found in northern Baluchistan and Seistan too, indicating links to the south and south-east.

Some of these trade contacts may have relied on large carts driven by camels and oxen, known from terracotta models of various sorts. In the following centuries, early cities used a buff-coloured pottery painted with intricate geometric designs resembling textiles, perhaps influenced by kilim and carpets, traditional pride of the nomadic tribes of this part of the world.

4. Private collection, *c.* 2600–2400 BC

A silver cup and its links with the Fullol treasure

The rise, in this period, of influential elites in the northern hinterland of Afghanistan is emphasized by the Fullol hoard, part of a large treasure of embossed or incised gold and silver vessels, some in a Mesopotamian-related style. The hoard or grave goods was found by chance and partially destroyed in an unknown context, perhaps within a large funerary mound.[38]

Many doubts persist concerning the nature of this find, and the chronology of the broken vessels ascribed to the deposit has been discussed at length, but a wonderful silver cup from a private collection, here published for the first time (Figures 4–13), has interesting links with some of the Fullol artefacts, and might have been manufactured in the same cultural and technical milieu.

A silver cup (Figures 4–13)

H 13.6 cm; max Diam 14.7 cm, Diam at the foot 2.9 cm. Weight: 128 g. Unbroken, with minor gaps filled with patches of copper-silver alloy. Embossed and incised with a continuous row of five bovines within a decorative field of scale-like patterns.

The cup (Figures 4 and 5), made by a single sheet, is well preserved, with minor gaps that correspond to the protruding areas of the embossed figures (such as the muscular masses of some legs and heads of the bulls) restored in recent times by over-casting limited patches of a copper-based alloy. The vase was certainly used for a long time, and several details are partially worn down by the handling. The incised figuration, however, in general, is in good condition: the outer surface of the silver sheet is covered by a uniform, stable silvery patina, while the interior one assumed a darker grey-violet shadow.

The outer surface is organized in a low foot-ring and three superimposed bands of increasing width (c.1.5, 1.9 and 3.9–4 cm) divided by three ridges in relief. The uppermost ridge runs c.6 mm below the edge of the vessel, and the resulting upper band hosts a fine pattern of little superimposed and intersecting arches made with a fine dotting technique. In some cases, part of the bisected area below each arch is filled with an irregular pattern of dots. The execution is in general competent but uneven; in more than one case, one notices

a clear transition from the work of a highly skilled silversmith to a much less experienced hand, often involved in the more menial, repetitive chasing operations (Figures 6 and 7). These variations lead us to suppose that the craft and its generational transmission were organized and managed within the boundaries of the nuclear family and might have been hereditary.

The upper and main embossed band has a row of five bovines proceeding within a field entirely covered by a continuous background

5

6

7

of small superimposed scales in low relief (Figure 6). Each scale is internally filled with sequences of 15–20 fine crescent-like impressions, left by the impact of a tool having a fine cylinder-like end, almost certainly made of copper or bronze. The shape of the scales varies from semicircular to almost hexagonal. While the edges of the scales were not usually chased, in some cases the craftsperson (a novice?) carelessly continued to work outside the central field.

The general effect of these scales, redundantly emphasized by the tiny, crescent tool marks, is clearly related to the inverted superimposed cone patterns which in Akkadian art, as well as in the iconography of the Halil Rud chlorite artefacts, clearly stands for a conventional mountain landscape.[39]

Below the main band with the five bovines, the lower ones, framed by their protruding ridges, bear only this conventional design. The size of the scales decreases almost imperceptibly from the main band to the lower ones, showing the great skill of the Oxus silversmiths.

The bovines (I will conventionally call them bulls, even if the sex is never represented) proceed in a row, in a clockwise direction (Figure 8). They seem to proceed calmly, the movement represented by the right front leg being put forward and slightly raised from the ideal plane of the other three; with the exception of one of the bulls (hereafter bull 1; the other four are consequently numbered in their anti-clockwise series) whose right leg is bent inwards. Such a quiet attitude contrasts with the scenes on the two cups of the Fullol hoard, where bovines seem to be engaged in a fight and in a herd run.

The heads of the animals are bent downwards. The eyes are prominent, ogival, with large and deep eyebrows, conveying and

8. The embossed and
incised figuration of the
cup of Figure 4

expression of serenity. Muzzle and nostrils are incised with very fine, delicate traits. Three bulls have both horns in sight, while two (bulls 3 and 5) show only one horn, imagined as superimposed, in profile, to the other. All horns are decorated with S-shaped or spiral-like incisions. The ear is a leaf-like bulging feature, decorated by a very fine fish-scale pattern resembling fur. The ears rise vertically from the rear of the jaw, but in a single case (bull 2), the ear sags down. The neck and throat region of every bull is decorated by wavy lines. The hooves are bisected and the sesamoid bone on the rear toes is shaped as a hemisphere. The tail is slightly lifted; the upper part is decorated by a spiral motif, and it ends in a tuft marked by a fish-scale design. Each bull has its own patterns on the rump and on the muscular masses of the front and rear legs.

Bull 1 (Figure 9)

As stated above, this is the only animal that seems to be moving, with a bent right leg, which allowed the artist to mark the knee with a small circle. The head is lowered, as in bulls 3, 4 and 5. Below the horns (undecorated) the front bears a thick series of lines resembling fur. The entire back of the animal is covered by a tight pattern of double concentric circles, the inner one with a single tiny dot in the centre, the outer one with a series of similar dots. This decoration, incised with exceptional skill, does not cover the muscular volume of the foreleg and part of the thigh; the lower end of this pattern is marked by a double wavy edge. The foreleg bears two similar lines.

Bull 2 (Figure 10)

The body is entirely decorated with a quite different design: large scale-like elements, made of three concentric arches filled with sequences of tiny dots. The pattern stretches

9

10

11

down to the belly, but leaves the hind leg and the foreleg undecorated; on the thigh, the scales form a long pointed tuft, that underlines the large, plain muscular mass. As stated above, the ear is bent downwards. Another minor difference is that the horns of this bull are covered with spiral lines.

Bull 3 (Figure 11)

The third bull is probably the least well-preserved. The details of the single horn, in fact, are scarcely visible, but it seems to be decorated with arch or spiral-like lines. The back was certainly covered in circles made with tiny dots, one beside the other; while the foreleg is plain, the hind leg is covered with an almond-like feature equally filled with impressed tiny dots.

Bull 4 (Figure 12)

The surface treatment of the two horns is unclear. The upper part of the tail seems to bear a hatched pattern. The rump was covered with curvilinear patterns that, again, are not well preserved. They could be superimposed concentric circles, like those featuring in bull 1, or superimposed scales, as in bull 2. In some points, what remains of the decoration might even suggest spirals. The belly, in contrast, is better preserved and was evidently widely covered by tiny, simple impressed points.

Bull 5 (Figure 13)

The horn of this last bull, like 2, 3 and possibly 4, is covered by spiral-like lines. The jaw is particularly prominent, and shows at the edge a triangular hatched feature.The rump is covered by a pattern of large parallel arch-like bands, filled alternately with rows of dots of variable size and circular impressions (left

12

13

by the same tool used to fill the large scales in the background). Along the lower belly, the pattern is delimited by a marginal row of dots. The foreleg and hind leg, in this case, are covered by almond-like or perhaps heart-shaped motifs, filled by similar concentric rows of dots.

The cup organically combines a naturalistic rendering of anatomical volumes (embossed) with purely abstract motifs (incised on their surface). There are explicit variations in the rendering of the bodily parts, and others, more subtle and less apparent, in the abstract motifs. These features provide

the cup with a sense of pleasant animation, and very lively forms.

Because of its good preservation, and the high quality of the embossed/incised figuration, this cup can be considered one of the masterpieces of the art of the ancient Oxus. Its immediate formal and stylistic references can be seen in some of the cups originally found in the hoard or treasure of Fullol (particularly those showing rows of bulls or bisons) which, however, so far have not been published with a sufficient level of detail.[40]

The hoard is made up of five gold vessels and 12 silver ones, found in obscure circumstances by farmers near the modern town of Fullol, south of Baghlan, in north-eastern Afghanistan. The objects were smashed and cut in the effort of sharing the precious metals, before being finally recovered (at least partially) by security forces. The finds had been reportedly excavated from a mound called Kosh Tepe, where a subsequent dig brought to light a skeleton in flexed position, that might, or might not, have been originally buried with the gold and silver pots.

The Fullol treasure is considered by most scholars a proof of the active links between Mesopotamia and the Afghan hinterland at the times of the great lapis lazuli trade of the third millennium BC, even though others have proposed a later dating.[41] However, in general, the craftsmanship behind this silver cup is much more refined than that of some of the Fullol artefacts or fragments.

The vessels were made by combining hammering and embossing. In general, in the cultural area under discussion, the bulls on vessels made of precious sheet metal of the third millennium BC have the rump and the frontal part rendered with fine dashes or scales, or with bands filled with geometric patterns and/or spirals or circles, while the muscular mass of the shoulder and the rear of the body is plain.[42] The conventional graphic signs for rendering the fleece of the bulls, in

the cases mentioned above, form a rather limited repertory. In contrast, in this cup, the bulls' bodies are entirely covered by different types of curvilinear and/or dotted patterns, in an evident effort to diversify the designs, not only in the position of each animal, but also in the decoration of the mantles.

Despite this different approach, several features link closely this masterpiece to the Fullol hoard, in particular to the gold vase of Dupree et al. 1971, vessel 4:[43] namely, the bisected hooves, the herringbone motif filling the ears, the alternate chevrons in one of the animals' tail tuft, and the almond or hearth-like framing of the chased decoration on the rear thigh.

The chronology of the finds of the Fullol treasure has been the subject of considerable debate: some scholars propose dating part of the finds around 3000 BC, other objects some centuries later; others suggested that everything was manufactured c.2000 BC, while a minority view propose the late second millennium BC. Following Tosi and Wardak, who provided substantial arguments for a dating of at least part of the Fullol artefacts within the second half of the third millennium BC, the formal comparanda outlined above would suggest for this rare find a plausible dating around or soon after the mid third millennium BC.

The Namazga V period, finally, coincides with the local Integration Era, a process of cultural homogenization led by the major early cities of Namazga Depe and Altyn Depe, while imposing fortified cities or citadels were constructed in the peripheral regions of the Oxus Civilization. The elites of this era used the same unpainted pottery and the same valuable status symbols across an area of not less – approximately speaking – than 1,000 x 200 km.

The traditional interpretation by Russian scholars is that the inner delta of the Murghab was deserted, until people abandoned the cities of the Kopet Dagh foothills and migrated there in the wake of a general, large-scale drought. Current research stresses instead the overlapping of the last phases of settlement of Namazga Depe and Altyn Depe with the earliest palatial phases in the Murghab delta; moreover, it is becoming more and more clear that the apparent absence of settlement layers of the early Bronze Age and of the late Chalcolithic in the Murghab are due to substantial floods, that have covered the sites in question.[44] Even the Murghab delta, in short, was gradually populated at least from the end of the fourth millennium BC; the flourishing agriculture of the delta in the late third millennium BC (based upon wheat, barley, millet, lentils, chickpeas and peas, and on fruit orchards with apples, pears, cherry plums, cherries, grapes and melons), as well as cattle breeding, was founded on centuries of local experience.

Some scholars, based upon the fact that the peopling of this vast, heterogeneous region proceeded from the foothills, then apparently to the Tedjen and Murghab deltas, then to Bactria (in other words from west to east), see the palatial developments of the Oxus Civilization as the result of a gradual interference by, and influx of, groups of nomadic herders coming from the north. These groups might have interfered with the settled population, and, led by influential tribal elites, become prominent in the economy and ways of life of agriculturalists by mastering advanced metallurgical techniques and by trade exchanges. The pressure they brought was eventually crowned by rapid conquests, and by the founding of new, albeit ephemeral dynasties.

This reconstruction of the events is controversial. Other scholars, in contrast, noted that only limited amounts of hand-made pottery of the nomadic tribes has actually been found in late third to early second millennium contexts in the cultivated plains, and that it therefore suggests temporary camps, episodic raids and explorations rather than systematic interaction. Furthermore, recent 14C datings would place the interaction around the mid-second millennium BC rather than in earlier centuries.[45] However, processes that were in some ways similar were taking place at the same time in upper Mesopotamia after the dramatic fall of the Ur III dynasty, when groups and aggressive tribal alliances of the Martu people in the west (nomads speaking Semitic languages) started to interfere heavily with the affairs of the city-states, until the house of Hammurabi, probably in the eighteenth century BC, seized power at Babylon and founded a new, powerful but ephemeral royal house.

The problem of ancient Tukrish

Tukrish was an eastern land and polity mentioned with a certain frequency by the cuneiform sources of Mesopotamia between c.2100 (early mentions appear in the cuneiform texts of the Ur III dynasty) and 1500 BC.[46] The land was famous in the West for its lapis lazuli and gold containers (gold being mined in a mountain called Harali), but also for ornaments and goods made of silver, stone and ivory (as mentioned in the later sources). Piotr Steinkeller, a Harvard professor and dogged explorer of the lost geography of the eastern neighbours of Mesopotamia, thinks that Tukrish is to be located on the shores of the Caspian Sea, and corresponded to at least a part of the Oxus Civilization,[47] a circumstance supported by the frequent find of vessels and well-crafted ornaments in gold and silver, sometimes inlaid with lapis lazuli and other stones, in the grave goods of the looted graves of Bactria, and in some rich, or even royal, burials excavated at Gonur in Margiana. In particular, Steinkeller quotes an ancient text from Syria mentioning a golden eagle imported from Tukrish, when ornaments of that description are common in the inventories of the Oxus centres. Other scholars disagree, as they would rather link the Oxus to the ancient names of Šimaški or Marhaši.[48] Steinkeller's hypothesis, at present, still has little material ground, but nonetheless remains, on the whole, the most likely.

III

The elites in life and death

Perhaps because of the composite genesis mentioned above, the development of urban forms in the Oxus Civilization is uneven and, when compared to that of other contemporary civilizations, quite idiosyncratic. In the middle Chalcolithic (3500–3200 BC) some centres of the Tedjen delta, even if made up only of a limited number of households and store-rooms, were already surrounded by walls and small round 'towers' (buildings that somehow, and superficially, resemble the *tholoi* of the earlier Halaf tradition in northern Mesopotamia). Such protected compounds, particularly if the round angular constructions were towers, might indicate a powerful, instinctive impulse for security but also – perhaps – the emerging power of local families of political leaders or khans, as they are called in the much later tradition of Central Asia. It is possible that the isolation, ecologically speaking, of the inland deltas favoured and accelerated local processes of political centralization.

In contrast, along the Kopet Dagh foothills in the late third millennium BC, there is no evidence of coherent systems of peripheral urban defences. Rather, the site of Altyn Depe, at some point in its history (conceivably around 2500 BC) seems to have been structured in a system of urban *insulae* on raised artificial platforms, including large square courts and divided by streets, all features of the major cities of the Indus Civilization. However, Altyn Depe at the time had a monumental gate flanked by two towers, and streets, the most important of which, at the entrance of the city, was subdivided in two pathways by a median mudbrick wall (a feature with no known equivalent in the archaeology of Central Asia).

In Margiana (the Murghab delta), the earliest fortified palaces appeared after 2300 BC: at Kelleli (a palace compound measuring 125 x 125 m, with square towers), then at Gonur, the most important place in the region. Gonur had two separate fortified compounds. Gonur North (Figure 14) is a unique city that measured more than 50 ha in extent (amounting, in theory, to *c.*25,000 inhabitants, though this area includes the monumental spaces of the palaces), within an irregular lozenge-shaped wall. The settlement had private houses, store-rooms, craft workshops, water basins and animal pens. At the centre stood a large palace of 150 x 140 m, protected by a double wall and provided with an axial corridor, two large courtyards, a large storage facility and inner living quarters (where the excavator identified audience halls and a throne room). Water reservoirs, sometimes provided with large pottery pipes, were arranged near the entrances to the palatial complex, perhaps signifying that visitors were supposed to enter the walled compound in a state of cleanliness and ritual purity.

The urban layout is concentric and obviously pivoted, even at a symbolic level, on the seat and role of the ruler. Both Kelleli and the palace of Gonur North were defended by imposing walls with square towers and bastions at regular distances, whereas around the fortified palaces of the following periods (end of the Integration Era, from *c.*2000 BC onward) the same towers were round or semicircular, as at Togolok and Gonur South (Figure 15). As stated above, the fortresses (and possibly the weapons deposited in the graves of other sites of the north-eastern Iranian Plateau, such as Tepe Hissar) indicate a time of growing hostilities and conflicts, and possibly of tension with the nomads of the outer steppes. These factors, together with ecological constraints, probably tightened the centralization of power in new institutional forms and the grip of a (perhaps military) elite on the general population of farmers and herders.

To the east, in the Bactrian plains, settlements were smaller. Each cluster of villages, in the last centuries of the third millennium BC, possessed a central rectangular or square fortress up to 1 ha in size that protected an elite residence or, according to other interpretations, a cultic building. The fortress, in turn, was surrounded by mudbrick walls with towers, circular at the corner, and semicircular along the perimeter (as at Dashli and other fortresses). Sandro Salvatori has pointed out (in a private communication) that in Uzbekistan, during the middle Bronze Age (late third millennium BC) small palatial buildings can be found with quadrangular towers; while recent research at Djarkutan revealed that such buildings actually arose, as at Gonur North, at the centre of urban settlements protected by much wider defensive walls. In the same urban compounds, another small palace was later built (in the Namazga VI period) with round towers, probably surrounded, in turn, by other residential constructions and its own defensive wall.

Two other similar structures were excavated at Dashli 3. One was a rectangular walled compound, measuring 130 x 150 m. Inside, dwellings were arranged in three concentric rings separated by two polygonal walls (the rudiments of a caste-like structure?), while in the centre stood a circular fortress with rectangular bastions. An inner construction, with a possible altar against the wall, supports the idea that it was a ceremonial centre, with houses and granaries. A second rectangular structure, 84 x 88 m, had a central courtyard, with storage facilities and a small house with altar-like structures and niches. Numerous pilasters decorated the outer walls, from which orthogonal T-shaped projections emerged. Sapalli, near Djarkutan, was another square fort 80 x 80 m (less than one hectare) that contained few individual houses. The defensive wall has series of asymmetric T-shaped projections,

14. Aerial view of part of the Gonur North complex, *c.*2400–1900 BC

15. A view of the ruins of the palace at Gonur North

that enclose rooms and form an intricate, labyrinthine pattern with the boundary wall. Sapalli was occupied only during the twentieth/nineteenth centuries BC. For an unknown reason (a symbolic reference to magical protection?), the ground plan of these forts resembles some of the common, contemporary types of intricate openwork copper stamp seals, as well as some traditional designs still very popular in the textile crafts of Central Asian nomads.

At the time of the court of Gonur North, the highest ranks of Oxus Civilization society lived in these impressive compounds, surrounded by the houses of the commoners that served the lords and their palatine court. The workshops of the bronzesmiths were active not far from the palace enclosures, while bronzesmiths, and presumably other specialists in humble crafts, lived in segregated clusters outside the central settlements. The cutters of semiprecious stones may have had an officially recognized status, as suggested by Grave 1200 at Gonur, nicknamed 'of the artisan' because, within a basket placed on the head of the dead, there were found no fewer than 131 fragments of semiprecious stones, including chalcedony and agate, magnesite, rock crystal, jasper, gypsum marble, steatite and other rocks,[49] together with

a half-finished stamp seal, a duck-weight of Sumerian type, a silver cone, marble disks, gold foil and other valuable small finds. Among these small objects six limestone arms were inventoried, evidently belonging to three pairs of limbs of the same size and with the same type of surface alteration.[50] The excavators write that these components are unfinished, but one wonders whether the basket may instead have contained three wooden figurines that had decayed (though against this hypothesis there is the fact that all the arms are of the same shape, clutched with the thumb onwards; usually on these statuettes the arms have a different hand posture).

The Gonur graveyard reveals that in death as in life, the lords and the commoners (craft specialists, servants and even the court dwarves) occupied segregated spaces.

Elite lifestyles

The silver vessels of the Oxus Civilization tell of an elite of males that had long hair and beards, with or without moustaches. Commoners often wore kilts, while individuals of the upper rank sometimes had tunic-like garments of the *kaunakes* type that left the right shoulder bare.[51] Their footwear was elegant: some images reproduce low, soft boot-like shoes, sometimes with an upturned end.[52] Proud of their chariots with four and two wheels,[53] pulled at a run by muscular bulls, the Oxus chiefs commanded organized armed corps, as suggested by the soldiers or guards visible in the pedestalled silver goblet illustrated below (see Figures 55–60), and other silver vessels.

Cylindrical silver vase, embossed (Figure 16)

This famous silver vessel shows a race of chariots with two and four wheels, pulled by bulls; in front, a bowman with a 'wine-skin'-like object from which hangs a sort of animal tail, and possibly a naked singer; below, another naked singer (?) flanked by two other naked persons, carrying heavy circular objects (possibly, large stone disks). The whole scene may be preliminarily interpreted as illustrating ceremonial games. The possibility cannot be excluded that such games took place during an elite funeral.

16. Louvre, Paris, *c.* 2200–1900 BC

The chariots were important personal properties and in the most lavish funerals they were buried, complete or dismantled, with their aristocratic owners.

The fighters of Bactria and Margiana were good archers. They used the traditional composite bent bow of the steppes, adopted from their northern neighbours,[54] and carried their arrows in quivers behind their back, held by decorated shoulder straps; but they were also provided with scabbards, daggers and axes. The Oxus art shows that they captured and cruelly killed their prisoners with daggers and maces.

17. Louvre, Paris, *c.* 2200–1900 BC

The local aristocracy, according to Viktor Sarianidi, may have also organized feasts involving communal eating near their palaces, open to various social ranks and identities, in order to confirm and legitimate their authority.[55] Other feasts and ceremonies might have been more private and seem to have taken place in gardens or open areas.

Silver *pyxis* with a banquet or ritual performance scene (Figure 17)

H 4.9 cm; Diam (max) 20 cm; lid: H 7.5 cm, Diam max (damaged) 21 cm. In this carefully embossed silver vessel, ladies dressed with a tufted garment, closely resembling the canonical 'Bactrian princesses', sit outdoors in the shadow of trees; one holds a child, while servants are busy with vessels and a large jar, in front of a table or altar. In this scene, the ladies seem to be members of the local aristocracy rather than divinities.[56]

The upper ranks of society were passionately fond of hunting, both on the mountain slopes where ibexes and other wild goats roamed, and within the riparian forests of the great river, inhabited by big wild boars. The love for hunting in this wild country was shared by people in lower social position, judging by a graffito with a wild boar hunting scene found on a less valuable ceramic sherd from the fort of Gonur South.[57]

Small silver 'trumpet' with a bulb-like swelling decorated with a male bearded face (Figure 18)

H *c.*12 cm. In this silver object, a tool or instrument, the rendering of the human face on the bulb is remarkably naturalistic. Made of a single silver sheet, this belongs to a series of similar objects that are generally interpreted as trumpets, but without positive confirmation. According to Bo Lawergren, these instruments may have been used by hunting parties, as their sound might imitate specific calls by female deer in their mating seasons.[58]

A series of objects that may be trumpets in bronze, silver and gold, sometimes richly figured, probably represents another important symbol of the elites. A few trumpets of this type were found in excavations at Gonur, Shahdad and Tepe Hissar, and many others have surfaced on the antiques market.[59] They could have been used in military parades, in horsemanship, but also for hunting signals, or for imitating the call of stags and other animals.[60] There is only one eastern Iranian Bronze Age image showing a trumpet being blown; coming from the Jiroft region, it might represent a celebration in which a kind of musical band took part,[61] but the instrument is not of exactly the same type.

18. Louvre, Paris, *c.* 2300–1900 BC

19. Louvre, Paris, *c.* 2200–1900 BC

The Oxus elites very much loved their hunting dogs, which are portrayed not only on embossed and incised silver vessels, but also in beads and figurines of gold and silver (Figure 19).[62] Dogs were also involved in special burial rituals. A bronze axe, published here for the first time (Figures 20–23), with its hunting scenes delightfully incised on both sides of the blade, well illustrates such concerns.

Two small silver figurines of dogs (Figure 19)

The figurines are pierced vertically, as if they were finials of a pin or of a similar object. The ears are raised in attention, the body, although stylized and bulky, seems to be contracted in an attitude of strength. The muzzle, collar and tail are decorated with a band of incised angles.

Copper or bronze axe, with an eagle-like protome, and hunting scenes incised on the blade (Figures 20–3)

L 15.60 cm; max H at blade 8.99 cm; max Th of blade 1.10 cm; min Th or Diam of shaft 2.65 cm. Weight: 399 g.

The axe, distinguished by an S-shaped appendix on the rear, is unbroken. It is covered on both sides by a uniform, stable patina of reddish cuprite, with minimal traces of green malachite.

The shaft is symmetrically pierced in the eye-like patterns and transversally crossed by a copper or bronze nail originally fixing the handle, the extremities of the nail being flattened and taking the place of pupils. The edges of the shaft and its end points are respectively emphasized with relief ridges and bulging eyelets. The interior of the shaft still retains traces of the wooden fibres of the axe's handle.

The edge of the blade, underlined by seven concentric ridges of variable height, is blunt, a feature qualifying the weapon as a symbolic or parade object (even more so because the axe is undamaged and was never sharpened). However, some parts of the surface of the object seem gently worn by use or handling.

The raptor's head protruding from the upper edge of the axe has round eyes, depressed on side 'a' (see below) and bulging on the opposite side 'b'. Around the eye, the rounded head has thin incised marks, almost effaced by wear; originally, they formed radial or angular patterns, now difficult to reconstruct. The curved beak is realistically represented with its lateral mid lines, while the bivalve casting seam is visible below.

The designs have been incised with a fine chisel after casting, with light, competent and secure lines; the animals are represented in run, the muscles of the foreleg emphasized with well executed contour lines. Defining 'a'

as the side where the edge of the blade is on the left, it shows a hardly visible hunting scene. A mastiff with a raised, curved tail and short ears pointing forwards, the legs spread at a run, is about to catch an unidentified long-tailed animal with long ears; the details of the muzzle are erased by corrosion. Three lines on the neck might indicate a collar. The mastiff's forepaw is already on the chest of the prey. The design was constructed using the lower edge of the blade as a base line. For the linear free style and the subject matter, this delicate incision may be compared with a wolf's head visible on the base of a silver cup in a private collection.[63]

On the opposite side 'b' (blade at right) a similar scene, better preserved, appears bottom up: the base line, in fact, is the upper edge of the blade. Here, a big spotted cat (a leopard?) is jumping on the back of a deer which turns to look backwards. The two scenes seem to oppose hunting by men (the mastiff) to natural hunting (the assault of a big cat); the opposition

20. Aron collection, London, *c.* 2200–1900 BC

seems further emphasized by the reversal of the scenes on the two sides of the axe. Hunting with dogs is one of the recurrent themes of Bronze Age Oxus art; the incisions also confirm the positive role of dogs in the display strategies of the local aristocracies. On the whole, the axe is an eloquent example of the great skill of the bronzesmiths of the late third millennium BC, and their socio-economic integration with their aristocratic clients.

The flared blade recalls examples known from Elam and Luristan in the early second millennium BC. For its basic, unmistakable form (consider the peculiar angle between the shaft and the blade, and the flaring tail) the axe is reminiscent of a number of similar weapons presumably found not only in Margiana and in Bactria (among others, the specimen from the Louvre collection reproduced as Figure 24),[64] but in Elam and in some sites of eastern Iran as well, such as Khinaman and Shahdad.[65] According to Piotr Steinkeller such axes, rather than being actual weapons, were badges of acquired authority that the kings of the polity known in Mesopotamia as Šimaški gave to their high-status officials.[66] The blunted blade, and comparison with an item depicted on the seal of Kuk-Simut, a high official under Idadu II, a ruler of Elam (Louvre, Sb 2294), demonstrates that at the royal courts similar weapons were prominent symbols of rank. These axes and hammers, in fact, although produced in the Oxus area, were evidently awarded by the rulers of Elam to dignitaries in recognition of particular merits.

The absence of any visible sign of impacts, too, supports the symbolic value of the axe, while traces of wooden fibres in the interior confirm that the axe had actually received a handle. Šimaški was a powerful polity that arose during the twenty-first century BC on the Iranian Plateau, north-east of Sumer and Susa, perhaps near contemporary Isfahan (although Daniel Potts, as already stated, instead identifies Šimaški with the Oxus Civilization).[67]

21

22

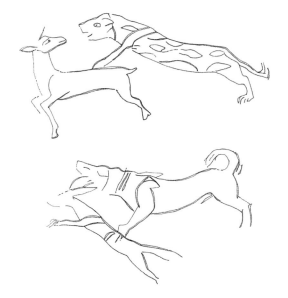

23. Copper axe (Figure 21): graphic recording of the incisions

Ceremonial axe in arsenical copper (Figure 24)

Very similar to the axe of Figures 20–23, this weapon has flared blade, concave sides, a blunt, thick edge, a haft-hole with oval section and a perforation where a rivet is still visible. The heel has a large wing with a scalloped margin. From the upper edge emerges the well-crafted head of a camel, that links this beautiful axe to Central Asia and to Margiana and Bactria in particular.[68]

24. Louvre, Paris, c. 2200–1900 BC

25. Louvre, Paris, *c.* 2100–2000 BC

Copper hammer with birds' heads looking backwards (Figure 25)

The inscription in Sumerian on this hammer-axe that hails King Shulgi as 'Powerful hero, King of Ur, King of Sumer and Akkad' places the weapon around the mid twenty-first century BC or shortly after. It was probably obtained at Susa, at the time firmly placed by the king under the control of Ur. The back terminates in feathers, suggesting a symbolic merging of the birds with the royal weapon.[69]

Copper or bronze flat cauldron embossed with figure of an ibex (Figures 26–8)

Max Diam at the mouth 25 cm; H 10.70 cm; a thick ridge in relief runs c.4.70 cm below the rim. Weight: 1362 g. The cauldron has a low carination, concave contour, a flat everted rim and the figure of an ibex embossed in relief on the interior. Damaged and restored on the base, particularly on the rear of the animal's horns.

The copper or bronze sheet is on average 2–3 mm thick; it is covered by a film of reddish cuprite, with localized patches of carbonates (malachite and, to a lesser extent, azurite). The bearded ibex, embossed in high relief and chased, is portrayed side-on, with a bulky body above two bent legs, while one of the forelegs is stretched in front, and is shorter in proportion than the others. Such position of the foreleg is commonly encountered also in other animal images, both two- and three-dimensional, ascribed to Bactrian art or the eastern Iranian Plateau in general.[70]

Ibexes and gazelles were the favourite game of the Oxus' hunting parties. The craftsmanship of this copper or bronze vessel is not extraordinary, but the animal's figure has its own harmony and strength. The head is distinguished by a disproportionate almond-like eye in low relief, and is crowned by a massive pair of crescent-like horns, and by raised pointed ears. Both ears and horns are bisected by incised lines, perhaps to suggest that these features are seen as superimposed in perspective. Bronze dishes with concave sides with gazelles, snakes and fish in high relief were found at Shahdad; a dish with a raptor appears among artefacts illegally excavated in the Halil Rud valley. There are also in the 'Bactrian' collection of the Louvre two large dishes with two bulls in the centre, one in bas-relief and the other almost in the round.[71]

26. Aron collection, London, c. 2500–1900 BC

27

28

Other animals that were certainly closely linked to these protohistoric elites were camels and horses, the former reproduced on clay pots, silver and gold vessels, and seals; the latter prominently featured as finials, for example on copper axes that were possibly used in parades, ceremonial exchanges of gifts and rituals. Some of the truncated cone-like cups made of gold found in the graves of Gonur are decorated on the underside with images of Bactrian camels accompanied by double-curvature bows (see Figure 3), possibly as badges of the nomadic, warlike ethnic or social background of a part of the Margianan elites, or more simply a sign of their alliances with the nomadic herders of the steppes.

Horses and camels, too, seem to have been ritually buried alongside their owners in the course of lavish ceremonies. Bronze heads of horses on axes or as finials leave little doubt that the Oxus was the first great civilization of Central Asia to confer a new social prestige upon horses, derived from the Central Asian hinterlands.[72]

The general picture can also now confirm what had been hinted at by the scattering of wonderful objects that appeared on the antiques market after the looting of the graveyards in Bactria: the elites of this people loved astonishingly beautiful jewels made of precious metals and semiprecious stones, but also of finely crafted white-fired steatite, and of brightly coloured, contrasting faience inlays.

Two necklaces of fired steatite, turquoise and other materials (Figure 29)

The necklaces in these pictures were probably assembled by antiques dealers from beads collected on the surface of ancient Bronze Age sites or found in looted graves of northern Afghanistan and southern Turkmenistan. Although several of these beads probably belong to later periods, many of them, particularly the largest ones that faithfully reproduce the forms and patterns of bifacial seals, and the rectangular or square beads decorated with dotted circles, all in white-fired steatite, are probably original creations of the Oxus craftspeople.

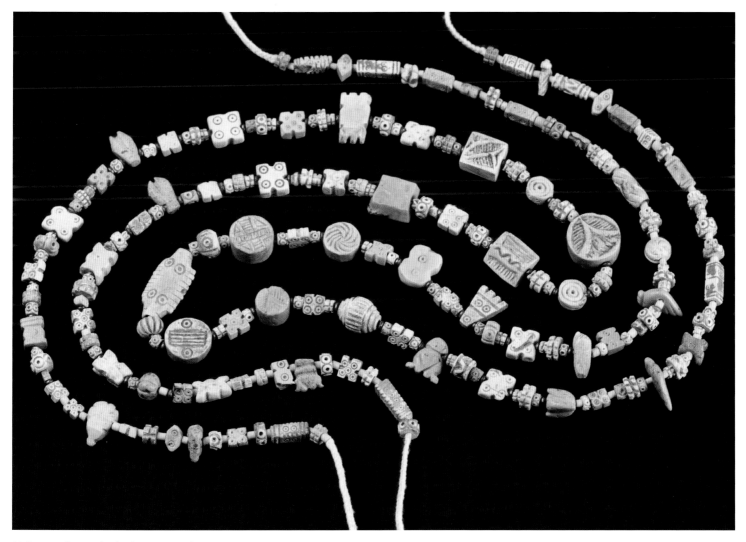

29. Private collection, beads of various periods

Carnelian, agate and multicoloured jasper beads (Figure 30)

Scattered around western collections, beautiful beads like these are frequently said to come from Bactria. Although their source is unknown, and some of the beads may be later, or may come from various locations, beads like these (particularly the large and flat oval ones) are comparable with those found in controlled excavations at Gonur in Margiana. Other beads closely resemble stone ornaments found in the Indus valley. They witness the taste of the elites of the Oxus Civilization for showy, variegated semiprecious stones.[73]

In particular, the iconography of the few published silver vessels may suggest that elite males used to wear necklaces of small beads of semiprecious stones, endowed with a single, large and flat central bead or pendant, something confirmed by the treasures from the looted cemeteries of Bactria.[74]

They also lived in luxury, surrounded by well-crafted inlaid furniture, chests and movable objects, and attended public ceremonies accompanied by cart races, bull fighting and sports. The images on their silver vessels reveal that they loved drinking while listening to music. Their passion for wine is demonstrated not only by archaeo-botanic finds and scenes of banquets and drinking on silver vessels and seals, but also

by a necklace with beads of copper in the form of vine leaves.[75] Through banquets, funerals and other public ceremonies, wealth was represented by possession of precious prestige goods and their public display, accompanied by the ritual killing of large animals and human lives, thus stressing at the same time economic and socio-political inequality.[76]

The Oxus elites were also fond of gaming, as ivory sticks and tokens of Indian type and even inlaid gaming boards have been found both in high-status graves and in the ruins of the Margiana palaces. Women, at least those of the uppermost ranks, seem to have enjoyed a particularly high status, compared with what we know

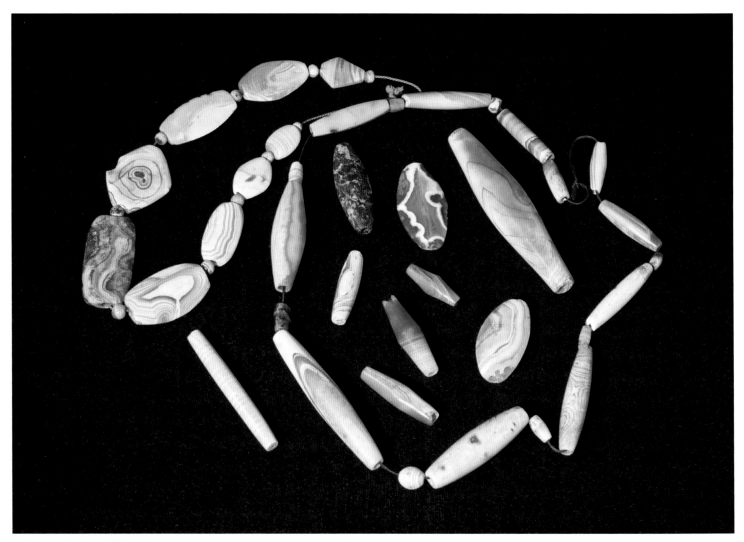

30. Private collection, *c.* 2500–1900 BC

of other contemporary civilizations. Both men and women probably used coloured cosmetics, contained within bronze or chlorite flagons found by the hundreds in numberless looted graves.[77] Current research on cosmetics found in the eastern Iranian sites of Shahdad and Shahr-i Sokhta suggest that some white and blue cosmetic substances, as later in Egypt, were made with a complicated wet-chemical process – hinting at the ancient roots of today's industrial chemistry. The cosmetics holders of the Oxus, made of copper or bronze and dark green chlorites, sometimes preciously inlaid with other contrasting materials, are probably the most sophisticated of their time.

Copper or bronze holder for cosmetics or perfumes in the form of a bull (Figure 31)

The holder bears an everted concave neck on the animal's shoulder. Slight damage to one horn tip and to one of the forelegs. L 11.41 cm, Max H at the edge of the neck 9.82 cm; Max Th at the shoulder 3.84 cm; Max Diam of the mouth of the neck 3.20 cm. Weight: 365 g. The casting is of high quality, with minimal traces of fine filing visible on the sides, on the back and at the base of the neck. The object is covered to a great extent by a uniform surface or patina of cuprite, but discontinuous patches of light green malachite are visible on the back, on the forelegs, on parts of the muzzle, and cover entirely the inner surface of the neck. The horns are short and curve inwards above the ears. The eyes, set laterally, flank an inverted trapeze-like front; the muzzle is short and bears incised dots for the nostrils and a horizontal line for the mouth. The bull has a thick collar in relief represented as spirally twisted; the legs, slightly curved, project onwards and end in well-fashioned hooves. On the back, a short, flat tail descends to cover the rear of the testicles.

31. Private collection, *c.* 2500–1900 BC

By the late fourth millennium BC, the production and trading across Central Asia of lead and copper-based cosmetic substances had become an important economic activity. Cosmetic containers are a wide, diversified class of small copper/bronze receptacles very common in the Oxus region.[78] Their contents are 'most likely black paint made of a lead-based paste. Many of them still contain a white, powdery, oxidized residue of the ointment'.[79] This white substance, in the light of our present knowledge, should be lead carbonate (cerussite/hydrocerussite) and/or phosgenite and laurionite, components of white foundations and eye-shadows artificially made by treating lead compounds in saline or carbonated solutions.[80]

Among this diverse class of containers, those shaped as bulls, with the flagon's mouth as the hump, are rather standard and not uncommon.[81]

32. Private collection, *c.* 2500–1900 BC

A set of small chlorite pots inlaid with limestone (Figure 32)

The following six small vessels, made of a dark green, fine-grained chlorite inlaid with limestone (?) share the same size, the same look and the same technical features, although the inlaid decorative patterns are individual.[82] They are also covered by the identical sediment, being heavily stained by the residues of a light grey-brown silty clay (7.5YR 8/2) hardened by

silicates. Most probably, the set was found as a unitary assemblage in a single grave.

Small cylindrical, canister-like pot in black chlorite, with scale-like inlays in white limestone

H 6.21 cm; mouth Diam 3.66 cm; base Diam 5.83 cm. Weight 194 g. This small pot is unbroken and perfectly preserved. It has a short cylindrical neck, modest swelling in the

middle, and a slightly everted rim. Under the corner point of the flat shoulder runs a frieze made of three rows of (respectively) 13, 14 and 13 scale-like inlays, measuring in length *c.*8.4–8.6 mm. The inlays alternate at regular distances, to form on this frieze 13 crosses. The same frieze is bounded on the shoulder by two thin parallel lines, incised with the utmost precision, and below, at about one third of its height, by three similar lines. For a good part of their extension, these lines seem to be filled with a light-coloured substance. Near the bottom runs a fourth band of 14 inlays of the same form, but slightly larger (on average 9.2–9.6 mm). In total there are 54 inlays.

The form recalls the so-called pottery canister jars of central-southern Baluchistan (Nal tradition); a small chlorite container, globular but decorated in an identical fashion, appeared for sale in the Kabul bazaar and was published by M.H. Pottier.[83] See also a squat restricted flagon in chlorite with white inlays of various shapes at the Louvre, illustrated in detail by Ligabue and Salvatori, and a more elaborate specimen in similar materials, made of superimposed parts.[84]

Small cylindrical, canister-like pot in black chlorite, with triangular inlays in white limestone

H 6.41 cm; mouth Diam 3.80 cm; base Diam 6.51 cm. Weight: 170.4 g. Equally well preserved, this second canister-like container (short cylindrical neck, modest swelling in the middle, and slightly everted rim) is an almost perfect replica of the first one: however, the two registers are of the same height and are framed by two subtle incised lines on top, three on the middle and two at the bottom. On the upper one, 32 opposed triangles (sides of c.5.8–6.2 mm) are set to suggest the corners of eight squares, while in the lower register 24 triangles of the same form alternate opposed in two rows; in total there are 56 inlaid pieces.

Cylindrical *pyxis* in black chlorite, with inverted triangular inlays in white limestone (with lid)

H (with lid) 5.40 cm; Diam 6.56 cm. Weight 187 g. Reconstructed from several fragments but complete, this precious container looks quite similar to the previous stone vessel and other artefacts now in private collections. The vessel is a perfect cylinder. The lid is a flat disk with a narrow ledge for fitting with the rim, apparently made with a large tubular drill. The lid hosts 28 triangular inlays (height c.5.6–6.1 mm) set in four concentric series and pointing towards the rim, giving the final impression of a radiating star. On the exterior, 72 inverted triangular inlays are arranged in six rows of twelve triangles each, with the same alternating geometric pattern of the scales of the canister-like pot described above. The total number of inlays is 100.

Small restricted globular jar with a cylindrical neck in black chlorite, with oval inlays in white limestone

H 6.32 cm; mouth Diam 4.03 cm; max Diam 6.66 cm; base Diam 3.24 cm. Weight 124.6 g. Unbroken and in good condition, this small jar has a strongly everted rim, and a slightly raised disc-like base, apparently made with a copper tubular drill. The decoration is a frieze running on the shoulder, framed by three parallel lines at the joint with the neck and the same number at the point of greatest width. Within this band run 33 oval inlays (height c.8.56–8.98 mm) arranged in three parallel rows, alternating at regular distances.

Small restricted globular jar with a cylindrical neck in black chlorite, with inverted triangular inlays in white limestone

H 6.36 cm; mouth Diam 4.10 cm; max Diam 6.51 cm; base Diam 3.23 cm. Weight 95.2 g. Regarding the form and the field of decoration, this small jar is very similar to the previous one, but the limestone inlays are instead identical to those of the lidded cylindrical *pyxis*. The disc-like base, too, was similarly made with a copper tubular drill. The shoulder frieze is made up of four rows of inverted triangles, with a total of 80 inlays, alternating at regular distances, giving the impression of diagonal lines or cross-like patterns.

Small restricted globular jar with a cylindrical neck in black chlorite, with lozenge-like inlays in white limestone

H 6.44 cm; mouth Diam 3.52 cm; max Diam 5.89 cm; base Diam 2.31 cm. Weight 109 g. The form is that of the two small-necked jars just described, but the body is slightly more elongated. The field of decoration, on the shoulder, is equally framed by two bands of three subtle parallel incised lines. The decorative pattern is composed of two rows of lozenges on the top and bottom at regular distances (height c.5.3–5.4 mm), for a total of 64 inlays; these two rows frame a series of crosses made of smaller lozenges, about 4.1–4.2 mm high.

A small truncated-cone container with a semicircular section, with an intricate inlaid design (Figure 33)

H 6.70 cm; max Diam (mouth) 5.34 cm;
W of the base 3.17 cm. Weight: 106.4 g.

This container, as unusual as it is complex, has a flat, plain face on the back (?) bearing two flanked passing holes; while on the exterior, on four registers, triangular inlays and round pieces, framed within lozenges (now missing), alternated in a rhythmic fashion. A similar pattern was carved on the bottom, adding another problem to the interpretation of this object. Most of the inlays are lost, and filled with an orange-coloured sediment (5YR 6/6) and in some of the cavities there is a well-preserved bright red mastic, possibly made with a fine ochre (reddish brown, 5YR 4/2).

33. Private collection, *c.* 2500–1900 BC

Three small receptacles made of different stones (Figure 34)

From left: a squat spherical bowl of light green chlorite. H 4 cm, mouth Diam 3.7 cm. The edge is decorated with a row of oblique traits, somewhat resembling the mouth of a fine basket, underlined by three parallel lines.

A miniature pot made of a high-quality lapis lazuli. H 2.8 cm, mouth and base Diam 2 cm. The slightly raised base seems to have been shaped using a tubular drill of copper. Pots entirely made of lapis lazuli are extremely rare for the third millennium BC, and, as witnessed by a famous spouted vessel found in the Royal Cemetery at Ur,[85] were owned by the highest social ranks.

A cubic flagon with a cylindrical neck, made of a soft, porous white limestone. H 5.7 cm, mouth Diam 4 cm.

Small and medium-sized lapis lazuli receptacles have already been published as coming from the Oxus region.[86] Containers of these three types might well have been used for unguents, perfumes and cosmetics.

It seems that the relationships and alliances with the Indus merchants and craft groups were crucial for representing the superior social status of the Oxus elites. In order to be provided with these exclusive symbols of status and power, their palaces may have hosted traders and craftspeople from the Indus valley, as some beads and other valuable products were made with technology and models familiar from the Indus tradition, but following local types and forms.

34. Private collection, c. 2500–1900 BC

Burial practices and rituals

Those western collections of antiquities where many precious jewels, silver and gold vessels and finely crafted bronze weapons and utensils have ended up offer an indirect but eloquent proof of the luxury and drama of elite funerals of the Oxus people. In spite of the general recent destruction of Bronze Age cemeteries (that had already been damaged in the late Bronze Age), excavations in southern Turkmenistan and Margiana have revealed important aspects of the burial practices and rituals of the Oxus Civilization.

Cemeteries of variously ranked groups were often located in the ruins of peripheral settlements, or (as at Altyn Depe) on abandoned lots within the urban area. Both at Altyn Depe and at Gonur North the Russian excavators claim that rooms

35. Grave 3497, necropolis of Gonur, *c.*2400–1900 BC

of abandoned houses and of the palace were converted into collective burial spaces for fractional burials.[87] However, poor stratigraphic control and intensive depositional and/or post-depositional disturbances do not support this far-fetched interpretation. While in the Chalcolithic period extended families used collective graves for generations, expressing the ideological prominence given to complex kinship ties, the burials of the third millennium BC, as a rule, contain isolated skeletons, often flexed on their right sides; in other cases, bodies were buried in a peculiar contracted position. According to Pottier:

---

il existe trois sortes d'inhumations: principalement des inhumations individuelles, mais aussi des inhumations doubles ou multiples des cenotaphes; les tombes sont creusées en pleine terre et consistent en une sorte de chambre funéraire creusée au fond d'un puits plus ou moins profond: la chambre peut étre située à l'aplomb de celui-ci ou latéralement. En surface, les tombes sont fréquemment recouvertes de briques [et] contenantes du mobilier en quantité variable: les vases en céramique sont souvent très nombreux (jusqu'à une vingtaine dans une seule tombe) mais l'on trouve aussi épingles, miroirs, bouteilles, bracelets, lames en cuivre, colonnettes, vases, perles en pierre, cachets ... [There are three sorts of burials: first and foremost individual burials, but also double burials or multiple burials and cenotaphs; the tombs are dug in open ground and consist of of sort of funeral chamber dug out at the bottom of a shaft of greater or lesser depth: the chamber can be situated directly below this or laterally. The tomb surfaces are often lined with bricks [and] contain grave goods in variable quantities: ceramic vases are often present in great number (as many as twenty or so in a single tomb), but finds have also included pins, mirrors, bottles, bracelets, copper blades, 'miniature columns', vases, precious beads, tablets, etc.][88]

As a general rule,[89] individual graves at Gonur host a single person, crouched on his or her right side, the head towards the north or north-west, and the grave goods (mostly pottery vessels, numbering up to three dozen) grouped near the head or beside the skeleton (Figure 35). Women very often wore stamp seals in various materials, while men were buried with bundles of arrows tipped with well-fashioned heads.

In the same graveyard, where about 80 per cent of the graves had been systematically plundered at the end of the Integration

Era, about 85 per cent of the excavated graves turned out to be of the shaft or 'catacomb' type, recurrent in many proto-historical sites of the eastern Iranian Plateau and Central Asia. Small chambers were laterally dug into the subsoil from a vertical shaft, closed off at the end of the burial ceremony with mudbricks or with covers of perishable material. Sarianidi reports traces of fires or models of hearths within the shaft or catacomb graves, often under the body of the deceased. Once the pits had been refilled, a small rectangular pit could be dug on top, filled with burnt wood and finally sealed with plaster. Many shaft graves, even if undisturbed, revealed only minimal, highly fragmented, parts of the skeletons. This suggested to Sarianidi that in some cases bodily remains might have been moved to other locations after decomposing. Some of the shaft graves contained stone sceptres, columns, bronze axes, valuable personal ornaments and other belongings.

In contrast, simple pits, apparently dug for the commoners, amounted to around 10 per cent of the total. They were furnished with some pottery and few personal ornaments. Sarianidi named a frequent variant (c.7.5 per cent of the total) 'burnt pits', because the pit walls are marked by the exposure to fire. Sarianidi notes that such burials 'included skeletons of people with some clearly apparent defects (dwarfs, hydrocephalics, armless and so on). Perhaps this explains the premeditated burial of these people separate from the other dead.'[90]

That dwarfs, probably in various roles, could have been part of the royal courts of late third-millennium Central Asia is confirmed by the iconography found on seals from the Elamite world and the regions further east.[91]

Other graves (little more than 2 per cent of the total), called cists, were rectangular chambers made of mudbricks, with or without a vault, built, according to the excavator, at ground level. They contained skeletons and in many cases quite valuable artefacts, but only one was found intact. Similarly rare are chamber graves that represent 'models of houses or more precisely of bedrooms. The main characteristics of these tombs are stepped entrances blocked by bricks, walled fireplaces and models of double hearths.'[92]

Chamber graves were similar to cists, but were collective burials used for more people over longer periods. The largest were elite family 'mausoleums' with inner partitions, niches and benches (Figure 36), that presumably contained shelves, wooden furniture and a great deal of precious property, including ceramics, ornaments, stone objects and vessels in bronze, silver and gold (Figures 37–8), weapons, composite statuettes, boxes decorated with geometric mosaics made with tiny coloured

36. Mausoleum 3235, necropolis of Gonur, c.2400–1900 BC

37. Gonur necropolis, a silver vessel with a Bactrian camel (left) and a gold flask (right) from a royal mausoleum c.2400–1900 BC

38. A Turkmen girl wears the jewellery found in the Gonur necropolis, c.2400–1900 BC

39. Inlays in stone and faience originally applied as a mosaic on furniture, as found in the Gonur necropolis, *c*.2400–1900 BC

40. Copper claddings of the wooden wheels of a dismantled cart, from one of the graves of the Gonur necropolis, *c*.2400–1900 BC

stone tesserae, and wooden furniture inlaid with geometric and animalistic insets in multicoloured faience (Figure 39).[93]

Similar to the cists and chamber graves are certain rich burials found (in disturbed condition) at Altyn Depe, below the Kopet Dagh foothills. Some contained precious stone and metal objects, including lyres with golden heads of a wolf and a bull, probably the local versions of the great lyres in copper, silver and gold found in the Royal Cemetery of Ur by Leonard Woolley.

The so-called 'Priestess burial' in the centre of the court of the complex of Togolok 1 had also been plundered soon after deposition. It was a brick-lined chamber containing the dead, a pile of more than 100 ceramic vessels, some precious objects and the skeletons of two bulls and of the driver of the wagon, possibly killed with his hands tied behind his back. As at Ur, at least in some cases, in the graveyards of Margiana the ritual killing of human beings might have accompanied the funerals of the elites, together with the sacrifice and formal interments, sometimes with rich furnishings, of camels, horses, dogs, rams, goats and lambs. One of the graves excavated at Gonur hosted the remains of a pair of male and female sheep accompanied by a lamb, buried along with jewels.[94]

At Gonur, a group of twelve particularly rich chamber graves with inner partitions was identified and excavated within the city wall. In spite of intensive and systematic plundering, three of these graves still contained four-wheeled wagons (Figure 40), like those in the richest graves of Ur and Kish, in Mesopotamia, one of which was driven by a camel. Also found in the shafts were gold, silver and copper vessels, a bronze mirror, objects decorated with mosaics, silver cosmetic flagons, ivory objects, long staffs of schist and other objects and containers in alabaster and chlorite, ornaments in faience, semiprecious stones and gold, and skeletons of horses and dogs. This funerary cluster, dated *c*.2200–2000 BC, is linked by Sarianidi to the ruling class of the city.[95] Inequality is expressed here in terms of the amount of lives and wealth wasted, as well as in those of a strict spatial segregation.

In the Margiana cemeteries there are also other variations – for example, some people were buried in large jars or *pythoi* covered with smaller vessels. Sarianidi also mentions 'cenotaphs' or simple pits in the burial grounds containing only vessels piled up in the ground before being refilled, and a few cases of secondary fractional interments.[96] The unusual and ample variety of Gonur's different grave structures and 'multivariant burial rituals',[97] is the reflection on one hand of a long developmental time span and on the other of a composite ideological landscape, probably due not only to the articulation of different social statuses, but also, perhaps, to persistent cultural differences within the urban societies.

IV

Contacts with other regions and the Indus

From the northern edge of Iran and the plains of northern Afghanistan, the Oxus Civilization also spread to southern Uzbekistan and to south-west Tajikistan; and to the south, in the north-eastern corner of the Iranian plateau, it affected the valleys of Khorasan. The use in the Oxus region of some classes of greyware pottery might indicate further connections with the northern Iranian cultures.

The Oxus elites had unmistakable connections with ancient Mesopotamia: many precious artefacts found in the middle Bronze Age centres of southern Central Asia are stylistically and thematically linked with the civilizations to the west, and a cylinder seal found in a grave at Gonur, made of a shell fished from the coastal waters of the Indian Ocean, bore the Akkadian inscription of a cup-bearer. The material culture, moreover, has many iconographic elements in common with Susa, in the Iranian province of Khuzestan, and the Elamite sphere in the south-western Iranian Plateau. Consistent and frequent, too, are the contacts with the Halil Rud valley or Marhaši Civilization, recently discovered near the modern town of Jiroft, near Kerman.[98]

The silver goblet illustrated for the first time in this book (Figures 55–60) almost certainly shows a ruler of Marhaši wounded and handcuffed in a ceremonial Bactrian procession, demonstrating that these contacts were far from peaceful and that military expeditions, at least in form of raids, could cross the Iranian Plateau

for hundreds, or even a thousand or more, kilometres. In the late third millennium BC, enigmatic stone artefacts such as the famous 'miniature columns' of variegated stone with grooves on top (Figure 41), weights or stone sceptres – all commonly found in sites in Margiana – were also to be encountered in distant lands. Columns, for example, were discovered not only in the ruins of a presumed cultic building at Tureng Tepe (Gorgan plains, north-eastern Iran) but also in different elite burials in Baluchistan, on the edges of the Dasht-i Lut, and in a recently discovered cemetery near Nikshar (Iran), not far from the shores of the Strait of Hormuz.[99] Although the use and the symbolic implications of these peculiar objects are unknown, there is little doubt that their diffusion marks the extent of a sphere of influence of the Oxus people towards the south and south-east. However, it is impossible, at the moment, to speculate on the precise nature of this influence.

The apparent frequency with which weights of different types and materials have appeared on the antiques market supports the theory that these objects, or some types of suspended weights, had a role in the funerals of the Oxus elites. On the other hand, the surface of the middle Chalcolithic site of Ilgynly Depe in Turkmenistan was littered with finished and unfinished objects bearing holes and grooves, suggesting that the use of this at present poorly studied class of artefacts was common over the course of almost one thousand years in the settlements of the Oxus.

41. Stone miniature column, ceramics and a yellow pigment from one of the common graves of the Gonur necropolis, *c.*2400–1900 BC

42. Private collection, third millennium BC

A grooved weight in travertine (Figure 42)

H 26.5 cm, W (base) 15 cm. The groove (deeper on one side than on the opposite one) hosted a cord that somehow suspended the weight for an unknown purpose. Many different weights with grooves for suspension have been found in sites of Central Asia, dating from the fourth millennium BC onward.

A pierced weight in chloritic
breccia, with calcitic inclusions
(Figure 43)

H 20.8 cm, W (base) 14.2 cm. The holes
converge in a V-like fashion, and are heavily
worn on the interior surfaces.

43. Private collection, third millennium BC

How 'miniature columns' might have changed over time

Although these mysterious stone objects have been frequently found in illegal, and more rarely in scientific, digs across several cemeteries, monumental compounds and settlements of third-millennium Central Asia, their functions and symbolism remain unclear.[100] So far, there have been no systematic studies on their forms, surface modifications, raw materials and precise location in the limited number of graves that have been properly excavated and recorded. They come from the most important sites of the Oxus Civilization, from southern Central Asia to north-eastern Iran, Seistan and southwards to the wide areas of south-western Baluchistan that are still largely unexplored; the limit of their western distribution seems to be the Halil Rud valley (the ancient country of Marhaši). Archaeologists in general consider these items a marker of the gradual spread southwards of the spheres of influence of the Oxus seats of power. The contexts where these 'miniature columns' have been found confirm a general dating to the whole second half of the third millennium BC and possibly to the early centuries of the following one.

Without forgetting that illegal digs caused permanent and irreparable damage, the advantages of working with private collections, besides a greater freedom in accessing and handling the objects, is the freedom to group, sort and reassemble the materials, without worrying about mixing up or losing information about their provenance: the latter is indeed already lost forever. One of the collections I have had the chance to study contained no less than a dozen of these peculiar artefacts, and this gave me the opportunity to attempt a preliminary typology and hypothesize – on purely conjectural grounds – how they could have changed in time.

The 'columns' that we could label as Type A (Figure 44) are sturdy, and in the shape of a truncated cone. Their height, in the small collection of samples studied, varies from around 26 to 29 cm, and their lower and larger base from 13 to 18 cm. They are made of variegated sedimentary stones, ranging in colour from buff to yellowish red (limestone with or without fossil inclusions, breccia or marly sandstone), with large grooves running continuously on the two flat extremities and along the sides. These grooves have trapeze-like or round sections and bear evident wear marks suggesting that perhaps some kind of fibre or leather cord used to run in their tracks; moreover, they seem to have been subjected to cycles of wearing away and renovation, when their inner surface was coarsened again or rejuvenated by light hammering with a pointed tool. The surface was polished but not intensively. In short, the evidence shows that Type A 'columns' might have had a prolonged use, unknown but practical, possibly in funerary rituals.

Type B 'columns' are in general taller (from c.25 to more than 33 cm), while the bases have similar maximum diameters (Figure 45). Their profile has a distinctive tapering; the polishing of the 'columns' is more intensive and the stones are somewhat more visibly variegated (the group in Figure 45 has three specimens made of light brown fossiliferous or metamorphosed limestone with red inclusions and ferrous bands; another is made of a dark green chloritic breccia). Type B is distinguished by wide and relatively deep grooves running from the flat top and bottom surfaces to part way along the sides, but not reaching as far as the middle, the point of maximum inflection. As in Type A, the grooves are relatively large, have trapeze-like or crescent-like sections and show evident signs of intensive wear possibly made by cords; in some cases, inside the wider grooves there are strongly polished tracks that seem to have been left by (leather?) laces about 4–5 mm wide.

Type C columns, finally, are shorter and smaller, with a height ranging from 16 to 23 cm, and a base of around 10 cm in diameter. The specimens of Figure 46 are made of dark brown or grey heavily metamorphosed marbles and breccias, with quite visible red veins and others made of spatic calcite filling ancient fractures and stress lines. Their polychromy is enhanced by heavy polishing. The grooves (flat, more rarely round in section) are narrow, shallow and highly polished on the inside. More importantly, they are found only on the flat top and bottom surfaces of the 'columns', and in some cases they are not aligned – that is the axes on the bottom and on the top are around five degrees apart. The grooves of Type C seem to show some degree of inner wear, but much less than in Types A and B.

44. Private collection, *c.* 2600–2500 BC (?)

Three column-like objects with a cylindrical contour and a continuous groove running from the flat ends to the sides (Type A) (Figure 44)

From left: 'Column' in fine-grained marly sandstone with yellow and reddish-yellow bands. H 28.7 cm, max Diam (base) 17.4 cm. Strong grooves with crescent-like section.

'Column' in reddish breccia with white fossil inclusions. H 26.3 cm, max Diam (base) 15.3 cm. Strong grooves with crescent-like section, which have been restored to function by an intensive and extensive light hammering, with a pointed tool, within their surfaces.

'Column' in brown limestone with fine ferrous veins. H 29 cm, max Diam (base) 13.2 cm. Flat grooves on the ends, with crescent-like section on the sides, highly worn, particularly at the edges.

Four column-like objects with a cylindrical tapering contour and grooves extending from the flat ends to part of the sides (Type B) (Figure 45)

From left: 'Column' in metamorphosed light brown limestone, with ferrous-like reddish veins. H 32.5 cm, max Diam (base) 16.6 cm. Partial grooves on the flat ends, with sections from trapeze to crescent-like and a partial inner wear.

'Column' in light brown fossiliferous limestone with reddish veins and inclusions (fossils are *Turritella*-like and bivalves). The grooves are flat, with inner deeper (wear?) marks *c*.4–5 mm in width.

'Column' in chlorite. H 25.5 cm, max Diam (base) 15.2 cm. Discontinuous grooves seem to develop from flat to crescent-like in section, and have been restored by light hammering with a pointed tool. Unusually, the wear is much more developed on one of the long sides than on the opposite, as if the object was hanging on its long side.

'Column' in light brown fossiliferous limestone or breccia (with bivalves). H 33.5 cm, max Diam (base) 16 cm. Flat grooves becoming crescent-like in section after intensive use. In this case, too, within the main grooves are visible inner, deeper furrows, highly polished and 4–5 mm in width.

45. Private collection, *c.* 2500–2400 BC (?)

46. Private collection, *c.* 2400–1900 BC (?)

Four smaller column-like objects with a tapering contour and shallow, flat grooves on the flat ends to the sides (Type C) (Figure 46)

From left: 'Column' in metamorphosed breccia with inclusions of various reddish-brown shadows, and intrusive veins of spatic calcite. H 15.9 cm, max Diam (base) 9.7 cm. Very limited wear, mainly on the edges.

'Column' in polychrome reddish marble, containing part of coarse breccia, highly metamorphosed. H 23 cm, max Diam (base) 11.2 cm. Strong wear only on the basal groove, crescent-like in section.

'Column' in brown-red marble with parallel veins and stress lines filled with spatic calcite. H 25.5 cm, max Diam (base) 12.2 cm. Shallow grooves, trapeze-like in section, with little or no wear.

'Column' in brownish grey marble, with parallel stress line and pockets filled with spatic calcite. H 23.3 cm, max Diam (base) 14 cm. The grooves have crescent-like sections and limited wear at the edges.

This evidence may suggest, as a preliminary hypothesis, that 'miniature columns' entered the rituals of the Oxus funerary practices, and eventually the graves, having previously performed a very practical function that involved strong laces running all around, that caused intensive wear to the grooves especially on their extremities. This practical use, whatever it was, later gradually became limited and the stone 'columns' grew more and more symbolic: this trend might be manifested in the selection of variegated marbles and breccias of contrasting colours and in the increasing intensity of the surface polishing, while the displaced axes of the lower and upper grooves indicates a major change.

Obviously enough, this suggestion, entirely based on the recurrence of formal and surface features of the objects, and not on the archaeological contexts, is purely conjectural. Future evidence from controlled excavations might fully dismiss the idea – but a preliminary hypothesis is always better than no hypothesis at all.

Seals and sealings

In the view of many scholars, the seals and sealings of the Oxus Civilization help to complete the picture of its long-distance contacts. They show links with western Asia, but mostly – through the bronze compartmented seals – with the eastern and south-eastern Iranian Plateau: specimens of the same type of seals, indeed, were found in variable numbers in Syria, at Shahr-i Sokhta in Seistan, around the Dasht-i Lut in Baluchistan, at Harappa in Punjab and Mohenjo-Daro in Sindh (Pakistan) and even, and in large quantities, in the Ordos region of China. At the end of the third millennium BC, strong similarities among the graves of Shahdad and Khinaman on the western Lut and Dhadar-Sibri in northern Baluchistan with materials found in Bactria and Margiana have been interpreted as the result of movements of Indo-Aryan speakers towards the south-east,[101] or, alternatively, as the product of enclaves of foreign craft communities settled at the edges of the Oxus sphere of control. Sandro Salvatori, for example, identified Shahdad as an Oxus *karum*, an outpost that might have thrived like the Old Assyrian colony of Kültepe-Kaneš, but ascribed the similarities among the objects found along the south-eastern boundaries of the Oxus region to the interaction between traders and craftsmen of the local cultures.[102]

Furthermore, Indus steatite stamp seals with animal images were found at Gonur in Margiana, together with transport and storage jars made in the styles of the Indus, precious beads in carnelian, jasper and other stones, small stone composite animal sculptures and ivory gaming pieces presumably imported from the Indus valley.[103] Other late Indus seals were found at Altyn Depe in southern Turkmenistan. Besides this, a few Oxus seals or seal impressions were found in relatively late layers at Mohenjo-Daro,[104] demonstrating a two-way movement of officials in charge of trade or on diplomatic or information-gathering missions, or more simply of bilocal kinship groups.

A prism seal found in the enclosure of Gonur South bears on one side a griffin, on the other a lion and on the third a three-headed creature with animal heads of unmistakable Indus inspiration.[105] Bovines – in particular powerful short-horned bulls with lowered heads, in what looks like an aggressive, charging posture – frequently appear in the iconography of the Oxus Civilization. In some cases, the graphic model is openly derived from Indus ones. Indeed, similar bovines are found (albeit relatively infrequently) in the standard series of steatite stamp seals from the early Indus urban sites of Pakistan and India; it is generally thought that the bovine represented on these seals is the *gaur* or *mithan* (*Bos gaurus*), a powerful, semi-domesticated species common in wide regions of South and South-East Asia.

The same animal appears very frequently on Indus seals, or Indus-inspired ones, found west of the natural boundaries of the Indus valley, on the Iranian Plateau and in Mesopotamia. The same bovine, in the twenty-first century BC, features on the so-called Gulf-type seals, a kind of round steatite stamp seal used for a short period by the local trade communities at Dilmun (Bahrain) on the southern coast of the Persian Gulf, where the animal emblem is associated with texts written in Indus characters but apparently bearing names, or other information, in a different, non-Indus language.[106] The reason why the Indus-related seals found west of Baluchistan featured almost exclusively the short-horned bull, or *gaur*, as an emblem remains a mystery. The only possible explanation suggested so far is that this animal somehow represented or symbolized the Indus families that had established their business in the western urban cores, outside their motherland; but this hypothesis is still not demonstrated. In the Oxus region, this animal was also celebrated through larger stone sculptures. A beautiful bull statue is now in possession of the Louvre (Figure 50). Another, previously unpublished, has been tracked down in a private collection (Figures 47–9).

47. Private collection, *c.* 2400–1900 BC (?)

Fragmentary large statuette of a male humped bovine in green and white layered onyx (Figures 47–9)

L 27.2 cm; H 16.6 cm; max Th at the chest 10.4 cm. Weight: 5187 g. The horns and legs of this large statuette are missing. The stone was cut along the direction of its natural layered bands, so that a series of thin, attractive white lines runs all along the back. Varieties of this type of green and white banded onyx are still extensively mined in south-eastern Iran, particularly on the northern slopes of the Chagai chain, nowadays at the political border between the

Helmand province of southern Afghanistan and Pakistani Baluchistan. However, rocks of identical aspect are reported from caves in eastern Turkmenistan.[107] Note that onyx is a commercial, rather than mineralogical term, and that this stone is probably a variety of calcium sulphate, not a silicate.

Leaving aside its beauty, the authenticity of this extraordinary sculpture is out of question, because its left side is uniformly worn by aeolian erosion, easily recognizable to every archaeologist that has worked on the field in the desert regions of Central Asia and the eastern Iranian Plateau. The statuette must have rested for five or four thousand years with the right flank exposed

to the wind, and the opposite side protected by sediments, before its discovery. We do not know much about the shape and the length of the horns, or about the legs, but what is left suggests that the posture of the bovine, dominated by an imposing angular hump, must have been quite dynamic: the left front leg moving forward, while the opposite one stood straight. The thighs, now absent, must have counterbalanced the push.

The fracture patterns of both thighs, in spite of the surface abrasion, indicate that they must have been intentionally chipped and removed, perhaps in an attempt to prepare the piece for a subsequent stage of processing and recycling.

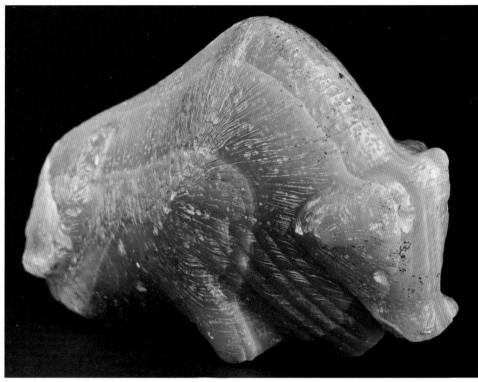

48

49

The powerful, triangular head, underlined by the straight, conventional line of the jaw, is lowered in an aggressive position; the muzzle is carved with a sharp contour, and the nostrils are two symmetric notches at its edge. The triangular ears are lowered, and it is possible that two thick horns pointed forwards. Even the thick tail, curled above the animal's back and ending in a thick flock, suggests the nervous movements before charging. The eyes are round and deep. A short but thick penis, with a triangular section, leaves no doubt about the sex of the animal. Between the jaw and the muscular mass of the foreleg, five vertical ridges in strong relief distinguish the bull's dewlap.

The most astonishing feature of this sculpture is the fine detailing of the fur, preserved only on the right flank where the statuette was protected from erosion. The subtle incisions, thanks also to the translucent stone, are hard to see, even in a photograph and with the help of oblique light. A point on the front edge of the foreleg is the centre of a regular, very fine pattern of radial lines, extending to the whole hump and covering the ridged-and-grooved surface of the dewlap. The muzzle is treated with a similar pattern of fine incised lines. While the belly is similarly treated with vertical lines; on the foreleg, the fur is divided into two diverging curved series of tufts. The sculptor paid the most attention to the upper back, where the same thin, well-incised vertical lines end in quite naturalistic tufts.

In the charging position, the curled tail and the rendering of the anatomical details, the statuette recalls closely a powerful bull in profile on a double-face chlorite seal, coated with gold, in the Ligabue collection, in which a charging, short-horned bovine is portrayed above a sledge-like object of uncertain meaning.[108] Another powerful bull of the same type and posture, although more schematic, appears on a round seal found in the fortified construction of Gonur South.[109]

Fragmentary statuette of a humped bovine in dark steatite (Figure 50)

Possibly found at Susa, this small, dark steatite statuette at the Louvre was bought in 1924 and dated on stylistic grounds to the Akkadian period.[110] For the lowered position of the head and the posture of the tail, and the balance between naturalistic and geometric modes in the bodily masses, it may be compared with the onyx sculpture of Figures 47–9, and hypothetically ascribed to the artistic traditions of the Oxus centres.

50. Louvre, *c.* 2300–2000 BC

Even the intricate pattern of intersecting circles on the upper part of the silver goblet of Figures 55–60 is a well-known Indus pattern, one of the most revealing cases of the penetration of the Indus culture into the elite groups of Central Asia. Besides decorative motifs and raw materials, the Indus valley and the Oxus undoubtedly shared the knowledge of the complex techniques (still poorly understood) needed to glaze and turn white steatite seals and beads, and of the production of coloured faience. At the time of writing, detailed archaeometric studies regarding the drilling of Bactrian beads are trying to assess whether these ornaments were produced with Indus tools and techniques, or through local adaptations, influenced by the transfer of specialized industrial know-how.

Finally, we have to mention another mystery – that of the so-called 'Priest King'. The name is purely conventional; nobody knows who or what the statue originally represented. The fragmentary stone statuette that bears this name, found in the lower town of Mohenjo-Daro, is universally recognized as a masterpiece and a symbol of the Indus Civilization. It is the most finished of a series of similar figures, generally poorly preserved, if not intentionally vandalized, representing probably the same kneeling male personage, with one knee down and the other up, sometimes bearded, with a tunic-like dress that left the right shoulder bare.[111] Once it is compared with the bearded males that appear on the Oxus silver vessels in the precise same position, the strong similarity of the 'Priest King' to these images is beyond dispute. Moreover, a fragment of the lower part of a statue in the same position was found by Viktor Sarianidi at Gonur North.[112]

In the Indus region, these peculiar sculptures were uncovered at Mohenjo-Daro in Sindh and (in one case) at Dholavira in Kutch, always in the most recent layers of the two cities. Fragments of partially similar statuettes are also known from third-millennium sites of the Seistan basin, on the eastern fringe of the Iranian Plateau.[113] On the whole, it seems justifiable to ascribe these images to the southwards expanding influence of the Oxus cultures and ideologies in the late third or early second millennium BC, rather than to the Indus cultures. However, this would not solve the problem of the identity of these enigmatic figures.

The increasing interaction of the Oxus with the Indus worlds, in the last centuries of the third millennium BC, was part of a more generalized intensification of cultural contacts and interregional links.[114] Some scholars have recognized in this process the opening of a prehistoric 'silk road', controlled at its western end by Oxus merchants and political leaders. Studies and discoveries point to the existence of important copper and tin-mining districts in the territory of present Uzbekistan (the Zeravshan valley) and central Kazakhstan,[115] while the traditional notion of the presence of valuable tin deposits in Afghanistan exploited in the third millennium BC has recently been questioned. Thus, one of the reasons of the sudden explosion of the Oxus polities might have been the control of the tin trade, that, judging from the available data on copper alloys, superseded the traditional arsenic alloys and became suddenly crucial in the last two centuries of the third millennium BC.[116] This will surely be one of the most intriguing future lines of enquiry for the study of the Oxus Civilization.

V

Intricacy of craft
technologies

n the middle Bronze Age, the Oxus Civilization, like that of the Indus valley, was distinguished by a high standard of both culture and technology, and by the surprising luxury of the material culture of the elites.[117] Unpainted vessels, whose regular forms are somewhat reminiscent of those in metal, were made on the wheel and fired in vertical kilns. Metallurgists, smiths and jewellers worked to a very high standard at Gonur and in the other palatial or early urban compounds. In the words of H.-P. Francfort:

La taille, fonte, la ciselure, le cloisonné, la granulation(?), le travail à la bouterolle, la soudure, le rivetage faisaient partie des techniques maîtrisées dans le échoppes de Bactriane. [Cutting, casting, chasing, cloisonné, granulation, chisel work, soldering and riveting: these are some of the techniques that were mastered in the workshops of Bactria.][118]

The copper/bronze inventories include a striking variety of copper vessels, axes, sickles, mirrors, pins terminating in human figurines or in clutched hands or in heads of various animals, and beautiful cosmetic flagons; there are also swords, spearheads and battleaxes inlaid and in relief, or cast and incised all round as lions, tigers, griffins, eagles and other natural or mythological figures. The axe (Figures 20–22), the cosmetic flagon in shape of a bull (Figure 31) and the copper dish embossed with the image of an ibex in high relief (Figures 26–8), are good, but partial, examples of the notable technical skill of the metalsmiths employed by the Oxus courts.

The production of copper stamps, often filigree seals like the one on page 90, with geometric, anthropomorphic or theriomorphic patterns, had also become intensive. Metal seals were produced with single lost-wax moulds, found still partially intact in a copper/bronze casting workshop at Gonur North, near the great palace.[119] The technology of copper/bronze seals deserves further attention.[120] If the metal was available, such seals could be produced and reproduced more easily than stone ones, even, if needed, serially, with simple procedures of moulding and indirect casting. In this way, the serial production and reproduction of these stamps well fitted the needs of expanding trade networks: groups or families of traders could easily equip their members with the same seal, in order to represent their activities in new caravan and trade routes or in newly explored territories.

As is testified by the grave goods, gold and silver were used for making precious vessels (perhaps those mentioned by the cuneiform sources as coming from the exotic land of Tukrish, for which see above), sometimes embossed with elaborate group scenes, as well as seals and jewels encasing various semiprecious stones; gold sheets were used to coat wooden statuettes, and for creating complex, composite ornaments with stone and faience insets.

In some rich graves at Gonur in Margiana, unbaked clay and wooden artefacts, certainly including pieces of wooden furniture, were inlaid with figures in faience and other materials, in the shape of geometric patterns, dragons, snakes, felines and so on, in work of almost incomparable beauty. Many necklaces found in illegal digs combine the use of copper and precious metals with that of artificially coloured materials (multicoloured faience inlays). As the Oxus people had a privileged access to crucial source areas, such as those where lapis lazuli and turquoise were mined, their love for faience and artificial products in general – certainly shared with the Indus craftsmen – puts paid to the simplistic idea that these blue materials were substitutes for precious stones.

Different types of marble and limestone were used to create weights and the well-fashioned, enigmatic miniature columns with grooves on the extremities, that were frequently deposited into the graves. Many have been found in the ruins of the fortified settlements of Margiana, for example at Togolok 21.[121] As discussed above, miniature columns, of unknown function and meaning (Figures 44-6), appear in graves or settlements of the mid-third millennium BC in north-eastern Iran, eastern Iran and Baluchistan, possibly marking the southern limit of the sphere of influence of some aspects of the religious beliefs or ritual practices of the Oxus people. Together with these mysterious objects, we also find shafts or sceptres in schist, and precious containers in alabaster or banded travertine, chlorite and steatite.

51. Private collection, third millennium BC

Four vases in banded calcite or travertine (Figure 51)

From left: high stemmed cup. H 16.4 cm, Diam (at widest point) 11.1 cm.

Ovoidal pot. H 8.8 cm, max Diam (mouth) 8.3 cm.

Low pedestalled cone-like beaker. H 6.2 cm, max Diam (mouth) 6.1 cm.

Truncated cone-shaped bowl. H 8.4 cm, max Diam 16.5 cm.

Thousands of vessels in banded travertine were found in, and stolen from graves illegally excavated in Margiana, Bactria and in other eastern regions of the Iranian Plateau, in Afghanistan and Baluchistan.[122] No systematic search and/or analytical study of the sources of these stones has so far been attempted.

Four sub-cylindrical vases in banded calcite or travertine (Figure 52)

From left: H 6.6 cm, max Diam (mouth) 7.4 cm; H 5.7 cm, max Diam (mouth) 7.9 cm; H 10.9 cm, max Diam (mouth) 9.1 cm; H 4.5 cm, max Diam (mouth) 8.3 cm.

52. Private collection, third millennium BC

53. Private collection, third millennium BC

A large, ovoid pot made of light yellowish-cream coloured limestone (Figure 53)

H 29 cm, Diam (mouth) 15 cm, Diam (base) 6 cm. Remarkable for the elegance of its essential form, this vessel is an outstanding example of the high levels of craftsmanship of the stonecutters from the north-eastern regions of the Iranian Plateau.

Funerary deposits also contain (or contained, given the generalized plundering of the Oxus graveyards) distinctive composite figurines of sitting females or 'princesses', now a universal symbol of the Oxus Civilization: the bodies finely carved in a dark chlorite to represent flocks of wool, and the heads in a light-coloured marble, covered with finely carved wigs, also in chlorite. As we will see later, it is now evident that the 'Bactrian princesses' were manufactured in different styles and fashions and ritually used for several centuries. A growing number of these figurines can now be found scattered around private collections across Europe, the Middle East, the New World and Japan. They are generally linked by specialists to images of *balafrés* (in French, 'scarred men') that might, or might not, belong to the workshops of the Oxus valley (these sculptures are illustrated and discussed in greater detail later on).

Since there are no large-sized artworks or heavy stone statues in the repertory of Oxus craftspeople, but only portable objects (even if sometimes massive), some scholars have ascribed this feature to the nomadic roots of the civilization; however the same simplistic argument does not hold for the Indus, which presents a similar and even more marked preference for portable artefacts.

VI

Shadows of lost beliefs

The late archaeologist Viktor Sarianidi (1929–2013), in the course of a long and quite fortunate career, first in the Soviet period at Leningrad, later – after Turkmenistan gained independence in post-Soviet times – at Ashgabat, had the distinction of discovering a great unknown civilization. But perhaps, sad to say, he must also stand accused of having carried out excavations far below acceptable scientific standards.[123] Sarianidi excavated Gonur with little or no stratigraphic control, truncating with caterpillars the uppermost layers of the late Bronze Age architectural compounds, where the signs of interaction with the Andronovo nomads would most likely be expected to have appeared.[124] Ceramics excavated, so far, have been documented and described only in very small quantities, without stratigraphy and quantitative estimates.

Furthermore, Sarianidi imposed a far-fetched and quite subjective historical interpretation upon his finds. He supported the rising nationalistic pride of the new nation of Turkmenistan by popularizing the idea that ancient Margiana was a core of the ancient Iranian world, and the cradle of Zoroastrianism. Indeed, he recognized within the palace of Gonur special rooms where, he stated, sacred intoxicating drinks such as *soma* (Rgvedic Sanskrit) or *haoma* (Avestan) were prepared; other rooms for ritually preparing bodies for the funerals; and special constructions labelled 'fire temples'. Although these notions were rapidly accepted in popular culture through the internet, they are probably not true, and – even worse – they will never be scientifically tested, because the relevant archaeological contexts have not been properly recorded and are now completely destroyed.

There is little doubt that some of the excavated buildings might have included rooms with religious functions, but they were not recognized as such on the basis of sound evidence. This is not uncommon in the archaeology of protohistoric Middle and South Asia: in the large contemporary cities of the Indus valley, for example, temples and shrines have never been identified with certainty.

Proto-Zoroastrianism in the Oxus Civilization, at present, is only a historical fantasy (and probably will remain so). In the words of C. C. Lamberg-Karlovsky, 'Sarianidi's rich interpretive narrative is simply not supported by the evidence. His is a narrative tale, rich in detail, but representing a complete disconnect between evidence and interpretation.'[125]

Did the Oxus people recognize an organized hierarchical priesthood? Royal houses, and centralized powers in general, often promote, support and control hierarchical religious organizations, that in turn play an active political role in justifying their power. It is possible (although far from certain) that some artworks of the Oxus region did represent individuals involved in official religious roles and practices. For example, a type of male figurine with shaved head, in a 'worshipping' or 'praying' position, the hand clasped on the chest, found in the ruins of the great palace of Gonur, may represent an individual of this kind. An almost identical statuette, but made in an attractive peach-coloured alabaster (Figure 54), that has ended up in a private collection, seems to support this impression.

Statuette (monolithic) of personage sitting on a stool, made of pinkish-orange banded calcite (Figure 54)

H 10.33 cm; W (at the base) 5.75 x 5.39 cm. Weight: 446 g. The personage sits on a low stool with concave sides; on the rear, the corners are damaged. The head, above a short concave neck, is egg-shaped, with an isolated V-shaped tuft of hair (?) on top. The bald head and this peculiar tuft suggest a ritual or religious identity.

The face protrudes in a staring attitude, emphasized by the large incised oval eyelids and their orbital arches, converging at the root of the nose. This latter, slightly damaged and polished by wear, is long and triangular, ending above a short curvilinear mouth. The ears are simple crescents in relief.

The torso is an inverted trapezium, elegantly curved at the large shoulders and along the arms; the curved hands are superimposed and joined on the chest. The fingers are sketched, rather than represented, with a few incised lines. This small sculpture was skilfully planned, orienting the parallel bands of the calcite pre-form so that they would coincide with the two folds of the dress visible on the lap. In this way, in front but also on the sides, the same folds turn out slightly lighter in colour than the rest of the figure. The thighs are inflated, but, as in the 'princesses', the body merges with the stool without a clear distinction; in front, a hemispherical cavity suggests at the same time the space between the feet and possible wooden legs.

This statuette might come from the graveyard of Gonur or from another contemporary cemetery of Margiana, as it is identical to another small sculpture found in Grave 115 of Gonur (defined as a '*transposition en terre cuit*' of composite stone statuettes).[126] Another identical image, and fragmentary or complete terracotta figures of the same general type, but

54. Private collection, *c.* 2300–2100 BC

with variants, were recovered from the ruins of the palace of Gonur North, a context approximately datable to the twenty-third–twenty-second century BC.[127] A terracotta variant also comes from Grave 560 at Gonur.[128]

Silver pedestalled goblet, with
a cortege scene with a captive
prisoner and intersecting circles
pattern incised on the upper part
(private collection)
(Figures 55–60)

H 16 cm, Diam (mouth) 9.6 cm, Diam at the
central ridge 9.5 cm, Diam (foot) 4.6 cm.
Weight: 159 g. Damaged in one point, restored
by overcasting and filing the overcast fillings.

Pedestalled goblets of this general type
are represented with several variants in the
ceramics of Gonur, the most explored cemetery
of the Oxus Civilization for the last centuries of
the third millennium BC.[129] Our silver specimen
is certainly formally linked to types that inspired
the fine, wheel-made ceramic replicas found
by the French excavators of Mehrgarh in the
cenotaphs of site MR 1, period VIII, South
cemetery, approximately dated between 2100
and 1900 BC.[130]

Even though the silver goblet is in a reasonable state of preservation, it was originally
fragmented. It was reassembled with minor
local integrations (on the edge of the foot,
probably at the joint between the pedestal and
the lower body, and in some points of the body
itself, apparently by casting a silver-copper
alloy (?) on the gaps. The incised figuration, to a
large extent, is very well preserved, as the silver
sheet is covered by a uniform, stable oxidizing
patina. The exception is an area of about 4.3
x 1.8 cm corresponding to Individual 2 of the
cortege (see below), which, as a consequence,
is scarcely preserved; all the rest is perfectly
legible. The interior, in contrast, is a rough
irregular surface where copper-like corrosion
products alternate with the effects of the
modern recent restoration.

The base and body were probably made
with two individual silver sheets, folded one
onto the other after engraving the outer one.
The foot is made with a single sheet (c.1.5 mm
thick), creating a flat ridge expanding below

55. Private collection, c. 2300–2200 BC

56

the joint. The body, in contrast, was made with a double sheet folded back on itself, so that it is thicker at the rim (by 2 mm or more). On the body, the edge where the double sheet joined on itself is partially preserved above the major damaged area of Individual 2. The entire surface of the foot, including the ridge, is covered by a continuous herringbone-like pattern of extremely fine oblique traits, arranged in alternating rows.

The body of the goblet is subdivided into two bands. The upper has a motif of circles intersecting in leaf-like patterns (two and a half superimposed registers), with an inner fishbone pattern that stands for the leaves' nervation. The lozenge-shaped designs within the four leaves is decorated with a cross-hatched design. The incision is extremely detailed and competent, even though discontinuous: in general, the nervation of the leaves of the upper registers ends in rows of tiny impressed dots, apparently forgotten in several of the lower leaves. The circles result from expert geometrical perception and spatial planning, as they are formed by tracing individual crescents, and not continuous circumferences.

The pattern incised on the upper body is, obviously enough, a re-elaboration and an enrichment of a common Indus motif, which is instead filled with a simpler hatching. A similar motif probably appeared on a globular metal vessel of the famous Asterabad treasure:[131] its graphic recording looks like a simplification made by the draughtsman of a design of the same type. Moreover, a band with a quite similar design runs below the edge of a silver cup from Grave 3235 at Gonur.[132]

A flat horizontal ridge, similar to that on the foot, separates the upper body of the goblet from the lower one. This second horizontal protruding ridge is covered by the same exceedingly fine herringbone pattern visible on the foot (three rows on top of the ridge, two below); the same motif extends to the lower body of the goblet where it forms the background to the seven incised human figures of the main figuration, an advancing cortege.

The human figures are miniatures, being on average not more than 6.4 cm high; however, in spite of their size, and with the exception of the badly damaged Individual 2, they retain, as we shall see, clear and often crucial iconographic details. For the stylistic details of the incisions, the frieze is closely linked to the famous, though limited in number, series of 'Bactrian' silver beakers with narrative figuration, including the *gobelet au banquet*,[133] the *gobelet à la bataille*,[134] the *gobelet à la chasse*,[135] the *gobelet à la procession*[136] and the *gobelet au labour et au banquet*.[137] Human figures in these friezes are so stylistically coherent, and characterized with the same codes, that they must come from the same royal court or individual silversmithing workshops.

The goblet has been consistently worn by handling in ancient times, particularly in a band of two or three centimetres below the horizontal ridge, suggesting that it had been the proud private possession of an individual or a family for a long time before presumably being deposited in a rich grave.

A detailed description follows of each incised figure, numbered for sake of clarity from 1 to 7 (Figure 58, from right). The order is given by the figuration itself, as the cortege is evidently opened by a leading character, Individual 1. All the personages are male; they are portrayed with the head in profile, but with the torso in frontal prospect; they move in a row in the same direction, towards the right. Following the stylistic conventions of other human figures on Bactrian-Margianan art, the bodies are rendered frontally, but the heads in profile; beards are rendered with thick sequences of straight vertical lines, extending to moustaches that reach the base of the nose; staring eyes are shaped like almonds and surmounted by wide eyebrow arches. Shoulders are often emphasized as round bulging features, beyond any realism. The torso, in some cases, narrows at the waist and is distinguished by conventional parallel curved lines that stand for the ribs;

the muscular volumes of the legs are sketched with short parallel strokes.

Individual 1

The cortege is headed by a bare-chested character with hair falling on the neck and a beard, both rendered with a sequence of simple vertical lines. The nose protrudes at a sharp angle in front of a large lozenge-like eye; the ear is absent or worn. In the left hand Individual 1 holds a vertical object that looks like a staff, or possibly a torch, while the right arm is bent to the chest with a clenched fist; under the elbow can be seen the end of an unidentified object carried by Individual 2. The pointed end of the vertical object might suggest a torch. However, if it was meant to represent a staff or a sceptre, it might be one of the long staffs in schist or similar metamorphic stones found in the graves of the late Namazga V cemeteries of Gonur, Tepe Hissar, Sibri and Shahdad, dated to around the last two or three centuries of the third millennium BC (considering that those found at Gonur have a very visible finial made of a grooved white or translucent semiprecious stone or of copper, although different in shape). These sceptres' tops are believed to be 'items of prestige that emphasised the high status of their owners'.[138]

Individual 1 is also distinguished from all the others by his peculiar and showy dress, a kind of long gown starting with a hatched strip or a belt at the height of the belly and going down to the calf, ending in two bands embellished by vertical lines, hatched patterns and an arch. (See also the discussion in the present section on the possible existence of an organized clergy in the Oxus Civilization.)

Individual 2

Badly preserved and heavily impacted by modern restoration, Individual 2 was another bearded personage. Details of the face and beard are almost completely erased. He advances behind Individual 1 holding in the left hand and carrying on the shoulder a double S-shaped object, that ends below the elbow of Individual 1; above the clenched hand, from the same object hangs some kind of net. The same composite object was also visible behind the man's back, probably in form of an elongated ogival projection, but details are blurred. The nature of this object is unknown. The man wears a kilt marked with a thick herringbone pattern. Individual 2 is unbalanced, the right leg is behind and its foot at a higher level than the left one. The right foot therefore seems to lean on a rectangular feature – it is not clear if this is just a graphic expedient or if the detail had an unknown meaning.

Individual 3

This man – hair divided in front in two wavy bands, and falling on the neck; beard incised with thin vertical lines – like Individual 1, has a strong angular projecting nose and a wide lozenge-like eye, with a marked dot as the iris and pupil. The ear is a small crescent that divides hair from beard. Individual 3 is bare-chested, with a narrow torso marked by emphasized ribs, unnaturally located at the height of the belly. His kilt is plain. In the left hand he holds, above the shoulder, a weapon distinguished by a round protruding blade and by a handle, apparently ending with a point. This weapon appears to be an axe or a kind of curved sword. The right hand holds one of the enigmatic objects resembling animal tails (this time forked in two points) that in Bactrian art hang from other objects such as wineskins and quivers. On his back, he carries a large bulging

57

object resembling a wineskin with a pending lap, while a purse or another compact round package seems to hang from the belt. Both loads are cross-hatched, and it is hard to say if this means that they were enveloped in some kind of cloth or net, or we should rather think of stylistic convention. Finally, Individual 3, like 7 who ends the cortege, wears an oblique band or strap on which sequences of six vertical lines are visible. The same bands, in other depictions on silver vessels, hold the quiver on the back of bowmen. The general context, in this case, suggests rather that these bands are a military emblem (see also the discussion of Individual 7).

Individual 4 (Figure 57)

In the middle of the cortege, Individual 4 is its central focus. He has conventional facial traits similar to 1 and 3 – thick beard, auricle, projecting angular nose, this time with marked nostril on the nasal base, and wide open lozenge-like eye with pupil under a strong eyebrow – but the head is covered by what looks like a helmet. This latter is rendered – uniquely in the whole group – by a grid of lines whose small squares are filled with triangular dots. This feature falls vertically on the rear of the neck, where it is fastened in what looks like a short hair bun. The form closely recalls the fashion of Meskalamdug's gold helmet found in the Royal Cemetery of Ur (but one cannot exclude, in principle, that the incision was meant to represent a hair dressing, rather than a helmet). Individual 4, like many other characters featuring in Bactrian-Margianan art, wears a tunic dress that leaves a shoulder (emphasized as a bulging round feature) and half of the chest naked. The tunic is covered with a continuous pattern of wavy lines, that probably hints at a *kaunakes* – the well-known tufted ritual dress of the Mesopotamian and Oxus traditions – and might qualify 4 as a personage with a ritual role.

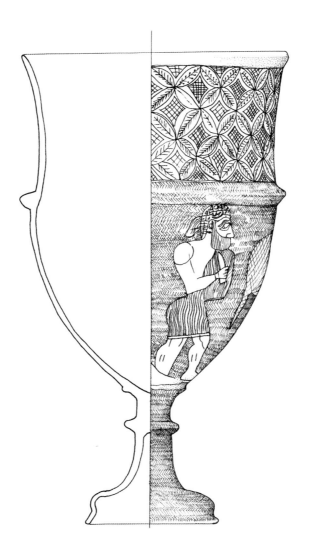

58. Graphic representation of the main frieze of the goblet of Figure 55

Indeed, Individual 4 holds in his right hand, in clear sight, a knife, while the left is concealed to the side. In the light of all this, the impression is that Individual 4 is the ritual executioner of the prisoner, Individual 6.

Individual 5 (Figure 59)

The facial features of the 5th individual are rather similar to those of the previous characters: like in 3, the hair is divided in front by a wavy line, but the nose falls on the same plane of the chin, and, despite the marked nostril, it is less evident. The right hand, seems to grasp a large container made of fur or skin. The same container appears in the famous silver vessel with the cart race at the Louvre (the *gobelet à la procession*, mentioned above). Steinkeller considers this item to be a quiver,[139] but this seems contradicted by the oblique arrow behind the man's back: evidently the quiver is imagined there. Looking at other Bactrian-Margianan silver drinking vessels, for example at the *gobelet à la bataille*, also mentioned above, it is clear that the quivers of archers are held on the back through an oblique shoulder strap.

The object carried by Individual 5 should rather be considered a kind of wineskin, although I have no good explanation for the hanging animal tail; the opposite extremity of an identical object seems to emerge from the rear, behind the right shoulder. It is not clear if the silversmith here meant to represent a single bag held under the right arm, and omitted to draw the parts that would have joined the front to the rear, or intended that the man was carrying two bags at the same time, one in front and one on the shoulder, tied by a strap. This second possibility is supported by the net-like pattern clearly visible only on the right shoulder – perhaps both bags were enfolded in a cloth or net balanced on the right shoulder. In the case of the loads of both 5 and 3, cross-hatching might be viewed as carrying

59

a suspended load. Likewise, Individuals 3 and 5 perhaps represent soldiers carrying in the cortege the booty of a successful military raid. However, as the container or containers are dotted with round spots, this pattern might equally well represent the skin of a spotted (young?) animal (see also the spotted deer in the famous *gobelet à la bataille*). In classical Greek art, spotted skins alluded to those of young deer, a particularly soft and appreciated material.[140]

A vertical band bearing a zigzag pattern seems to hang from the fist; this band appears to pass under a thin belt distinguished by oblique strokes. The kilt of Individual 5, like those of 2 and 7, is covered by a continuous herringbone pattern.

Individual 6 (Figure 60)

The implications of 6 are rather indisputable. The man's arms are bound behind the back by shackles in form of a double clamp, whose extremities are loaded with stone or lead balls (three are visible, the fourth is imagined behind the back). The prisoner is brought, or pushed on, through a cord or another type of bond by Individual 7, perhaps another guard (see below).

The hair is rendered in front as in 3 and 5, with the auricle in full sight, and a strong nose with a large nostril. But the beard and hairstyle are completely different: the beard is long and pointed, and a thick vertical braid falls on the shoulder. This feature is a standard attribute of male characters in the iconography on stone and on copper stamp seals of the Halil Rud Civilization.[141]

That Individual 6 is ethnically typified as a captive from the Halil Rud or Marhaši (in this we follow, with absolute trust, Piotr Steinkeller) is confirmed in this case by his cross-hatched kilt that opens in front like an inverted 'V', exactly as it appears in several human figures from the carved chlorite vessels tradition (for example, in the chlorite bowl reportedly found

60

at Khafajah, now at the British Museum).[142] A closer look at the man's body parts reveals a tightly packed random cluster of scratches on the right shoulder; similar longer scratches fall from an oblique cut on the inner calf of the left leg. These signs certainly represent wounds and blood and make perfectly clear that the captive was wounded in battle or tortured. Such graphic attention to the signs of physical damage and suffering is the same (wounds, vomited blood) that appears in the *gobelet à la bataille*.[143] The left side of the lozenge of the eye, under the eyebrow, is almost entirely occupied by a large void.

Individual 7

The cortege is closed by a guard, whose facial features are very similar to those of 3 (for the projecting nose, open lozenge-like eye with pupil and eyebrow, thick beard marked with parallel vertical lines; the hair on the neck is shorter). With a raised left hand he holds the cord with the shackles of the prisoner, and, at the same time, a kind of double-pointed weapon on the left shoulder. That the two objects are not the same is evident from the shift between their axes, above and below the clutched hand. Individual 7 shares with 3 the oblique strap decorated with vertical traits crossing the chest (but hanging in the opposite direction) and the characterization of the chest, with the ribs unnaturally marked above the belt. The kilt is covered by herringbone patterns, exactly like those worn by Individuals 2 and 5.

This silver pedestalled goblet, perhaps the first Bactrian metal vessel to celebrate a historical and military event, witnesses the Bactrian version of a military clash, or more probably a sudden raid of conquest, carried out by an armed group moving from the Oxus basin to the south. It probably belonged to a king, commander or chief who had defeated, captured and probably executed a chief of

the Halil Rud polity (ancient Marhaši), or of a community under the direct influence of Marhaši itself. He was so proud of this accomplishment that for a long time he enjoyed drinking wine in a goblet that celebrated his victory. The cortege is lead by an important personage, perhaps carrying a sceptre, who has no evident military features, nor any royal characterization, and this – together with the unusual, showy decorated dress – leaves open the possibility that he was a priest, or an officer invested with a particularly relevant ritual, as the killing of a powerful defeated enemy might have been.

The second important character is the man probably dressed in a *kaunakes*,[144] wearing a helmet and advancing with a knife – almost certainly, as stated above, a ritual specialist and executioner. The other figures might well be soldiers carrying booty, or food and wine for the ritual banquet that followed the execution.

Most probably this artefact was not isolated. In a recent auction at Paris there appeared a small silver embossed beaker, cylinder-like with a short everted rim, with the representation of a similar cortege.[145] Although this second beaker is heavily encrusted and/or corroded, and restored near the mouth, the frieze is partially readable. It shows a procession of six personages, two of which reproduce exactly, and in the same position, our Individuals 3 and 4; while another couple closely corresponds to the guard and prisoner in shackles labelled above as Individuals 6 and 7 (but the details of the prisoner are unclear, and nothing can be said about his hypothetical ethnicity). A quite sinister aspect is that behind Individual 4 one sees what looks like a child, apparently with grotesque features, with the arms tied behind its back and a cord around its neck. Not much can be said here about this second 'war' beaker, but it is clear that the two pieces, despite the different techniques of manufacturing and the different forms, were inspired

by the same, possibly canonical model of representation of the military bravery of the king or chief, and the crushing of the enemies and their families.

The dating of this possible event remains an open question. Even if we could have reliable archaeological evidence of the context of discovery, the goblet remained in use for a long time before being (presumably) buried, and its actual age would be questionable. Because of the apparent similarity of the bun-like helmet (or hair dressing) with Meskalamdug's gold casket, it might fall in the (much discussed) chronological range of the Ur Royal Cemetery, EDIIIA-EDIIIB, more probably at the lowermost limit, let us say about 2300 BC. Another scene of execution of bound prisoners on a famous bronze axe from Bactria is ascribed by H.-P. Francfort to a direct Akkadian influence.[146] On the other hand, the intersecting circles motif and leaves are common on Indus pottery, best represented and formally well expressed from periods Harappa IIIA (*c.*2600–2450 BC) to Harappa IIIB (*c.*2450–2200 BC), while in later periods its complex geometry loses coherence and organization, to the extent of becoming almost indistinguishable. The processions on this goblet and on the Bergé beaker, hinting at the ritual killing of enemies, like the prisoners killed on the bronze axes, show the extent to which the Oxus chiefs were proud of public executions accompanied by drinking and banquets, as complementary aspects of the representation and legitimization of their power. A similar ideology shows through the Karashamb silver goblet found in a kurgan on the Tsalka plateau, southern Georgia, where the beheading of prisoners features alongside fighters, a feasting scene with a lyre player and an Anzu-like lion-headed eagle.[147] The Karashamb beaker and the kurgans of the middle Bronze Age Trialeti culture have been recently redated to the last three centuries of the third millennium BC,[148] in a partial, but indisputably meaningful, overlap with the burials of the Royal Cemetery of Ur and the Gonur royal graves, and it is not by chance that all three elite cemeteries share the interment of large four-wheeled wagons.

The highest point of Akkadian militaristic pressure on the eastern polities dates to the campaigns of Sargon and Rimush that, following Reade's low chronology,[149] fits well (in general terms) with the same chronological horizon. The adoption of the 'enemy in shackles' motif by the Oxus elites is an eloquent proof of the depth of the cultural interaction between Bactria-Margiana and the Indus valley in the late third millennium BC.

On the whole, the silver goblet may be ascribed to the early Akkadian period, when captives from Jiroft also appeared in shackles on semiprecious stone vessels, that presumably were proudly exhibited at the Mesopotamian court.[150] It is clear that around 2300 BC, or soon after, the early state of Marhaši had become so influential and powerful that it represented a real threat to both its western and northern neighbours.

WD-XRF elemental analysis of the alloy

The silver goblet was analysed at ISCR (Istituto Superiore per la Conservazione e il Restauro, Rome) by X-ray fluorescence.[151] The results are semi-quantitative, and the artefact was not fully cleaned, so composition refers to parts of the surface that retained films of clay sediments, or that were partially contaminated by the material applied by modern restorers. However, the analysis gave a consistent picture of the vessel's constitutive materials. On average, and grossly speaking, the alloy seems to be around 90–92 per cent silver, 3.5 per cent copper, 1.5 per cent gold, the rest being minor impurities. This alloy is different from that reported by Deborah Freeman for two Bactrian and/or eastern Iranian silver vessels (roughly 98 per cent silver and 1–1.5 per cent copper, traces of lead and no gold).[152] In our case the silver/gold association and their relative proportions, together with the scarcity of lead, suggest the use of native or placer-mined metals, rather than the extraction of silver from galena. In the restored parts there is less silver and much more copper. It is probably a kind of stucco with high amounts of silicon, iron and particularly titanium; perhaps one of the components was a modern emery powder.

If you look at the frieze of the silver goblet illustrated in Figures 55–60, the personage that leads the procession is distinguished by a long, richly decorated dress, but has no royal or military insignia. He seems to hold a kind of staff or sceptre with a cone-like finial. Staves or sceptres of a similar description have been found in a number of rich graves at Gonur, both intact and plundered.[153] Two personages with richly decorated woven dresses, one of whom holds a long staff with a finial in a highly formal posture, are embossed with great skill on a pair of damaged silver plaques of unknown provenance in the Al-Sabah collection.[154]

We argue that the cortege leader might have been a high priest heading a victory parade or even the formal execution of an enemy, a scenario not unknown in the Oxus Civilization.

Some scholars, mainly on the basis of the architectural organization of the late Bronze Age forts, have added that the supreme power was theocratic in nature as was the case in the formative stage of other early civilizations. In other words, the clan leader and military chief would have also performed priestly functions, compatible with the ritual prescriptions and social hierarchies described in the religious hymns of the Rgveda (for the Indo-Pakistani subcontinent) and in the Gatha of Avesta, the sacred book of the Zoroastrian faith (for Iran). This intriguing hypothesis cannot be proven at present. However, a scene of double ritual killing of naked prisoners, in one case at least with a mace, features on a 'parade' copper/bronze axe in the Ligabue collection.[155]

Two staves in dark grey mica schist (Figure 61)

Left (fragmentary): H c.80 cm, max Diam 8.2 cm; right, H 110 cm, Diam max 6.2 cm. The sceptre on the left is broken at one end, and has strong signs of reuse on the opposite end. The function of these objects, found in late third-millennium graves at Gonur in Margiana, in the cenotaphs of Sibri near Mehrgarh (Pakistan) and at Tepe Hissar and Shahdad in eastern Iran, is still unknown: they must have been used for some specific task, because their functional end, as a rule, is worn, and finally deposed in the graves after the funerals.[156]

61. Private collection, c. 2400–1800 BC

62. Gonur necropolis, excavating 'Death Pit' 3900, *c*.2400–1900 BC

At any rate, if we are right in recognizing a schist staff or sceptre in the hand of the leading personage of the silver goblet of Figures 55–60, figures of the same role or rank might have been involved also in solemn animal sacrifices, probably linked to funerals of members of the elites. Animal burials, in fact, are an important feature of the Oxus Civilization.[157] The 'burial of the lamb' at Gonur North reveals in three rooms the sacrifice of a lamb, still bearing a small knife stuck in its spine, a hoard of 20 vessels, and the intact skeletons of two camels with parts of two goats. The animals were buried with miniature stone columns, an imposing schist sceptre over 1 m long capped by a copper finial, a famous silver pin with the figure of a 'Bactrian princess' in a *kaunakes* and other valuable items.[158] The performance of sacrificial rituals might also be suggested by the heavy mace-head in lead with figures of ibexes in the round illustrated below (Figures 63–4).

The most impressive evidence concerning such probable rituals is that recovered at Gonur, from Round Pit 3900 (Figure 62). This grave is not particularly rich in treasures, but contained a large four-wheeled cart with wooden wheels fitted with copper, and two long, carefully fashioned schist staves. There were also the remains of seven young men or sub-adults, some of whom had their arms tied behind their back, two camels, two donkeys and seven large dogs. A large carinated bronze cauldron might have been used in the last feasting. Two of the dogs had been buried when the large round pit had been completely filled in, as if they were guarding the mouth of the grave; the copper shovel that had been used to seal the site of this cruel ceremony, was found discarded nearby. Perhaps Pit 3900 contains the cart and part of the funerary cortege that had accompanied a king or a queen to their last resting place.

Mace-head in lead with ibexes in the round (Figures 63–4)

H 11.22 cm; max Width of head 15.31 cm; max Diam of shaft, on top, 5.41 cm; max Diam of shaft, at the base, 4.3 cm. The mace-head features four hemispherical protrusions, cross-shaped in section, with ibex figures between the arms, with their head downwards. The ibexes measure about 4.7–5 cm in length and 2.7–2.9 cm in height.

This heavy mace-head was cast within a double mould whose seam joints are well recognizable in the finished object (one mould had three ibexes and two arms of the cross, the opposite with one ibex and two arms) and a cylinder taking the place of the shaft. After casting, the mace-head was rectified by light hammering and finally with limited use of a large chisel, evidence of which is still recognizable between the forelegs of the standing ibexes. These latter are distinguished by a short conical muzzle, short pointed ears bent backwards (in three of the figures) and crescent-like horns curved towards the base of the neck. The body is elongated and ends in a short, flat tail variously shaped on the back (two animals have a short, oblique tail in the round; in the other two images, the tail is hammered flat).

The weapon was probably actually used, as demonstrated by the flattening of the top and the hammer blows on the lower extremity, certainly meant to fix the object to the extremity of a handle. Furthermore, a careful scrutiny of the edges of the four lobes reveals two major areas of impact and a general condition of diffuse edge damage. The

63. Private collection, c. 2500–1800 BC

64

described features might be compatible with
the use of the mace as a sacrificial weapon.
However, we cannot exclude the possibility
that this piece was a decorative-symbolic finial
of a stone sceptre like those found in the Gonur
graveyard.[159]

Although we are not aware of any
identical artefacts, animal images in the
round frequently appear on the rear of copper
axes and pins of the Oxus Civilization, as
well as some copper/bronze containers for
cosmetics.[160] The ibexes of this lead artefact
are rather similar to the caprid of a copper/
bronze pin and a bronze ibex illustrated by
Ligabue and Rossi Osmida.[161]

Small copper figurine of an ibex,
with pierced body
(Figure 65)

H 4.2 cm, L 4.3 cm, W 1.3 cm. This figurine,
possibly the finial of a pin or another
composite object, is stylistically rather similar
to the ibexes cast on the large mace-head of
Figures 63 and 64.

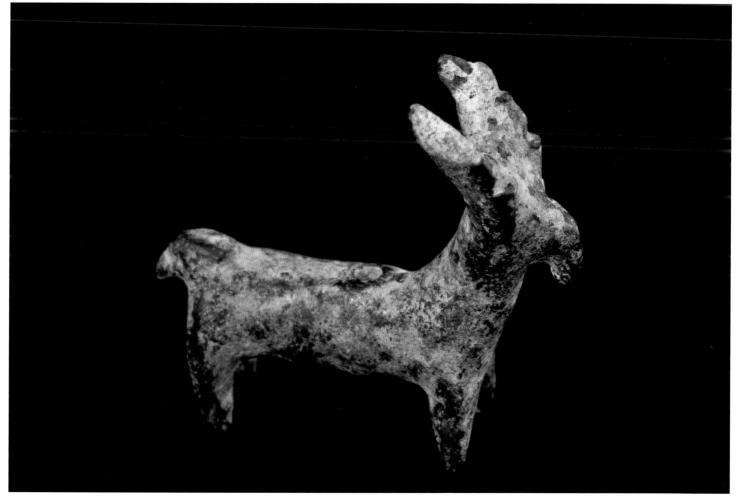

65. Private collection, c. 2500–1800 BC

Viktor Sarianidi lists a long series of possible sacred deities and symbolic icons found in the art of the Oxus, including masters or mistresses of animals, deities of vegetation, enthroned or kneeling anthropomorphic deities, heroes fighting winged monsters, dragons and snakes, lions, birds and the Tree of Life with animals, suggesting links with the religious-mythological imagery of contemporary northern Syria and the Anatolian word.[162] The belief in powerful female deities might be reflected in the many flat terracotta figurines with stylized facial features, applied breasts and emphasized pubic triangle common in Margiana as well as in the centres along the Kopet Dagh foothills.[163] At another level, female deities might figure on more formal and precious artefacts in stone. As we will argue in a later section, it is possible (but not demonstrated, as there are alternative explanations) that the composite female statuettes with the dressed body in chlorite or steatite, and with heads, arms and legs in calcite, placed in graves (as witnessed by the find of a few composite statuettes discovered *in situ* in the graves of Gonur) were images of a powerful female deity of fertility, vegetation and water, and possibly of mountains, analogous to her Elamite (or even Sumerian) counterparts, as argued by Henri-Paul Francfort.[164] The same great goddess, some scholars propose, would also appear on rare cylinder seals, silver vessels, pins and stamp seals (particularly in silver and gold). On the seals, one or more similar powerful female deities would sometimes appear with wings, seated on dragons or big felines, but there is no certainty that they were representations of a single female goddess.

Other statuettes in chlorite and calcite (but with inverted parts: dress in calcite, body parts in chlorite) represent a man with reptilian skin, a deep scar through the face, and a pot held under his arm. Because of the scar, this image is commonly called *balafré* ('scarred man' or 'Narbenmann' in German) and freighted, as a man-dragon, with demoniac significance. At the time of writing, at least 16 complete or fragmentary statuettes of this personage are known (see below), although none comes from a proper excavation or from an objectively confirmed location or context.

Some other hitherto unknown examples of these rare *balafrés* are held in private collections and published here for the first time (Figures 145–68). Although formally and technically quite different from each other, these peculiar statuettes do represent the same personage. Their meaning and precise cultural ascription, discussed in more detail at the end of this volume, remain at present an open question.

Vessels in precious metals show complex group scenes with personages (male and female) dressed in the same way, that might represent rituals, and even, in one case, a truly mysterious scene of cremation (or execution by burning).

Copper weapons and stamp seals in copper and other materials show aggressive animals (scorpions, snakes, lions, vultures, griffins, bulls) and personages with mythological features – often human bodies with heads of raptors and with wings – that might be demons or divinities. One important mythological or divine being is a muscular male character with two raptor heads, winged and with the limbs ending in powerful claws. In a cylinder seal, he is portrayed standing above a big snake.[165] He also appears in a few masterpieces of Bactrian art, including the famous and beautiful gold and silver axe at the Metropolitan Museum in New York. On this axe, the man-eagle appears in a heraldic position touching both a winged dragon and a wild boar at the same time. Does the scene illustrate a popular story – the fight of a hero with two destructive and powerful creatures? Another possibility is that the double-headed man-eagle was portrayed in this context as separating primordial elements (setting apart the mighty boar, linked to earth and water, from the dragon that might suggest air and fire). The suggestion is reinforced by its material context, an axe, a powerful weapon that physically divides and splits. In some metal stamp seals, the same supernatural being is also portrayed fighting or devouring dangerous snakes.

Stamp seal in copper and lead with figurated handle and anthropomorphic-avian character (Figures 66–7)

Round stamp seal with toothed edge and a winged anthropomorphic character with two raptor heads. Max Diam 4.08 cm; Th at the handle 0.95 cm. The handle is finely crafted as a crouching gazelle with the head turned backwards. The main character on the opposite side is a male being, with bulging thoracic muscles, with two eagle-like heads marked by a large round eye and short curved beak, surmounted by pointed vertical ears. The torso, wings and arms are represented frontally, the heads and the lower limbs in profile. Arms and legs end in talons fashioned like sharp claws. The figure wears a short kilt and has the right knee down, the left lifted up. From the beaks two vipers hang down. The eagle-headed personage, with some variants, is not uncommon in the Oxus iconography and he is frequently engaged in mortal combats with snakes and other dangerous beings. The most famous example is the silver and gold foil axe at the Metropolitan Museum, New York, where a similar demon, or mythological hero, fights a wild boar and a dragon.[166] In a round steatite seal, an anthropomorphic character with single crested avian head and similarly crouched legs holds two tigers by the tail.[167]

66. Private collection, *c.* 2300–1800 BC

67

An attempt to frame this polythetic and fragmentary scenario into a unified Bronze Age ontology was made by Francfort, who, on the basis of a structuralistic approach, wrote:

> [L]e corpus est très riche et varié. Il nous permet de séparer, en des hiérarchies parallèles à trois degrés, les images du monde des hommes de celui des divinités et des êtres mythiques composites, mais dans une dualité qui semble opposer régulièrement la fécondité-fertilité à la mort. Un couple déesse-dragon est central dans la mythologie de l'Oxus. [The corpus is very rich and varied. It allows us to separate into parallel hierarchies of three degrees the images of the world of men from that of divine beings and of composite mythical beings, but in a duality which seems regularly to oppose fecundity/fertility to death. One couple, a goddess/dragon, is central to the Oxus mythology.][168]

Actually, this construction is quite conjectural, as it assumes that the 'Bactrian princesses' were images of a mighty, pervasive female deity and that dragons, or better men-dragons (as represented, according to some scholars, in the statuettes of the *balafrés*: see below) were contemporary with them, allowing them to play an opposed symbolic role in the same contexts. Nowadays, this view is hardly acceptable, because no *balafré* has ever been discovered in a controlled archaeological context, nor were they ever found in association with their supposed mythological female partners. However, although so far there is no credible evidence that *balafrés* came from Bactria and/or Margiana, this view is supported by the stylistic similarities between some details of the rendering of the 'princesses' and the *balafrés*, particularly the alternation of limestone and marble with chlorite parts, the detailed rendering of the hair and the systems of mortise-and-tenon joints in statuettes assembled from different pieces.

VII

Form of government,
administration, writing

M any scholars believe that these societies were ruled by powerful tribal chiefs with some of the prerogatives of the later khans, with the authority to mediate between nomad chiefs and the politics of settled groups, as recorded for much later historical periods.[169] Historical khanates in Central Asia, in the Iron Age and later, built citadels and enclosures fortified with towers that, at least superficially, look rather similar to those that appeared for the first time in the late third millennium BC. Khanates, in the later history of Central Asia, became effective systems of political control and collective labour management, but, as everything depended on the personal charismatic prestige of the chief and the consensus of his closest kin, they could also be very fragile, if flexible, social organizations.

At any rate, the work by Sandro Salvatori on the changing settlement systems of protohistoric Margiana shows that in the last two or three centuries of the third millennium BC the inner deltaic region had been politically unified and was ruled by a single royal house, whose fixed, central nucleus was at Gonur. A state-level organization had been certainly reached, but it did not last long, because in the Localization Era (2000–1800 BC and later) the Murghab delta was again fragmented into a mosaic of smaller fortresses settled by minor, independent seats of power. The precise role played in this change by the pressure of the powerful nomadic tribes of the time is still unclear.

At the same time, with the expansion of long-distance trade, when palaces and fortresses acted as caravanserais, seals and tokens could be used to check and manage the loads of goods entering and leaving the storage facilities. The Oxus elites and merchants used a surprising variety of seals in a range of materials (natural and fired stones, copper/bronze and sometimes precious metals) and forms (openwork and solid stamps in copper/bronze and stone, some extremely elaborate, others limited to coarse geometric patterns, triangular prisms, lens-shaped rectangular cachet and, more rarely, cylinder seals). Elaborate stamp seals in silver and gold, like a few of the most beautiful weapons, might represent deities and mythological groups in fight, and were perhaps the exclusive properties of the highest ranks. Large and thick stamp seals in steatite of various shades of green, as a rule carved on both faces, sometimes fired white at temperatures approaching 1000°C, bore images of aggressive creatures such as eagles, dragons, griffins, coiling vipers, felines and bovines, sometimes combined with intricate geometric designs.

Lozenge-shaped seal in light green steatite, with toothed sides and bifacial animal images
(Figures 68–9)

Sides 3.97 x 3.98 cm, Th 0.74 cm. Weight 17 g. Light green to white, partially fired steatite. The seal, perforated at one apex, is finely carved in depth. On one face, it bears the image of a running winged dragon with a raised crest and wide open fangs. A spiral-like feature extends from the top of the wing. The body is entirely hatched with bands of vertical segments and angular designs. Winding features below the throat and under the belly of the monster might represent snakes. The opposite face shows a running caprid with long notched horns turned backwards; the body is hatched in the same style. Beside and below the animal can be seen stylized filling designs of vegetal and/or possibly animal inspiration.

68. Private collection, *c.* 2300–1800 BC

69

Lozenge-shaped seal in light green steatite, with toothed sides and bifacial patterns
(Figures 70–1)

Sides 2.83 x 2.81 cm, Th 0.87 cm. Weight 13 g. Light green, perhaps partially fired steatite. Perforated at one apex; this seal is finely carved in the same style as the previous one. One face has a very stylized crouching griffin, turned to face backwards. The beak is curved and the ear is straight. The wings and the body are filled with regular hatched segments. On the opposite side, a curved and an angular band, filled with similar hatchings, alternate with stylized vegetal patterns and, on a single side, with a wavy feature.

70. Private collection, *c.* 2300–1800 BC

71

Rectangular seal in white-fired steatite, with animal figures (Figures 72–3)

L 2.54 cm, W 2.27 cm, Th 0.77 cm. Weight 6g. The seal is rectangular, with a lens-shaped section and deep carvings on both faces. The perforation follows the main axis of the object. One side shows a griffin, with a short curved beak, a round eye and a raised, pointed ear, looking backwards. On the back of the fantastic creature, the wings are suggested by different features, hatched or not. The space between the animal and the edges is filled with lines and other abstract carvings. On the opposite face, a bull in a dynamic posture, with the horns in profile, lifts its head upwards. Above the back of the animal there are incised filaments that may or may not allude to wings.

72. Private collection, *c.* 2300–1800 BC

73

74. Private collection, *c.* 2300–1800 BC

Round seal in green steatite, with winged monster and a geometrical design on the back (Figures 74–5)

Diam 2.55 cm, Th 0.58 cm. Weight 9 g. The seal is diametrally perforated on the edge by two converging holes. The main side shows a composite monster with an ophidian head, round eye, open fangs and possibly a protruding tongue. The body is hatched, with the exception of the bare hindquarters. From the neck and the back of the creature erupt at least three sinuous wings, equally finely hatched, and two vegetal branches. The tail is held erect. On the back, two concentric bands are filled with oblique lines hatched in opposed directions; in the centre is a six-petal rosette in relief.

75

Round seal in white-fired, glazed steatite, with animal carvings on both faces (Figures 76–7)

Diam 2.51 cm, Th 0.93 cm. Weight 13 g. This seal, lenticular in section, is perforated axially at the maximum diameter. The carvings are deep, regular and quite competent. One face shows a snake coiled on itself, some abstract or vegetal fillings and, along the edge, a running animal in profile (a lion or a canid). On the opposite face, the sinuous figure of a tall caprid in profile, perhaps an ibex, is carved on the interior with elegant, curved traits. Moreover, the creature is surrounded by simple vegetal signs that might allude to grass, spikes and a flower.

76. Private collection, *c.* 2300–1800 BC

77

A copper stamp seal from Gonur. Its concentric geometry recalls the planning of the bronze age fortresses and palaces. Private collection, c. 2300–1800 BC

The collections of seals and possibly amulets from the Oxus basin published by Sarianidi include hundreds of smaller and simpler stamp seals that might have belonged to common households and to the lowest-ranking trading families. Recent discoveries have added to this inventory of local seals imports from the Indus valley, from Mesopotamia and possibly from the Iranian Plateau, that testify to the role of the early cities of Bactria and Margiana as crucial nodes on long-distance routes.

Since only a few seal impressions on clay from regularly excavated Oxus sites have been published, some scholars doubt their actual use in common administrative practices.[170] While this might be a simple accident of preservation in the buried deposits and poor excavation standards, it is clear that in the Oxus palaces different information technologies and various levels of administrative control were in play. Near one of the entrances of the palace of Gonur North, in Margiana, was found a small hoard of clay tokens bearing incised signs evidently used in the described fashion.[171] The tokens had been probably abandoned within a bag or another perishable container. According to Sarianidi, 'they were used for the taking stock of food and cattle. An inspector could make this easier standing at the gates of the citadel.' It seems

that an archaic recording technology, directly inherited from the earliest Neolithic, was still perfectly functional in a well-organized Bronze Age palace.

As far as we can tell, the Oxus was a civilization without writing. Soviet archaeologists tried to interpret a limited system of incised signs appearing on female terracotta figurines of the Integration Era (2500–2000 BC), particularly along the Kopet Dagh foothills, as a form of proto-writing. Actually, these signs are probably a limited set of religious symbols and have little to do with centralized and standardized writing technologies. The Oxus Civilization, it seems, was illiterate, with the exception of a few Linear Elamite inscriptions – perhaps on ceramics, certainly on silver vessels manufactured in their styles,[172] and of the Indus characters found on the stamp seals of Gonur. This very limited, and anyhow specialized, use of writing could be explained assuming that the peculiar form of centralized government of the Oxus Civilization was supported, and not undermined, by the maintenance of crucial kinship relationships. In other words, people knew each other and each others' lineages very well, and their reciprocal obligations, inherited through kinship ties, were so clear and generally acknowledged that it prevented the need of a formalized bureaucratic control: writing, at the times, might have been simply, at least in the majority of contingencies, unnecessary (obviously enough, the future discovery of an archive of tablets would totally subvert this argument *ex absentia*). However, objects with Linear Elamite, cuneiform and Indus inscriptions circulated at court, enhancing the aura of prestige of the rulers and stressing a cultural boundary with foreign traders and diplomatic messengers.

The linguistic background

Some consider the birth of cattle breeding and the beginning of the domestication of the horse as fifth-to-fourth-millennium Chalcolithic developments that took place in the Russian/Ukrainian steppes, which they believe is the original homeland of the proto-Indo-European linguistic community. The Indo-Iranian languages were a single common language group prior to its division into two main branches, or embryonic linguistic communities, often called the Iranian and Indo-Aryan languages.

The Iranian branch, through Old Iranian or Avestan, is the source of Middle Iranian and ultimately of various languages presently spoken in Iran (Farsi), Kurdistan (Kurdish), Pakistan and Iran (Baluch), Afghanistan and northern Pakistan (Pashto), Tadjikistan (Tadjik) and others. Indo-Aryan was rather closely related to Vedic Sanskrit and ancestral to the Dardic or Kohistani ('Kafir') languages of the Hindu Kush, and less directly to ancient Pali, and to contemporary Sindhi, Hindustani, Bengali, Bojpuri, Marathi, Romany (the language of the Gipsy tribes) and many other languages of the Indo-Pakistani subcontinent. Rgvedic Sanskrit (the language of the Rgveda, the ten oldest books or *mandalas* of India's religious tradition) and Avestan (the language of the Gatha, the oldest scripts of the Zoroastrian Avesta, supposedly composed by Zarathustra in person) are the oldest specimens of Indo-Iranian languages of which we have evidence. As they have many words, constructs and concepts in common, they must have been orally composed at a very early time, not long after their division at the end of the middle Bronze Age or Integration Era.

Opinions diverge widely, but linguists, who have their methods for calculating the relative chronology of language formation processes according to their rates of change in time, place the first ingression of groups speaking Iranian languages into the northern Iranian Plateau in the second millennium BC, and the separation of the Indo-Aryan-speaking groups to the same range of time or slightly earlier. By the mid second millennium BC at least, a group that spoke and formally used

words and concepts common to Indo-Aryan languages had reached the lands of what would become upper Assyria in the West and on the eastern margin the northern Indus plains (the Rgvedic religious elites).[173]

In Middle and South Asia this process would coincide with the end of the Integration and the rise of the Localization Eras; and in the steppes of Central Asia, with the spread of nomadic pastoral and marginally agricultural communities, such as the so-called Timber Grave or Srubna, Sintashta-Arkaim and Andronovo cultures (from *c.*2200/2000 BC onwards). The Sintashta settlement in Chelyabinsk Oblast, Russia,[174] a double ring of wooden houses of the same size, is centred on a common open round court that contrasts with the central elite residences of the late Integration Era in Margiana and Bactria, suggesting a quite different social structure.

Since the hand-made, heavily incised ceramics of the nomads are found in Margiana, on the edges of the last Bronze Age settled areas, these nomadic cultures are almost universally linked by Russian archaeologists with the speakers of Indo-Iranian languages, before their division into the two linguistic branches of Indo-Aryans and Iranians. But since the unmistakable Andronovo ceramics have never been found in Pakistan or India, and hardly encountered along the supposed route of migration, it is hard to consider such pottery a reliable marker of the hypothesized migrating groups or 'peoples'. The question, like many others is still pending, and subject to continuous revision.[175]

In the light of all this, which languages did the occupants of the early cities, palaces and fortified settlements of the Oxus Civilization actually speak? Some scholars believe that in the late Integration Era or during the conflictual events of the first Localization Era, the urbanized communities spoke a non-Indo-European language. The Bactrian-Margianan settlements were gradually surrounded by nomads of the Andronovo and related cultures (see below), that spoke Proto-Indo-Iranic languages. These groups might have interacted with the fortified settlements, absorbing part of the culture, religious views and social institutions, and probably introduced the horse into the palaces' ideology. However, the nomads would have maintained their language or languages, which in just a few centuries became the lingua franca, spoken among the tribes and the fortified oases.

The last Bactrian-Margianan settlements of the Localization Era would have been invaded, in about the mid second millennium BC, by successive waves of Proto-Indo-Aryan or Indo-Aryan speakers, on their enduring migratory route to the southern plains of the subcontinent.[176] This would explain why the later Rgvedic hymns celebrated, although in widely metaphoric terms, the destruction of the concentric walled compounds inhabited by 'impure' indigenous groups called *Dasas* or *Dasyus*, imagined as hidden in intricate fortresses and described with contempt as darker-skinned people with a different language and ethically reprehensible habits.[177]

Another possibility is that the urban elites of the Oxus may have originally spoken one or more unknown, isolated languages, now lost. Assuming that different waves of nomadic pastoral communities from northern Central Asia had been in close contact with the Oxus Civilization core areas for some centuries, linguists have made lists of words of Indo-Iranian and Indo-Aryan languages borrowed from extraneous urban and agricultural environments: interestingly, such lists include not only the camel and the donkey, but also the words relating to cereals and bread-making (such as bread, ploughshare, seed, sheaf, yeast), waterworks (canal, well), architecture (brick, house, pillar, wooden peg), tools or weapons (axe, club), textiles and garments (cloak, cloth, coarse garment, hem, needle), the words for wine, honey and intoxicating drinks and a few important domesticated plants including hemp and mustard.[178]

It is important to stress that all the cultures and civilizations involved in the hypothesized contacts (nomadic Srubna, Sintashta-Arkaim, Andronovo and other nomadic or semi-nomadic traditions, and the settled communities of the Oxus) are dated to 1000–1200 years before any textual evidence, and without texts all these constructions and hypotheses remain highly speculative and (needless to say) await future discoveries; equally hypothetical is any possible link between this linguistic background and the material culture emerging from the excavations.

VIII

Collapse

S ites and cemeteries of the late Bronze Age or Localization Era of the Oxus Civilization have been identified from the western Kopet Dagh foothills to Bactria, and southwards in the valley of the Atrek river in north-eastern Iran; but the main settlement cores may have developed in Margiana. Important changes occurred in Middle, Central and South Asia between the last two centuries of the third and the early second millennium BC, when archaeologists report a general decline of proto-urban cultures. Although well-stratified and scientifically excavated sites are few, and the general picture is still blurred, it is clear that the largest urban centres were depopulated or abandoned; metallurgy, glyptic artefacts (the seals), and all the important symbols of power and prestige became less lavish or disappeared completely; and regional and long-distance contacts decreased.

Among the reasons advocated for the collapse of the Oxus is the hypothesis of climatic change, with the sudden emergence of strong conditions of aridity. In fact, there is a growing consensus among palaeoclimatologists and archaeologists that a major general drought might have suddenly affected wide regions of southern Eurasia, from the eastern shores of the Mediterranean to the Iranian Plateau and the Indus valley.[179] In the words of Harvey Weiss, in summary:

The collapse and abandonment of Akkadian imperialized Khabur plains settlement, and adjacent dry farming domains in the Aegean and West Asia, were a function of 4.2–3.9 ka BP megadrought abruptness (onset over not less than five years), magnitude (30–50% precipitation reduction) and duration (200–300 years) that reduced dry farming agriculture. In the absence of available technological innovation or regional subsistence relief, the region-wide regional adaptations were collapse, abandonment, habitat-tracking to agricultural refugia, and nomadism.[180]

How far this deterministic picture is valid for southern Central Asia and the Oxus region will be verified by future dedicated research. Other critical and possibly co-occurrent factors might have been demographic pressure that stretched the capacity of the local agricultural districts, leading to harsh social

Aerial view of the Gonur South complex, c.1900–1600 BC

conflicts and, in turn, to political decentralization. In the case of such a major climatic change, nomadic or semi-nomadic societies, unlike sedentary agriculturalists, would have been capable at least to a certain extent of intensifying the movements of their living wealth without changing their way of life and subsistence completely. Certainly, the quite rapid diffusion of horse-mounted nomadic pastoralism in the time range under consideration allowed new communities to manage larger mixed herds (cattle, sheep, horse, camels and dogs) and to bring them efficiently across the Kyzylkum and the Karakum for the first time. These deserts, according to Philip Kohl:

> functioned as a more effective cultural barrier until roughly the end of the third millennium BC, when the semisedentary cattle herders in the Volga and Ural river basins and even farther east were regularly able to cross the extensive arid expanses by developing ever more mobile means of transportation with the help of horses and, most likely, Bactrian camels, which had earlier been harnessed to wagons and probably used to haul goods and worked for draft purposes in southern Central Asia and eastern Iran ... The continuous arrival of 'cowboys' with wheeled vehicles, horses and tin-bronze weapons and tools from the steppes must have disrupted – particularly at some points as their number increased – sedentary life throughout the low-lying irrigated plains of 'civilised' southern Central Asia ... The smaller fortified manors or qalas that dotted Margiana at the end of the Bronze Age bespeak unsettled times.[181]

The limitations of such dramatic narratives are that they are scarcely supported by direct, material sources of archaeological information. In Margiana, given also the large-scale damage to the uppermost layers of the great Bronze Age palatial compounds made by professional archaeologists, the evidence of the interaction between the immigrants and the sedentary communities is scanty and poorly understood.[182] Furthermore, as a rule nomadic settlements containing potsherds of the steppes types date to the mid second millennium BC rather than to the late Bronze Age, and were recorded far from the irrigated areas of agricultural interest.[183]

However, many agree that nomadic communities would have given birth to the Srubna and Andronovo cultures of the second millennium BC, generally considered – as stated above – to be speakers of proto-Indo-Iranian and/or Iranian languages.[184]

Other models envisage, together with the ingression of nomads from the northern steppes, a shift in the tin trade, when a powerful Šimaškian state or confederation rose between southern Central Asia and the Mesopotamian markets. At the same time, Hammurabi's state and other eastern partners, in a socio-political landscape of gradual deurbanization, started to import tin from Cyprus, rather than along the traditional eastern caravan routes. To complete the list of of historical conjectures, Daniel Potts, who would rather identify the Oxus polity (or polities) as the land or nation of Šimaški abundantly quoted by the cuneiform texts of the late third millennium BC, adds a raid led on the Iranian Plateau by king Shu-Shin of the Ur III dynasty to the elements that might have deeply unbalanced, with a domino-like effect, the local powers.[185]

Whatever the contingencies and/or primal causes, around 2000 BC the Margiana settlement pattern, formerly pivoted on a large directional court and city distinguished by an outstanding concentration and ritual waste of material wealth, collapsed in a radical cultural and political transformation.[186]

All the seats of power of Margiana apparently shifted to new locations, and palaces and fortresses that had been previously defended by wall systems with squares or rectangular bastions were replaced by others with round or semicircular towers. It has been proposed that together with power fragmentation, a change in the diet is suggested by a reduction of caries and other dental diseases, possibly 'connected with a decrease in the intake of fermentable carbohydrates in the later Gonur population',[187] as if centrally managed extensive agriculture and the centralized redistribution of cereals to the population surrounding the palace had come to a sudden halt.

Another effect of this change was that the great Gonur cemetery was systematically plundered at the end of the Integration Era, and there is evidence at Togolok 21,[188] and possibly at other sites, that previously respected and valuable stone objects such as miniature columns were gathered in storerooms or craft workshops to be recycled and cut into smaller, less valuable items. To the same period may be dated some hoards outside Bactria and Margiana, containing valuable, but fragmentary, status symbols of the old elites, such as the famous deposit discovered by chance at Quetta, Pakistan while digging for building the local Serena Hotel, that contained the lower body of a badly damaged 'Bactrian princess' of our Type 3a (for the classification, see below).[189]

The re-excavation of whole cemeteries, including the burials of its kings, queens and chiefs, signals a dramatic crisis of the very bases of local political authority. The signs of reworking and recycling as raw materials, but sometimes also as tools, of part of the stone artworks from private collections considered here (for example, see Figures 103 and 149–51) might be explained along the same lines (even though we cannot exclude the possibility that recycling in some cases happened much later).

Eventually, in the late second millennium, through a new cycle of urbanization, the Yaz, or earliest Iron Age, culture emerged. With it came an increasing sedentarization of nomads, the resurrection of monumental architecture, newly founded settlements, and new painted pottery with parallels to Susa in Iran and Pirak in Baluchistan.

IX

The mysterious
'Bactrian princesses'

Given the disastrous plundering of numberless cemeteries in northern Afghanistan and presumably in the nearby regions, 'Bactrian princesses', their iconographic and ritual implications, and their formal and stylistic variations and evolution remain, to a large extent, open questions, or open lines of enquiry. Beyond the irreparable loss of contexts, there is some evidence that some of the statuettes placed in graves had perishable parts in wood, that did not survive post-depositional decay.

Illegal and shabbily run excavations may have frequently caused the loss of the applied parts of the statuettes; moreover, in the vagaries of bazaars, auctions and private sales some of the applied parts (in particular the limestone heads) have freely moved from one figure to another, so that now only a small proportion of the 'princesses' still feature their original applied parts. Even in the collection presented here, a number of the statuettes have heads and/or headdresses that are not original, thus blurring the perception of their stylistic identity.

This growing uncertainty notwithstanding, recent excavations in Margiana made abundantly clear that the 'Bactrian princesses' were made, and circulated, in the central seats of power of Margiana of the middle-to-late Bronze Age, and presumably in the Bactrian courts as well. The following table summarizes the finds of statuettes or their parts in more or less reliable archaeological contexts in the Murghab delta.

The impression is that these figures played a crucial role in the funerals of the elites for a long time, possibly from the mid-third to the beginning of the second millennium BC. While the number of 'princesses' that have surfaced so far on the unstable waters of the antiques market is growing exponentially, their multiple morphological and stylistic variations have been described and commented only on a piece-by-piece basis, and, up till now, no attempt has been made at a classification of their morphological changes over time, at least on the basis of preliminary stylistic considerations.

Table 2. The 'Bactrian princesses' so far found in reliable archaeological contexts and published

Part of statuette	Site and context	Reference
Limestone head, schematic Part of the body with fleece	Togolok 21, room 148	Sarianidi 1998: Figs 17, 10; Hiebert 1994a, 150, Figs 9–12
Two limestone heads with wig	Adji Kui, surface and trench	Ligabue and Rossi Osmida 2007, Fig. 20 Rossi Osmida 2011, 176–180
Limestone hands or feet	Togolok 21	Sarianidi 1988: Figs 17, 11 and 12
Limestone head, schematic	Entrance of Gonur South	Sarianidi 1988: Figs 17, 11 and 12
Limestone head and wig	Gonur, Grave 3210	Sarianidi and Dubova 2013: Fig. 137
Limestone hand or foot	Gonur North	Sarianidi 1998: Figs 18, 8
Chlorite torso of Type 3a	Gonur North	Sarianidi 2007, 118–119; Ligabue and Rossi Osmida 2007, 169; Rossi Osmida 2002, 100
Three sets of limestone right arms and other pieces	Gonur, Grave 1200	Sarianidi 2002, 140; 2007, Figs 38–39
Complete composite statuette	Gonur, Grave 2900	Sarianidi 2008, Fig. 141 Ligabue and Rossi Osmida 2007, Fig. 21
Complete composite statuette	Gonur, Grave 1022	Sarianidi 2007, 74, Fig. 56
Complete composite statuette	Gonur, Grave 1799	Sarianidi 2007, 74, Fig. 54
Headless composite statuette with marble arms	Gonur, Grave 1028	Sarianidi 2007, 74, Fig. 55
Arms and headdress	Gonur, Grave 2780	Sarianidi 2007, Figs 57–59
Fragment of a *kaunakes* dress	Gonur, Grave 2655[190]	Sarianidi 2007, 75, Fig. 60
Complete composite statuette	Nishapur, Iran (in grave?)	Khaniki 2003[191]

Looking for an identity

The 'Bactrian princesses', composite statuettes made of a variable number of detachable parts (heads, wigs and limbs), were undoubtedly produced and used in the central seats of power of the Oxus Civilization (see above). It is presumed that some kind of adhesive was used to fix the parts, and despite Agnès Benoit's and my observation of residues of a red material, usually under the necks, and patches of some other extraneous materials in correspondence of the joints, the evidence on this important aspect of the statuette's materiality is still inconclusive. Indeed, these red substances are easily mistaken for or mixed up with clay residues from the dig. An additional problem is that dealers and restorers often applied to the composite statuettes modern materials such as plasticine and the like, so that the chances of finding uncontaminated original adhesives are very low.

The stones most commonly used were different types of green to black talc-based rocks and minerals such as chlorite and steatite (not always reliably recognized by archaeologists without a mineralogical analysis) and white, or light-coloured, marble or calcite. Usually, the green rocks were used for the dress masking the seated body, for the headdress and hair, while the white stones were used for the uncovered body parts (usually, head, arms and hands, as only few specimens had visible legs and feet). While Benoit stresses the presence of traces of colours and applied pigments to enhance the anatomical details of the face,[192] the 'princesses' from private collections we have so far examined did not confirm this hypothesis.

The statuettes, in most cases, are rather small, from 8 to 15 cm in height. The attractive contrast between the green, dark green or blackish dress and the white body parts is undoubtedly the most evident and distinguishing aesthetic trait of these figures, together with the variable stylized rendering of their *kaunakes*, the Mesopotamian ritual garment that consisted of a sheepskin with woollen tufts sewn on. The same fundamental contrast (black/green to white) supports the hypothesis of a structural opposition and inversion between the 'princesses' and the images of the *balafrés* (white kilt and shoes, green chlorite bodies) whose origin is still shrouded in mystery.

However, the inventory of those statuettes that have been published so far and considered in the present study, or temporarily exhibited in the auction houses, includes some sculptures that are larger or smaller, unconventional and made of quite different materials (think of the heavy black metamorphic stone of the unusual statuette, Figures 108–110, or the massive rose quartz body parts of the one illustrated in Figure 129, little less

than 30 cm high; or to the isolated stretched body in bitumen, Figure 142); moreover, on some statuettes the usual *mèches* (lozenges) or *kaunakes* tufts are accompanied, and eventually replaced, by geometric ornamentation and leaf patterns. In spite of their anomalous or even bizarre look, the present author believes that the sculptures described in the following resumé are most probably authentic. This would expand the production and the repertory of the 'princesses' to forms, styles and materials a long way beyond those more commonly published (for example by Benoit) and support the hypothesis that these fascinating sculptures were manufactured and circulated for a longer time and come from a wider cultural area than previously thought.[193]

What was the ideological role of these small sculptures, and how did they relate to the contemporary iconography of the eastern fringe of the Iranian Plateau? If we limit ourselves to the ascertained facts:

The seated female figure in a voluminous skirt appears in the glyptic art of south-eastern Iran from Shahdad, as well as on a silver vessel said to have been found in the province of Fars, in south-western Iran, both assigned to the latter half of the third millennium, around the time of the Akkadian Empire. The motif occurs later on Iranian cylinder seals. A number of clay impressions of cylinder seals with this same female figure have been found at Tall-i Malyan, ancient Anshan, in Fars; and at Susa, in Khuzistan. These are dated by stratigraphic and epigraphic evidence to the dynasty of the Sukkalmah (c.1900–1450? BC).[194]

In these words Holly Pittman summarized the evidence that had accumulated after a long debate among the specialists on the archaeology of these intriguing images. Pierre Amiet, among others, noted that the composite stone statuettes of the Oxus tradition have close formal links with images of seated female characters in the iconography of Shahdad, Tepe Yahya and the centres of the Elamite sphere,[195] and Daniel Potts comes to the conclusion that 'it seems justifiable to suggest that the appearance of similar figures on "Anshanite" seals reflects Bactrian or Margianan influence on Anshan rather than Elamite influence in Bactria and Margiana'.[196]

On this view, we appear to be dealing with prestigious female images circulating in the Oxus basin, and 'translated' onto prestigious objects (silver vessels and seals) in the framework of a network of contacts and possibly long-distance gifts exchange (if not circulating booty) involving the elites of the times. Potts, referring also to the iconography of the seals found at Anshan, further stresses that:

These finds reflect a period of contact and inter-cultural communication between Elam/Anshan and Bactria/Margiana that lasted from the life time of Ur-Namma and Puzur-Inshushinak – with whom the Persepolis vessel is linked by virtue of its Linear Elamite inscription – to the sukkalmah or Kaftari/Old Babylonian period, when the Anshanite glyptic style flourished, or something over 200 years.[197]

In the late third millennium BC, Linear Elamite inscriptions of variable scope, importance and length appeared on metal vessels, seals, tablets and possibly ceramics from Elam eastwards to Margiana and the Halil Rud valley, which suggests that, at a time when certain important images and symbols were internationally recognized, Linear Elamite was possibly, for one or two centuries, a kind of eastern *scriptura franca*.

However, while in the western seals and on artefacts made on silver such female images seem to refer to actual women belonging to the local elites, in the case of the Oxus statuettes most authors, at least recently, are agreed that they were images of deities capable of pacifying the wild forces of nature personified by animals.[198]

Both Henri-Paul Francfort and Agnès Benoit strongly support the interpretation of the female composite statuettes as divine characters. The latter, at the end of her book, concludes that:

On peut donc se prononcer sur la fonction protectrice des représentations féminines incarnées dans la statuaire composite d'Asie centrale, protection qui s'exerce dans le monde des morts, mais aussi dans celui des vivants, même si les témoignages sont plus rares. Il faudrait donc renoncer à l'expression de 'princesses de Bactriane', et remplacer par 'divinités de l'Oxus': l'appellation y perdrait en poésie évocatrice, mais y gagnerait en exactitude. [It is therefore possible to pronounce in favour of a protective function for the female representations materialized in the composite statuary of Central Asia, protection which had force in the world of the dead, but also in that of the living, even if the evidence is rarer. We ought therefore to abandon the expression 'Bactrian princesses' and replace it with 'Oxus divinities': what the title lost in evocative poetry, it would gain in accuracy.][199]

In contrast, Amiet eventually came to consider the composite statuettes as *gracieuses mères* ('gracious, beneficent mothers'), ideally representing influential female personages of the courts of the outer Elamite sphere: leading characters who personified a '*matriarcat résiduel*' ('residual matriarchy') within the elite families and whose stone images would have accompanied the dead in the grave with protective functions.[200] Indeed, when the statuettes were found in undisturbed graves, they stood near the head of the deceased, looking at her or him; however, their protective role does not allow us to differentiate deities from beneficent mothers. At any rate, it is impossible to disagree with Élise Luneau when she writes that:

[L]'importance des figurations féminines dans l'iconographie bactrienne, comme dans le monde iranien, sur plusieurs types de support (figurines, « cachets », flacons) est à remarquer, telles les représentations de femmes de classe supérieure ou d'une déesse, les scènes de gynécée voire de cours féminines. Cette différence de genre dans le traitement iconographique n'est sans doute pas fortuite. Que ce soit sur le plan divin ou humain, les femmes semblent avoir bénéficié d'un prestige social fort. [The importance of female figurations in Bactrian iconography, as in the Iranian world, in several types of media (figurines, 'cachets', drinking vessels) is notable, be they the representations of elite women or of a goddess, scenes of a gynecaeum or even female education. This difference of genre in iconographic treatment is doubtless not a matter of chance. Whether on the divine or human plane, women seem to have benefited from strong social prestige.][201]

The symbolic implications of the statuette (from a private collection) reproduced as Figures 126–8 might also be important. On the well preserved mantle-robe, the trees with the winding outline would signify wilderness, the spikes that alternate with them the agricultural world. Both seem to converge on top of the statuette that, in its strongly triangular structure, suggests a mountain. In this light, it would be difficult to ignore the impression that, at least in this case, the 'princess' might have been a divinity – more precisely, a 'lady of the mountain' to whom vegetation, wild or domesticated, was sacred.

A very similar 'princess' – her torso covered by alternating spikes and wavy trees, the latter originating from the robed figure's lap – was recently auctioned in Paris;[202] evidently this type of representation was not unique, but belonged to an established type. The alternation between trees and cultivated cereals, on the other hand, is faithfully mirrored in a complex and badly preserved object found by Sarianidi at Gonur: a composite anthropomorphic image, presumably built on a cone of decayed wood, coated with figurated gold foil and flanked by a radial arrangement of a number of faience spikes of wheat fixed on copper rods, flanked by two larger pointed trees in the same materials, very similar in fashion to those featured on the Louvre's silver *pyxis* described above (Figure 17).[203]

Other associations with a sacred vegetal world would account for the appearance, in some other 'princesses' (presumably of a later age?) of leaves, rendered in naturalistic terms or in various stages of abstraction. If we were to base our judgement on this peculiar 'Bactrian princess', the identification of the statuettes with divine images would gain in plausibility.

The 'princesses' classified by material and formal features

What follows is a preliminary attempt at an overall classification based upon elementary material and formal features (monolithic as opposed to composite bodies, number of body parts, presence or absence of applied limbs made of different materials).

Type 1: Seated statuettes with monolithic body
   Type 1a: without evidence of arms
   Type 1b: with elongated, stretched body
   Type 1c: with arms sculpted in relief
   Type 1d: with applied limestone arms

Type 2: Standing, with monolithic body

Type 3: Seated statuettes with composite body
   Type 3a: seated, made of two superimposed parts (chest and legs) and other applied features
   Type 3b: seated, made of three superimposed parts and other applied features
   Type 3c: elongated seated statuettes made of three parts (lower legs, thighs, chest) and other applied features

Secondary variations are many: the base materials, style and sculptural details of the bodies and of the applied parts (first and foremost the heads and headdresses), the joints and the treatment of the dress.

Seated statuette with monolithic body, without arms (Type 1a) in dark green chlorite, white limestone head and dark green chlorite headdress (Figures 78–9)

Body: H 14.85 cm, W (at the base) 14.08 x 10.54 cm. Head: H 5.69 cm, W (at the base) 3.77 x 3.01 cm. Headdress: Diam on top 4.26 cm, H 3.53 cm, max W (at the base) 4.75 cm. Weights: body 3781 g, head 90.5 g, headdress 37.21 g. The three pieces are coherent and probably the original parts of the same sculpture (body and headdress are made of the same stone). In perfect condition but for some old, limited damage in front.

The modelling of the head is refined, careful and competent, with naturalistic features. The occipital area has a strong flat slope on which the headdress fits perfectly. The face is elongated, with a pointed chin, inflated cheeks and fleshy protruding lips; the strong nose is triangular when seen in front, and curved from the sides. The eyes are large, almond-shaped, with bulging hemispherical eye-globes. The ears are small, with round auricles in relief, round central cavities made by drilling, while the lobe below is a small bulging hemisphere. The low forehead is almost entirely covered by the fringe of the headdress: the base of the neck is almost flat.

78. Private collection, *c.* 2300–2200 BC

79

The headdress shows rows of flat tufts (three on top, two on rear) with simple vertical incisions, very similar in rendering to the tufts of the *kaunakes*.[204] The body is embellished by regular rows of large vertical, parallel tufts with rounded ends (two on the chest, two on the lap, while two last rows of larger elements run around the lower body: defined as *grandes languettes allongées* by Amiet). In a subtle play of lines, the shoulder row of tufts sags slightly at the centre, while the one below is minimally restricted and curved in the opposite direction. The volume of the whole chlorite body is gently, gradually curved, so that the naturalistic features of the head join it in a harmonious way.

On the statuette are still visible residues of a light yellowish brown fine sediment (Munsell 10YR 6/4), left from the excavation.

80. Louvre, *c.* 2300–2200 BC

'Bactrian princess' (Figure 80)

H 17.3 cm, W 16.1 cm. This famous statuette, whose tufted garment is an example of the '*Languettes*' style, might be a relatively early one. The asymmetrical decoration of the dress on the right side of the chest probably shows a woven stole worn above the right shoulder, exactly like those visible in the same position on the statuettes of Figures 102–7.

81. Private collection, *c.* 2100–2000 BC

Seated statuette with monolithic body, without arms (Type 1a) in dark green chlorite, a head of white marble with light brown veins, and dark green chlorite headdress (Figures 81–3)

Body: H 9.40 cm, W (at the base) 9.99 x 10.54 cm. Head: H 4.57 cm, W (at the base) 3.44 x 2.34 cm. Weights: body 1859 g, head 43.24 g, headdress 35.50 g. The three pieces (headdress, head and body) are probably original and coherent. In fair condition, with minor localized damage.

Below the neck, an inverted V-like décolleté is polished and slightly convex. The top of the head is flattened, slightly convex; the front is short and sloping, and ends in a curved, sharp angular nose. In front view, the face is sharply defined, with a polygonal contour, high cheekbones, and narrow, almond-shaped bulging eyeballs, surmounted

82

83

front and plain on the rear, possibly suggesting a gold crown. The body is massive, well formed, with a gentle slope between the chest and the lower part. On the dress or mantle, the tufts of a *kaunakes* are replaced by a dense, continuous pattern, with regular rows of lozenges filled in with alternating vertical and horizontal lines. In front, such lozenges (hereafter called, following Amiet and Benoit, by the French term *mèches*) were incised, organizing them within regular vertical bands, whereas on the rear similar but longer and less regular *mèches* were made by a criss-cross pattern of intersecting bands. The shoulders are entirely covered by two elongated heart-shaped leaves. All the carved patterns extend beyond the limits of the various prospect views, so that the volume and the thin incisions support each other in subtle aesthetic play.

The lower base, highly polished, shows faint concentric wear marks left by the manufacturing process.

Large, somewhat roughly carved leaf-like patterns surround the neckline of the composite statuette (Type 2a, with applied limestone arms) found in a quite damaged state in Grave 1799 at Gonur, as well as in another 'Bactrian princess' in a private collection; another statuette of the same general form was recently (2014) auctioned in Paris.[205] Leaves fall also on the knees of these statuettes, and cover patterns of *mèches* internally filled with concentric incised lines. One is tempted to assume that in the development of the dress, leaf-like patterns appeared first on the shoulders and as radial appendages of the neck-girdle, and expanded, perhaps later, to the whole surface of the robe.

by long eyebrow arches. The simplified ears are limited to the auricles, poorly defined, in the form of short crescents in relief alongside an elongated cavity. The base of the neck is slightly convex and fits exactly in its oval, carefully polished neckline.

The chlorite headdress retains on the interior traces of the burin-like copper or bronze tool

with which it was carved. It seems to represent a complicated hairdo: on the flat top, hair seems to be twisted in a braid wrapped around the head, with thick tresses emerging from the centre and falling down on the neck in vertical locks. The front and rear part are tied in a kind of tiara, which is incised with multiple lines in the

Seated statuette with monolithic body and no arms (Type 1a) in green chlorite or chloritoschist, rich in mica and possibly with darker veins, the head of fine white limestone (Figure 84)

Body: H 10.60 cm, W (at the base) 9.80 x 9.10 cm. Head: H 3.78 cm, W (at the base) 2.75 x 21.55 cm. Weights: body 1785 g, head 22.63 g. Body and head are probably assembled from different statuettes. In good condition, with limited damage to the shoulders.

The head of this statuette has a flat sloping occipital area; the face is massive, with a substantial triangular nose and marked nostrils. The almond-shaped eyes have bulging eyeballs; the rendering of the lips and chin is rather naturalistic. The ears are sketched with shallow elongated cavities at the top of the deep, oval neckline. The front side of the neckline, and a restricted area on the knee, have been modified by strong localized wear of uncertain origin.

The entire chest and lower body are covered by a freely incised pattern of *mèches* in form of lozenge-like leaves. Such *mèche*-leaves were rapidly incised with skill, the ends of the leaves pointing downwards and right, with the final result that they give the image a noticable rotational push. The head has abundant traces of a fine clay sediment, light yellowish brown (10YR 6/4).

84. Private collection, c. 2100–1800 BC

Seated statue with monolithic body and no evidence of arms (Type 1a) in massive dark green or black chlorite or steatite (Figure 85)

Body: H 18.20 cm, W (at the base) 20.52 x 19.30 cm. Weight 10950 g. The head is lost. In fairly good condition; the wide, shallow concave socket where the head was set shows traces of minor impacts, suggesting a limited reuse of the statue as an anvil. On the lower surface of the base, there are further traces left by modern tools in a recent reuse of the sculpture.

Judging from the maximum width of the socket (*c.*8 cm), and the proportions of other similar statuettes (see above) the head should have been more than 11 cm high (including the headdress). On the cavity of the head socket, a reddish film might be what remains of an adhesive. In this exceptionally large figure, the well-polished robe-mantle is entirely substituted by an unbroken pattern of finely carved leaves, with the leaf stalk on top. The leaves have from 15 to 20 veins departing from the middle; they are plastically rendered in low relief with great skill, and shown as if turning in a helicoidal clockwise movement. The lap of the sculpture is slightly sloping; where the chest joins the lap, the upper apexes of four leaves are undercut, leaving four angular depressions. It is impossible to know whether or not two of these depressions originally hosted the arms in limestone. At the base of the leaves of the 'robe', there is a fringe of vertical lines in relief, about 3.3 cm high.

86. Private collection, *c.* 2200–1800 BC

Seated statue with monolithic body and no arms (Type 1a) in light green micaceous chlorite (Figures 86–7)

Body: H 5.99 cm, W (at the base) 9.17 x 4.50 cm. Head: H 2.72 cm, W (at the base) 1.66 x 1.19 cm. Weights: body 395 g, head 7 g. The head is made of fine white saccharoid marble. Body and head, although reasonably in proportion, have been assembled from different statuettes.

Uniformly worn on surface, damaged at length along the edges of the base but generally in good condition.

The well-preserved head has a flat sloping occipital area; its flat surface – a unique feature in this collection – extends down to the rear base of the neck. The face is conventional and frontal, with a sub-triangular-oval contour. The triangular nose, without nostrils, is smoothed (possibly after being damaged). The frontal,

almond-shaped eyes are surmounted by incised lines, symmetrically balanced by other incisions on the infra-orbital margins. Both seem to suggest the eyelids, while the superciliary arches are finely expressed in slight volumes. The deep nasolabial sulci end in the mouth commissures. The ears, in relief, end in unusually pointed lobes, and the interiors have no cavities.

The socket is sub-rectangular-oval, shallow and highly worn. It has no evidence of extraneous substances. The back has a slope of around 80° to the plane of the base of the statue. There is no neck girdle or décolleté. The torso is semicircular, with a soft, round contour and a short lap. It is covered by a continuous pattern of deeply carved, thick naturalistic *mèches* in relief, large on the upper chest (where they are almost erased by wear) and longer on the shoulders. The *mèches* in relief are wavy, but the central and most prominent ones under the socket, both in front and on rear, were carved as sharp, larger triangles. The base retains fine linear traces of abrasion left in the last stages of the finishing process.

87

88. Private collection, *c.* 2200–1800 BC (?)

Small seated statue with monolithic body and no arms (Type 1a) in massive, homogeneous black chlorite or steatite (Figure 88)

Body: H 4.39 cm, W (at the base) 4.79 x 4.08 cm. Weight 114 g. The head is lost. Broken in two parts, reassembled; slight damage to the lower edges, otherwise in good condition. On the top, the upper socket for the insertion of the head is semicircular and deep. There are no traces of extraneous substances. The neck girdle is semicircular in front and triangular on the rear, whereas the contrary is more frequently observed. The flat torso and its elongated lap form a body with a distinctive

L-shaped section, unique in the collection. Torso and lap are covered with a continuous pattern of large, flame-like superimposed *mèches* made of lines incised on the flat surface, that closely resemble those on the statuette of Figure 130. Some of the abrasion lines left while finishing the base are concentric.

Small seated statue with
monolithic plain body and
no arms (Type 1a) in massive,
homogeneous black steatite
(Figure 89)

Body: H 4.47 cm; W (at the base) 6.53 x 2.56 cm.
Weight 121.8 g. Headless, unbroken; significant
damage limited to the lower lap, caused by the
prolonged use of the piece as a light hammer.
The base is slightly convex. The socket for
the neck is oval, undamaged and free from
extraneous substances. A shallow neck-girdle
is visible in front. There is no evidence of
attachments for the arms or of any surface
modification suggesting robe patterns.

89. Private collection, *c.* 2200–1800 BC

Statuette with monolithic stretched body and no arms (Type 1b) in dark green chlorite; head in white-cream saccharoid marble, and large fan-shaped headdress in dark green chlorite (same as the body) (Figure 90)

Body: L 18.05 cm, W 13.81 cm, Th 6.52 cm. Head: H 5.81 cm; W (at the base) 32.31 x 31.18 cm; Headdress: H 7.35 cm; max W (on top) 5.53 cm; Th (with rear projection) 3.52 cm. Weights: body 3292 g, head 68.48 g, headdress 73.55 g. The three pieces fit perfectly together, and there is no doubt that they belong to the same original statuette. The figurine is undamaged.

The head, on a slender neck, has a flat, sub-triangular face, featureless and impersonal. The almond-shaped eyes are convex and deeply marked by a double line on the edges. The nose, attached to the orbits, is thin and linear, larger at the root than at the base, without nostrils. Cheekbones are not emphasized. The mouth is an unusual featureless cavity, without lips. The ears have crescent-like auricles, with central holes made by drilling, and ending in a bulging hemisphere that might indicate a lobe. The base of the neck is convex, to fit the deep, round socket in the upper body.

The large fan-like headdress has a trapeze-like form. It is decorated with linear concentric frames and it is skilfully carved in a flat, slightly concave plane (there is no protruding occipital area). The hairdo seems to suggest crossed braids.

The body is massive, and deeply carved with linear designs. While the sides are covered by chevrons hatched in alternate directions, the rear bears vertical grooves. The top is bisected by an axial line incised in the middle, and along the sides runs a wavy frame, with triangles filled with three holes made with a tubular drill (Diam c.0.85 cm). The wavy frames meet a deep hemispherical

90. Private collection, *c.* 2000–1800 BC (?)

neckline. The sloping surface is entirely covered with a pattern of continuous oblique carved grooves on both sides of the central line; all corners are gently and harmoniously bent and accompany the volumetric development of the carved patterns.[206]

Because of its massive look, and the undecorated lower surface of the body, this statuette may be seen as transitional between the types so far reviewed and the peculiar specimens that follow.

91. Private collection, c. 2000–1800 BC (?)

Statuette with monolithic stretched body and no arms (Type 1b) in olive-green chlorite with abundant mica, carved on both sides (upper and lower); head in white-pinkish marble, and large fan-shaped headdress in light green chlorite (Figures 91–2)

Body: L 10.73 cm, W 9.20 cm, Th 3.37 cm. Head: H 3.74 cm, W (at the base) 1.95 x 1.43 cm; Headdress: H 4.86 cm, max W (on top) 4.04 cm, Th (with rear projection) 2.69 cm. Weights: body 515 g, head 16.84 g, headdress 28.85 g. While the head and the headdress fit reasonably (but not perfectly) together, they do not belong to the stretched body. The body is broken into two halves, with further damage on the edge and wide areas along the sides, due to being reused as a craft tool (see below).

The head is almost featureless, with a scarcely defined triangular nose, no eyes, no eyebrows and almost invisible ears in slight relief. The neck is more slender than in other heads, the base convex; and the angle formed by the base of the neck with the axis of the head (*c.* 60°) shows that this head actually belonged to a Type 1b statuette, albeit not this one. So the reassembling seen in Figure 91 only reflects the circumstance of the acquisition and does not have any archaeological implication.

The headdress reproduces a highly formal, fan-shaped hairdo, decorated with a concentric pattern of straight incised lines. This feature stands on a grid-like hairstyle visible on the top and on the rear, possibly representing braids.

The flat, triangular body is bisected by an axial line incised in the middle, both on top and on the base. Along the sides runs a wavy frame of juxtaposed, curvilinear locks, while other wavy incised lines entirely fill the centre. The same pattern is visible on both sides of the stretched body. These formal solutions are highly specific, and there is little doubt that they expressed a well encoded, shared template with precise symbolic and ritual implications. Regarding this type of 'Bactrian princess', Benoit writes:

Les ondulations divergentes de la robe supposée qui se substituent aux habituelles mèches de kaunakès nous incitent à séparer ce type de l'ensemble du corpus, car il est nettement associé au thème de l'eau. [The diverging wave-patterns of the supposed robe, which take the place of the usual *kaunakes mèches*, prompt us to differentiate this type from the main corpus, since it is clearly associated with the theme of water.][207]

And indeed it is difficult to avoid such a supposition.

The body was evidently reused as a percussion tool or an anvil, along both long sides. Damage by striking has changed the round edge into a pointed one, and it was probably the cause of the body's splitting into two large fragments.

93. Private collection, *c.* 2300–2200 BC

Statuette with monolithic stretched body and no arms (Type 1b) in olive-green chlorite with abundant mica, finely carved on both sides, above and below; head in fine white limestone, and finely carved chlorite headdress in light green chlorite (Figures 93–4)

Body: L 19.40 cm, W 15.07 cm, Th 5.20 cm. Head: H 3.77 cm, W (at the base) 3.90 x 3.12 cm; Headdress: H 1.76 cm, Max W (at the base) 2.74 cm; Th (hair projecting on rear) 0.63 cm. Weights: body 2387 g, head 30.82 g, headdress 12.20 g. Although the head apparently fits its socket well, the headdress does not. On the interior of the wig, on the neck, there is a fresh fine abrasion that indicates that the piece has been recently adapted to fit the head. The head, too, might have been slightly ground on the rear of its convex oval base to match the socket. The chlorite of the wig is much finer than that of the body and has a different colour. In short, most probably head and wig are not part of the same original sculpture,

and do not belong to the stretched body. This latter is unbroken and in perfect condition.

The head is a fine sculpture, probably one of the best in the collection (Figure 93). On the large oval base, convex on the lower surface, a short concave neck supports a sub-triangular face. The front is low, the occipital area is convex. The nose is short, triangular when seen in front, with a narrow root and large emphasized nostrils, straight in profile. A pronounced philtrum is visible above fleshy, naturalistic lips, the lower protruding more than the upper. The commissures of the lips are deep and slightly bent downward. The eyes are carefully carved in the form of drops, the point as the lateral commissures, and the lower eyelid outlined. The auricles, in relief, are a crescent surrounding an inner cavity, apparently made with a drill.

The body is a well-sculpted, perfect oval, bisected by a deep axial groove in the middle (Figure 94). The groove and the flocks appear both above and below the base. Both on top and bottom, along both edges runs a wavy

frame covered by a thin, accurate pattern of curvilinear or flame-like flocks, while the centre is entirely covered by other wavy incised lines departing orthogonally from the central groove. In front of the socket, there is an irregular spot measuring about 4 x 2.5 cm where the surface of the 'mantle' is worn and polished, suggesting that something was repeatedly placed in front of the statuette's face, perhaps as an offering. The right side of the stretched body, too, shows a slightly worn surface. A completely flat variant of Type 1b is revealed by a statuette auctioned at Paris in 2014 (whose head, however, is completely out of proportion, and does not belong to the body).[208]

94. Private collection, *c.* 2000–1800 BC (?)

Statuette with monolithic body and arms sculpted in low relief (Type 1c), in green chlorite, homogeneous and compact; head in fine white limestone, with remains of a transparent film on surface; headdress in very dark green chlorite (different from the stone of the body) (Figures 95–7)

Body: H 7.82 cm, W (at the base) 7.71 x 7.33 cm. Head: H 2.99 cm, W (at the base) 2.20 x 1.92 cm. Headdress: H 1.80 cm, max W (on top) 2.13 cm, max Th 2.81 cm. Weights: body 753 g, head 8.51 g, headdress 9.17 g. The head, although damaged at the edge of the neck base, fits very well into the oval depression of the neckline, and the headdress, although looking somehow larger than usual, fits well on the head (in particular, the auricles in relief seem to match exactly the inner lateral cavities on both sides of the headdress). For such reasons, and because of the general similarity to the following statuette (Figures 98–9), acquired together with this specimen, I would consider the three parts (body, head, headdress) as originally belonging to the same figure.

The body is intact and perfectly preserved.

The finely carved head has a flat sloping occipital area and a slender conical neck. The face has no forehead (being entirely covered by the headdress), a rather large triangular nose (damaged), eyes with slightly protruding eyeballs, elongated towards the temples. Eyebrows are suggested by deeply carved arches converging on top of the nose. The lips are fleshy and protruding; the ears two crescents in relief with a minimal inner cavity. From a preliminary study, the head was considered to be of fired steatite (a distinctively Indus base material) because of a transparent glaze or varnish on the neck, behind the ears and on small patches on the face, but an ESEM (Environmental Scanning Electron Microscope inspection) revealed

95. Private collection, c. 2100–1900 BC

96

97

that it is made of limestone; the nature of the varnish or glaze (possibly organic) remains unknown.

The headdress is thick and hemispherical, with hair combed over, or pulled back, and falling in two large locks on the neck; a frontal lock points to the nose. Inside the wig there are abundant traces of a red material, possibly an adhesive.

The upper socket for the head is oval, deep and well formed. Below, the angular décolleté is small and its inner surface is plain and polished. The body is entirely covered with a 'mantle' of *mèches*, finely carved lozenges with concentric angular motifs heading away

from the top ('*mèches imbriquées, couvertes de stries*' ['interlocking *mèches* covered in grooves'], as they are described by Amiet).[209] An unusual feature of the dress of this and the following statuette is that the *mèches* are carved in a reverted fashion, the lowermost being higher in relief than those of the rows above, whereas in other statuettes the relief of the hair tufts decreases from the top downwards.

These lozenges cover both arms in low relief without interrupting the regularity of the general pattern. The right arm seems almost concealed below the dress, while the relief of the left one is slightly higher, and ends in a

set of parallel lines that might suggest a hand stretched towards the lap. The asymmetric posture of the arms recalls the same formal arrangement found in other 'princesses', including those with arms applied in limestone. The geometric pattern of the *mèches* becomes irregular on the shoulders and on the lower left side, near the base. On the lower surface thin abrasion lines are visible following the edge in a round or concentric fashion.

Statuette with monolithic body and arms sculpted in low relief (Type 1c), in compact green chlorite; head in white fine limestone, with substantial traces of a transparent film on surface; long headdress in very dark green chlorite (very similar that of the body) (Figures 98–9)

Body: H 7.32 cm, W (at the base) 7.54 x 5.89 cm. Head: H 3.03 cm, W (at the base) 2.19 x 1.94 cm. Headdress: H 1.84 cm, max W (on top) 2.13 cm; max Th 2.81 cm. Weights: body 538 g, head 9.73 g, headdress, 10.76 g. The head, like in the previous statuette (Figures 95–7), fits precisely into the oval depression of the neckline. Similarly, the headdress, larger than what one would have expected in proportion to the body, fits reasonably well on the head and its deep lateral cavities for the auricles. Body, head and headdress (as argued for the previous specimen) are probably original parts of a single statuette.

The body is intact and well preserved.

Note how the measurements of the head, besides being made of the same material, point to the same stone-manufacturing workshop as the previous statuette. The occipital area with a double slope, the large, deeply carved eyes extending to the temples, the straight triangular nose and protruding lips look very similar to the previous sculpture too. This head, moreover, retains tiny holes for the nostrils. The long, bulging headdress seems parted in the middle, combed over, with a frontal lock pointing downward to the nose, and covers entirely the rear of the neck. In front, the décolleté – angular and internally polished – is also very similar to that of the former statuette, as is the deep oval socket for the head.

The dress, however, is rendered in a quite different way. The tufts or *mèches* are larger and resemble irregular wavy flames (Amiet's *mèches ondulées*),[210] filled with fine concentric lines; those on top (on the chest) are carved at deeper

98. Private collection, *c.* 2100–1900 BC

99

planes, while those on the lap and near the base are in higher relief. The carving is skilled and gives the statuette a lively, animated look.

The hands seem to emerge at different angles from the sleeves (the right oriented to the knee, the left to the lap); both are carved as rectangular projections. Along both arms, on the interior,

two vertical fringes made of oblique traits separate what looks like a mantle from a dress. The manufacturing traces on the lower base are comparable with those already described in the previous figure.

Statuette with monolithic body
and arms sculpted in low relief
(Type 1c), in compact green
chlorite; head in white-pinkish
marble with brown veins; long,
thick headdress in very dark green
chlorite (slightly darker than that
of the body) (Figures 100–1)

Body: H 7.32 cm, W (at the base) 7.96 x 6.66
cm. Head: H 2.82 cm, W (at the base) 2.15 x
2.03 cm. Headdress: H 3.29 cm; max W (at the
base of hair) 2.57 cm; max Th 0.90 cm. Weights:
body 716.5 g, head 10.53 g, headdress, 21.48
g. The head, like in the other two statuettes of
the same type just described, fits well into the
oval depression of the neckline. Furthermore,
the headdress, quite similar to that of the
other two statuettes but somewhat coarser,
fits reasonably well on the head and has two
rectangular lateral cavities for the auricles. In
this case too, body, head and headdress look to
be the original parts of a single statuette.

All parts are intact and well preserved. The
upper socket and the interior of the headdress
show the usual reddish films (plus traces of a
red plasticine). The head has a low forehead, a
flat sloping occipital area and the ears are two
simple crescents in relief. The face is triangular,
elongated. The nose is long, substantial
and straight when observed from the side.
Philtrum and lips are pronounced. The eyes
are deeply carved in almond shapes, and have
marked eyelids; they develop more laterally
than frontally. The headdress, quite similar
to those of the previous two statuettes, is
massive and bulging. The hair is combed over,
curving upwards at the base of the neck, with
two lateral, symmetric tufts combed back from
the centre of the forehead.

The décolleté is V-shaped, pointed in front
and round on the back. The lap is a sloping
platform on which two forearms emerging
from the sleeves rest in symmetric position.
If the statuette originally had hands applied

100. Private collection, c. 2100–1900 BC

in limestone, they have left no material evidence. The mantle is represented by a continuous pattern of well-carved lozenges filled with concentric segments. A peculiarity of this statuette is that the lozenges at the height of both wrists are wide elongated triangles pointing downwards, but merging harmoniously with the surrounding pattern. For the treatment of the *mèches* or tufts, the robe of the last three statuettes resembles that seen on a headless statuette published by Amiet.[211]

101

102. Private collection, *c.* 2300–2200 BC

Fragmentary, headless statuette with monolithic body and arms sculpted in relief (Type 1c?), in compact green chlorite (Figures 102–3)

H 9.50 cm, W (at the base) 9.20 x 6.70 cm (residual maximum width, the original size would have been c.13 cm); W at the waist 6.13 cm. Partial weight: 1244 g.

The body was intentionally broken in two halves by heavily hitting the base in the centre with a pick-like tool (about 15 impacts are still recognizable near the fracture edge). The statuette is largely covered with fine parallel abrasion marks (horizontal to oblique along the lower body); the upper socket, oval and deep, is also uniformly worn in a single direction. The evidence thus points to its reuse, for a long time, as an abrading tool for soft materials. The figure is distinguished by a truncated cone-like lower body, with a double row of long rectangular tufts (the upper

ones superimposed to the edges of the lower ones) ending in a fine fringe, and a horizontal platform for the lap. Each tuft is marked by three vertical, regular incisions.

The lap supported the converging arms, without hands. The vertical armholes are polished, but it is not clear if these surfaces were originally hidden by applied hands or not, also because of the bad state of preservation of the dress surface.

This statuette, in spite of its damaged state, is closely comparable to one of the best-sculpted specimens of the Louvre collection.[212] Like in the Louvre statuette (shown in Figure 80 of this book), what remains of the dress points to three superimposed garments, namely, from the inside out:

- a kind of light shirt or chemise with fine parallel creases, visible on both arms (possibly the representation of a linen one);

- what Benoit calls a dress-mantle (*robe-manteau*), covering the left shoulder, fixed with a belt visible on the back, and falling down in rigid tufts to form the gown;

- over the mantle, a kind of shawl, visible on the right part of the chest with alternating herringbone designs arranged in vertical bands. This shawl seems to have been pulled back on the right shoulder.

On the lower base, together with the aforementioned series of impacts along the edge of the fracture, multiple abrasion marks that follow the edge with variable angles are clearly visible.

104. Private collection, c. 2300–2200 BC

Statuette with monolithic body and arms incised in low relief on the chest (Type 1c), in compact black chlorite, head in fine-grained white limestone, and a finely carved headdress in dark green steatite (Figures 104–7)

H 15.30 cm; W (at the base) 14.07 x 10.79 cm; W at the waist 8.80 cm. Head H 4.65, W 3.29; wig H 2.15; W 3.72. Weights: body 3850 g, head 52 g, headdress 12 g. The three parts of this high quality composite sculpture are doubtless original, and provide a stylistically coherent model.

The forehead is low, and the head has an oval, convex base on which rises a short, sturdy neck with concave contour. The occipital area has a flat sloping surface; the face is oval to pentagonal (the lower corner forming the chin) and, on the whole, it is carved with soft, fleshy features. The nose is short, ending in two short superciliary arches; it looks triangular from the front and straight when observed in profile, with strong nostrils. The eyes with eyelids in relief have a drop-like shape, the points being the lateral commissures, almost on the temples. The philtrum below the nose is small but deep, and the serrated lips end in small commissures and protrude over a weak chin, almost concealed by round, heavy cheeks. The ears are two concentric round crescents in relief ending in short lobes; the cavity is drilled from an angle, thus leaving a tiny, semicircular inner cavity.

Its beautiful near-black steatite headdress is quite similar, in structure, to that described above for Figure 93, but carved even better: note the flat top and the realistic tufts of hair that cover the occipital area (but ending at the height of the ears) forming six or seven large tufts. A thick braid, carved in intricate detail (note the crossed hairdo in the centre) surrounds the upper part of the head. The front is covered by the usual tiara with multiple lines in front, with the beaded rim on top.

The body is well proportioned, with a short slightly sloping lap, and strongly polished. The usual *kaunakes* robe-mantle shows three rows of superimposed thick, stylized tufts in front, ending below in a wide basal strip as a continuous, wide fringe. The rows have subtle variations that are reminiscent of those (more clearly visible) in the statuette of Figures 78-9. The tufts are in form of wide, regular *languettes allongées*, each bearing three vertical, deeply incised lines. The robe-mantle is modified, on the rear, by a prominent *tournure*, that occupies entirely the first three rows of tufts and gives a pleasant movement to the otherwise massive volume of the figure. The torso shows a version of the complicated attire visible in the Louvre statuette of Figure 80,[213] but some details of the patterns in the front remain difficult to explain. This 'princess', in fact, has the same scarf or shawl with alternating herringbone designs arranged in six vertical bands, pulled back on the right shoulder. This garment, on the back, ends in two large lozenges and a grid of square elements. At the opposite end, on the chest (if indeed the cloth is continuous) the shawl maintains one of the herringbone bands, while other two, on the left, take the form of elongated tufts or *languettes*. A possible reconstruction of the shawl is given in the sketch of Figure 107.

On both sides of the torso, positioned symmetrically, two wide arch-like patterns in slight relief emerge from below the robe-mantle, internally filled with a thick sequence of parallel, orthogonal incisions. They could be perceived as stylized arms covered with a wrinkled, light cloth shirt (as proposed for the statuette of Figure 102) and converging on the belly, if not for the fact that two highly simplified hands are clearly recognizable in the upper left corner of the chest in a conflicting position. Note that here the position of the hands is not symmetrical

105

106

(one horizontal, the other pointing upwards), and therefore perhaps reflects the peculiar settings observed in other described specimens. Possibly, this statuette, too, had three superimposed cloths (shirt, mantle and shawl) but their representation, particularly as far as the setting of the arms is concerned, is conceptual, without any presumption of realism.

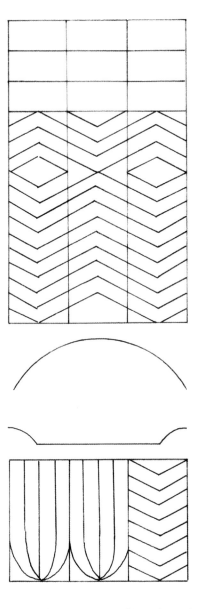

107. Graphic reconstruction of the stole worn by the 'princess' in Figure 104 (the part on the front is below)

108. Private collection, *c.* 2000–1800 BC

Statuette with monolithic body and sculpted lateral arms (Type 1c), in hard, heavy black metamorphic stone, and a head made of fine-grained, compact cream-coloured limestone (with micro-fossils) (Figures 108–10)

Body: H 6.30 cm, W (at the base) 7.54 x 5.93 cm.
Head: H 21.95, W (at the base) 1.85 x 1.79 cm.
Weights: body 533 g, head 8 g. Unbroken, in

perfect condition, and distinguished by a uniform, strong polishing. Head and body are probably original parts of the same statuette. The head has no neck, and looks upwards; there are no eyes, the nose is triangular, slightly curved in profile, with tiny nostrils; the auricles are carved in relief, around a small drilled hole. Lips and chin are delicately carved. Its base is strongly convex.

The arms are suggested by two symmetrical stumps projecting from the shoulders.

The statuette is basically a torso, the lap being suggested by a limited basal projection in the front. The head socket is highly polished like the rest of the figure: a round cavity with a peculiar nipple-like central feature. The décolleté is a V-shaped groove, and ends above what looks like a knot of a double belt in relief. Many clay figurines representing males, in the contemporary iconography of the general region, are similarly stylized.

This small sculpture is highly unusual – both as regards its materials and the forms – and has no comparanda among the artefacts of the same class known so far; although, for the general form and proportions between the head and its base, the head of this figure can be compared to an isolated example in the Ligabue collection, whose facial details, however, are well expressed.[214]

109

110

Seated statuette with monolithic body and sockets for holding arms (Type 1d); body made of dark green chlorite; head (which does not belong) in cream-coloured limestone (Figure 111)

Body: H 11.32 cm, W (at the base) 13.85 x 8.06 cm. Head: H 33.59, W (at the base) 2.48 x 1.75 cm. Weights: body 2888 g, head 15 g. Unbroken, in fair condition, strongly worn and bearing irregular impacts on the surface. Head and body do not belong to the same original statuette, and the reassembly illustrated here has no archaeological grounds.

The base of the head is convex. The head is slightly pear-shaped, with inflated cheeks. It has a convex occipital area, a long nose with large nostrils, curved in profile, above fleshy, naturalistic lips. The eyes are carefully carved, with convex eyeballs and outlined eyelids. The auricles, in relief, surround an inner cavity.

The décolleté is semicircular in front, and angular on the back; both inner surfaces are carefully polished and smooth, except for a semicircular cluster of pecked dots visible in the centre, below the neck. The head socket is oval and deep; the shoulders, beside the socket, are slightly raised. The dress or mantle is drafted with rough, cursory incisions in a pattern of large irregular lozenges, rapidly filled with equally rough parallel segments; but the wear on the surface has almost erased this design, particularly on the back.

On the sloping lap, there are two cone-like sockets manually carved with slow rotatory movements, that originally hosted two arms, presumably in white limestone. The one at the right is slightly higher; the main axis of the two cavities looks asymmetric, probably reflecting an equally asymmetric setting of the arms.

This type of 'Bactrian princess' is apparently one of the most common. A complete specimen, with limestone head and

111. Private collection, c. 1900–1800 BC

arms, was found in grave 2900 at Gonur.[215] Two examples of quite similar sculptures (one at the Louvre, another in a private collection) were published by Benoit.[216] Both appear in similar pictures with a schematic, featureless head without eyes and combine the same rough rendering of the dress with a large décolleté of the same kind. Another statuette like these is at the Metropolitan Museum of Art, New York.[217]

112. Private collection, *c.* 2100–1900 BC

113

Standing 'Bactrian princess', (Type 2) without hands (Figures 112–13)

This exceptional composite statuette, 25.3 cm high, has a garment covered by highly stylized tufts in the lozenge style. It is similar to the other two standing female figures published in this book (Figures 114–19). Like these latter, the Louvre Abu Dhabi statuette combines a very competent carving quality and a good sense of proportion with a partially conventional rendering of the facial features, that does not detract from the general beauty of the sculpture. It was acquired by Louvre Abu Dhabi in 2011, coming from the French market and reportedly belonging to dealers and private collections since 1950.[218]

Standing statuette with
monolithic body and arms in
relief (Type 2) without hands;
body made of green chlorite,
homogeneous and compact; head
in cream-coloured limestone;
headdress in dark green chlorite
or steatite (a finer stone, different
from that of the body)
(Figures 114–16)

Body: H 14.12 cm, W (at the base) 7.52 x
6.10 cm. Head: H 4.71 cm, W (at the base)
4.29 x 3.19 cm. The total height of the three
assembled parts is *c*.18 cm. Weights: body
3162 g, head 58 g, headdress 31 g. The three
parts (headdress, head and body) certainly
belong to the same original sculpture.
Unbroken, in perfect condition.

The body, entirely covered with a single
kaunakes robe-mantle (9.5 rows, from the
girdle to the base) is a solid, slender cylinder,
slightly curved inward at the waist and near
the base; slightly inflated below the neck, it
has an almost imperceptible slope backwards.
The light-coloured head and its headdress on
top, create an elegant contrast that attracts
the eye of the viewer. The face is an oval,
truncated on top by a wide flat surface; on
the back the occipital area has a short slope.
The facial traits are well carved but somewhat
schematic: a triangular nose, with enlarged
nostrils (without holes) ends in the arches of
the eyebrows; the eyes are almond-shaped,
with eyeballs in relief and a tiny drilled hole
for the pupils. The lips in relief are more
realistic: the oral commissures, slightly bent
downwards, give the figure a serious, if not
sad expression. A short cone-like neck joins
the head to a wide, semicircular base with
a strongly convex lower surface that fits
exactly in the wide, deep socket of the
neckline. On the base there are patches of a
bright red material. The headdress represents
an elaborate hairdo – on the top, the hair is

114. Private collection, *c.* 2100–1900 BC

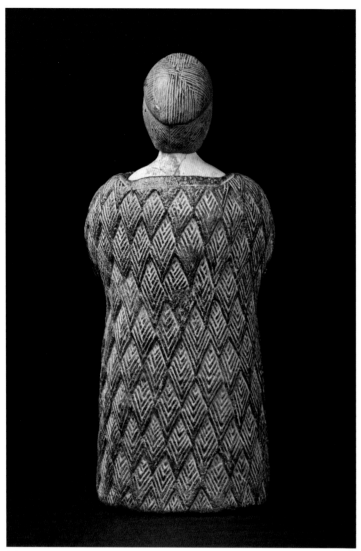

115

116

subdivided in a cross-shaped pattern; the upper part of the wig is bulging, as if retained by an invisible fillet; the lower part is parted, with three symmetrical pointed locks in the front, and two large tresses converging behind the neck. Two deep symmetrical cavities host the ears in relief, distinguished by elongated auricles in high relief with small cavities in their upper part.

The décolleté is a plain, polished undercut girdle, straight on the back and arch-shaped in the front. From this feature a series of radial triangular *mèches* runs down, filled with fine angular, concentric patterns. The carving is flawless, competent and highly standardized.

The arms are in high relief and end in two sleeves, with plain raised borders and flat arm-holes. The left arm was thicker and more prominent than the other. As in other similar cases, it is not clear whether the arm-holes supported hands in a different material or not; the *mèches* in between are perfectly formed, and the surfaces at the end of the sleeves are well polished; however, two shallow grooves between the sleeves and the dress lead us suspect that the space in between actually hosted an applied part. On the base, we find the usual pattern or fine abrasion lines following the inner edge. The only and already famous comparandum for this statuette, and for the following one, is

obviously the standing 'Bactrian Princess' at the Louvre Abu Dhabi (Figures 112–13).

Tall standing statuette with monolithic body and arms in relief (Type 2) without hands; body in green massive chlorite, homogeneous and compact; head in cream-coloured limestone; elongated headdress in dark green chlorite or steatite, very similar to that of the body (Figures 117–19)

Body: H 17.50 cm, W (at the base) 8.76 x 7.24 cm. Head: H 5.40 cm, W (at the base) 4.10 x 3.26 cm. The total height of the three assembled parts is *c.*23 cm. Weights: body 2184 g, head 72 g, headdress 36 g. The three parts (headdress, head and body) probably belong to the same original sculpture.[219] Unbroken, in perfect condition; the hands are lost.

When compared to the previous standing princess (Figures 114–16), the body, similarly covered with a single, continuous *kaunakes* robe-mantle of lozenge-like stylized tufts, is more slender and harmonious, thanks to a distinctive tapering at the waist that gives the lower body a distinctive hourglass shape. Like the previous statuette, this one is slightly inflated below the neck, and imperceptibly slopes backwards.

The light-coloured limestone head rises from a semicircular, convex base quite similar to that of the previous sculpture, but is distinguished by a longer, better balanced cylindrical neck. When refitted to the body, the head of this statuette gently accompanies the backwards sloping of the figure, and seems to be slightly inclined to her left. This latter asymmetry – intentional or not, it is hard to say – gives to the piece a quite peculiar lively, naturalistic look. The slender shape of head and neck is further stressed by the elongated form of the headdress or hairdo, enveloping the rear of the neck down to the joint with the shoulders. On the whole, the volumetric contrast between the body and the head is quite pleasant.

117. Private collection, *c.* 2100–1900 BC

118

The face is a neat oval, and truncated on the top by the wide flat surface made for hosting hair. The facial features are perfectly preserved and delicately sculpted. The eyes, more lateral than frontal, are almond-shaped, and marked only by deeply incised, fine eyelids. The nose is triangular, with minimal nostril holes on the base, and naturalistic philtrum and lips which are carved with notable skill. The simple ears in relief have marked lobes, and their inner cavities were made by drilling on top, and by incising a short vertical line below.

The headdress, for its elongated shape, resembles that seen in Figure 101, but looks quite elaborate. The hair tapers at the base of the neck, where it forms an angular swelling. It is combed, from the top, in a cross-like hairdo of wide strands, and fixed in the front with two diverging braids that might continue symmetrically in the back. Three fillets or fine braids, at the centre of the three tufts, seem to converge on the back in a single vertical feature. The rendering is fine and accurate; formally, it closely resembles the style of the hair of the *balafré* series in Figures 156, 160 and others. The internal surface, like in other cases, retains traces of a red film.

The *kaunakes* robe-mantle that covers the body without interruption was carved with 14 rows of spirally-arranged lozenge-like tufts or *mèches* filled with fine angular patterns, to which we should add a single row of smaller triangles in slightly higher relief, hanging from the neckline. Thus, on average, the tufts of this piece are smaller and finer than those of the previous standing statuette. The intricacy of the carving did not conceal, in this case, some expedients and accidents of the carving process. First of all, the first row of *mèches* hanging from the neck area was planned and executed by the stonecutter(s) by incising a continuous field around the girdle; its limits were not removed by subsequent work. Such triangular features are well carved in front, but quite clumsy on the back; and there is

119

Exactly as observed, the left arm, preserved up to a plain and rounded sleeve-edge, was thicker and more prominent than the right one. The match suggests that this feature was not casual, but specifically made for holding hands formed in a symmetrical position (probably the left hand was clutched above the right one). The inner surface of the end of the left sleeve has an ancient notch that might be due to a fracture (but we should suspend judgement on its nature).

The two standing statuettes presented for the first time in this book and the one at the Louvre Abu Dhabi (Figures 112–13) are very similar and form a coherent sub-group from a stylistic viewpoint.

an evident uncertainty in the way the upper row of triangles was joined and matched to the first row of lozenges immediately below. Like in other cases, the geometry of the *kaunakes* robe was planned by tracing on the figure's volume a spiral-like net of intersecting lines, but in some critical points (particularly under the elbows and at the shoulder joints) geometric reference was lost and the craftsperson had to arrange the inner filling how he/she could (i.e., chaotically). In short, comparing the two statuettes, the carving project of the second was definitely finer and more ambitious, but somehow less accurate.

Seated statuette in green, homogeneous chlorite, made of two superimposed parts (chest and lower body) (Type 3a), with a head in yellowish, red-veined fine limestone (Figures 120–1)

Body: H (total, the two parts assembled) 7.35 cm; H of the lower body, 3.06 cm, H of the chest, 4.21 cm; W (at the base) 8.89 x 5.20 cm. Head: H 3.78 cm; W (at the base) 2.34 x 2.26 cm. Weights: lower body 298 g, upper body 288 g, head, 20.70 g. The head does not belong to the body, but in terms of size and proportions it cannot be far off the original.

The base of the head is round and convex. The chest is fixed to the lower body by a slot joint that allows the upper part to slide frontally on the lower one. The head, highly polished, is finely carved; it has a smooth sub-triangular contour, with softly fashioned facial details in front view. The nose is wide, triangular and rather flat; the eyes are almond-like, with upper eyelids and wide eyebrow arches. The small lips are naturalistically rendered. The ears, on the contrary, have no anatomical reference: they are round solid projections, evidently meant to be out of sight in order to support a lost headdress.

The head socket is round and deep. The tufts of the *kaunakes* robe-mantle are suggested by a linear pattern of large lozenges, bisected by a middle line in form of large 'leaves'. Four of these leaves begin at the upper socket (in front, on the rear and on the shoulders). The perfect match of the lines on the chest and the lower body reveals that the motif was carefully incised on the two assembled parts.

The decoration on the back cannot be made out, because here the surface is almost entirely covered by a post-depositional film of copper carbonates showing that the statuette, in the grave, was probably contained in a copper or bronze container. Near the base, a ring of copper or bronze remained soldered by such corrosion films to the stone. In the socket, the same products of corrosion sealed a thin film of a bright red material (Munsell 7.5YR 5/6) that might have been the adhesive originally used to fix the head to the chest.

120. Private collection, *c.* 2200–1800 BC

121

122. Private collection, *c.* 2200–1800 BC

Upper part (chest) of statuette in green chlorite with diffuse darker mottling, originally made of two superimposed parts: chest and a lower body, now lost (probably Type 3a), with a head in white saccharoid limestone or marble (Figure 122)

Body: H: 2.90 cm, W (at the base) 7.47 x 2.18 cm; Head: H 2,76 cm, W (at the round, convex base) 1.69 x 1.65 cm. Weights: body 109 g, head 8.44 g. The head evidently does not belong to the body, therefore the assemblage illustrated has no archaeological basis.

The neck is cone-shaped, base of the head is round and slightly convex. The sculpture (chest) retains abundant residues of a light brown (Munsell 7.5YR 6/4) sediment; below the chest there are traces of a modern, light-coloured plastic substance.

The head, flat on top, has worn surfaces; the face is elongated, with a long prominent nose, curved when seen in profile, slightly inflated cheeks and prominent eyes. The ears, in high relief, are large and round, carved on the interior with round patterns.

The head socket is oval, the décolleté is narrow and limited to a shallow girdle, wider and more curved in front than on the back. What remains of the robe-mantle (on the chest section) was decorated with *mèches* of various forms and filled with different kind of deep incised lines in alternating directions. Probably the forearms were sculpted in low relief, like in the following statuette (Figures 123–5). A very similar torso (damaged) was found in a room of the palace of Gonur North.[220]

Seated statuette in a light green, homogeneous chlorite with blackish inclusions, made of two superimposed parts (chest and lower body) (Type 3a), with applied head and arms made of fine-grained white limestone, and a headdress made of the same stone as the two body parts (Figures 123–5)

H (total, the three parts assembled): c.14.00 cm. H of the lower body, 6.34 cm, W (at the base) 17.07 x 17.04 cm. H of the chest, 5.37 cm; W (at the base of the torso) 9.14 x 3.75 cm. Head: H 3.25 cm; W (at the base) 2.45 x 0.98 cm. Headdress H 3.20, W 3.01. Weights: upper body 352.4 g, lower body 2187 g, head 18.61 g, headdress, 18.05 g. Complete and in good condition, the surface being slightly and uniformly worn. The four body components are original parts of the same figure.

The base of the chest enters the lower body through a shallow slot of the same form. The head, partially flattened on top, and with a limited slope on the occipital area, is finely carved with fully naturalistic, even if stereotyped, features. The face is oval, cut and crowned by a low front, almost entirely covered by the fringe of the headdress. The elongated almond-shaped eyes have deep marked eyelids, around bas-relief eyeballs where tiny drilled pupils create the effect of a staring gaze. The cheeks are softly fashioned, and at the base of the strong nose, triangular in front and curved in profile, the nostrils are emphasized. Both the philtral ridge and the mentolabial sulcus are rendered with great skill in the proper proportions. The cylindrical neck gives way to a semicircular and convex base that fits its socket exactly.

The headdress, with deep lateral cavities for hosting the ears, is shaped like a helmet – the hair being combed, from top, in a cross-like hairdo, fixed on front with a thick angular

123. Private collection, c. 2200–2000 BC

fillet, and covering the neck with an angular bulge.

Viewed from the side, the sculpture has an L-shaped profile, with the lower part much thicker than the chest. This latter is trapeze-like: on the sides, the vertical arms, sculpted in low relief, end above the lower body in two shallow semicircular cavities. The undercut, pointed décolleté, shallow and carefully polished, is an inverted triangle in front, while on the rear is a simple girdle.

The lower body is a flat semicircular block, whose flat side corresponds to the rear of the statuette. The edges, on the rear, are marked by narrow bands in high relief carved with conventional chevrons. The dress, representing a single, continuous *kaunakes* robe-mantle of angular tufts, is rendered as curvilinear, flame-like *mèches*. Those on the chest and on the lower body were separately carved, but are partially adjusted, in front as well as on the back, by the match of the central *mèches*. Both on the flat rear and on the lap, the flaming *mèches* radiate from the centre towards the edges, in a visually fascinating movement that strongly contrasts with the rigid posture of this statuette.

It is not clear how the assembled arms in fine-grained, white limestone were materially attached and fixed to their cavities or sockets on the lap. The angles of the limbs, at the elbow, reveal their original anatomical setting: the right arm pointing to the knee, with the hand clutched; the other, stretched open on the lap with the palm downwards, fingers held together. Some statuettes of this type had a single foot emerging from their lower volume.[221] On the base there are the usual marks left around the edge by the last stages of the finishing process.

Some of the finest known examples of Bactrian princesses belong to Type 3a. In its general construction, with the flaming centripetal *mèches*, the form of the hairdress (even if hair is combed differently) and the band of chevrons in relief on the edges of the

back, this statuette closely resembles other high-quality composite sculptures that have appeared on the antiques market,[222] some of which eventually reached large private collections.[223]

The long *mèches* radiating from the neck girdle resemble those of the *kaunakes* robe of the sitting 'princesses' of the Persepolis silver vase,[224] whose body volumes, too, are divided into two superimposed parts. Also quite similar is the dress of a tiny silver female image (the terminal of a pin) in the Al-Sabah collection,[225] as well as that of another famous female 'princess' in a *kaunakes* reproduced as stamp-finial of another silver pin, discovered in one of the Gonur graves.

In its general form of being two blocks, along with the wig and the partially wavy *mèches*, this statuette also resembles a 'princess' auctioned at Paris in 2014.[226] The same band carved in relief along the rear edge also appears on the bottom part of the chlorite statuette buried with other artefacts in the Quetta Hoard.[227] The dating hypothesized for this composite statuette, and others of the same type, follows that proposed by Daniel Potts for the Persepolis silver vase: 'shortly before or around 2100 BC, within the Early Kaftari period (*c.*2200–1900 BC) at Tal-e Malyan, as defined by the excavator, W. M. Sumner'.[228]

125

126. Private collection, *c.* 2100–1900 BC

Seated statuette in a green, homogeneous chlorite, made of two superimposed parts (chest and lower body) (Type 3a), with applied head made of presumably banded pinkish white limestone, and a headdress made of the same stone as the two body parts (Figures 126–8)

H (total, the three parts assembled): *c.*14.00 cm. H of the lower body, 6.34 cm, W (at the base) 17.50 x 10.76 cm. H of the chest, 5.40 cm; W (at the base of the torso) 8.10 x 2.75 cm. Head: H 2.3 cm; W (at the base) 1.35 x 0.98 cm. Weights: upper body, 352.4 g, lower body, 2187 g, head, 18.61 g, headdress, 18.05 g. Complete and in good condition, the surface being slightly and uniformly worn. The four body components are original parts of the same figure.

The torso rests on the lower body without a socket or cavity; the contact is enhanced by a polished, worn surface with the usual traces of a red substance or sediment. Without a glue or mastic the two parts would have not stayed

put. The head, rather worn on the surface, has a double slope: flat, slightly oblique on top, and stronger on the occipital area, with stereotyped features. The face is sub-triangular with a low front, laterally covered by the fringe of the fine headdress. The eyes, expanded to the temples and touching the ears, are shaped like strongly bulging almonds. Stylistically, the simplified conventional traits of the face – but for the total absence of the mouth – share some of the features of the piece illustrated in Figure 116. The neck, distinguished by an elegant concave profile, rises on an oval, convex base that fits perfectly in its deep oval socket. Below, the well-polished undercut décolleté forms a rectangular opening in the front. The headdress, as in other cases, represents hair combed, from top, in a cross-like style, fixed in front with a wide braid-like hairdo parted in the middle, and covering the neck, down to its join to the shoulders, with an angular swelling. On the top, the hair shows the cross-like pattern observed in other specimens.

Like the previous 'princess' (Figures 123–5), when viewed laterally, the assembled image has an L-shaped contour, but the lower body is much thicker, in proportion to the size of the chest. The body is sub-vertical in front, and sloping with an angle of around 70° on the sides.

The lower body is thick, semicircular and entirely covered by a *kaunakes* robe-mantle of tufts, rendered as lozenge-like, internally hatched *mèches*. On the statuette's left side, the edge between the flank and the rear is emphasized by a vertical band in higher relief, whose original decoration, which interrupts the lozenges of the mantle, is now lost.

What renders this image unique is the sculptural pattern finely carved on the torso. While there is no hint of the arms (except for the slightly higher relief of the lateral edges), it is easy to recognize in its radial arrangement a sequence of wheat spikes, ending in a series of converging barbs, alternating with schematic trees. These latter, in higher relief, as if they were imagined as being in the foreground, are distinguished by a central winding log from which depart sequences of lateral symmetric, slightly curved branches. The general shape is reminiscent of cypresses or similar trees. The fact that the trees appear truncated on top seems to mean that the head of the anthropomorphic image (that takes the place of the trees' tops) would correspond to a sacred mountain peak.

127

128

129. Private collection, *c.* 2200–1800 BC

Massive seated statuette in rose quartz, made of two superimposed parts (chest and lower body) (type 3a), with a head made of fine pinkish-brown quartzite (Figure 129)

H (total, the three parts assembled): 27.36 cm. H of the lower body 12.94 cm, W (at the base) 17.35 x 15.35 cm. H of the chest 9.24 cm, W (at the base) 9.65 x 9.10 cm. Head: H 5.85 cm, W (at the base) 3.33 x 3.05 cm. Weights: lower body 9050 g, upper body 1862 g, head 119 g. Total Weight, 11.031 kg. Complete and in perfect condition. However, the head does not fit precisely in the upper socket and probably belonged to another sculpture. The original head should have been slightly larger; the assemblage illustrated therefore has no archaeological value, but the general look of the original statue was probably not far from it.

The base of the chest fits into the lower body through a shallow square depression of the same form. The head has a square face, with a sloping front, and sunken, deeply carved eyes, with eyelids and bulging eyeballs (the left one larger than the other). The nose is triangular from the front, curved when seen from the side, with a flat nasal base and no nostrils. The cheekbones, rather than cheeks, are emphasized; the chin and the mentolabial sulcus are in evidence, while the serrated, wide mouth is distinguished by the slight cavities of the oral commissures. The auricles are crescents in relief, closing onto themselves, and ending in a small hemispherical dot; above this latter, an inner tiny hole was made by drilling. The neck is cylinder-like and the round base is flat rather than convex.

In this sculpture, like in others of the collection, it is hard to say whether decorative motifs represent actual garments, or are just an abstract decoration. The lower body is a heavy square block with carefully rounded edges and corners; on three sides, it is covered by a pattern of alternate chevrons, filled with large, deeply carved parallel lines. In front, a similar inverted triangle hangs from the top; it is framed by a V-shaped band filled with a motif of curvilinear leaves, whose naturalistic rendering conflicts with the rigid geometry of the surrounding chevrons. The band of leaves ends, on both extremities, with a simple triangular chevron.

The upper cavity, or socket, that hosts the chest part was evidently made by drilling vertically the corner points with a copper tubular drill (Diam c.2.8–2.9 cm), as revealed by the typical undercutting of the edge of the hole below the perimeter of the frame.

The upper part (the chest section) is a smaller block, truncated pyramidal in form, that has a richer, more complex decorative pattern. In the front, the two arms in relief that converge towards the centre are prominent: they end in two flat surfaces bearing variously preserved oblique incisions that might indicate fingers. The chest is covered by three vertical bands filled with alternate chevrons, centred on a diamond or lozenge at the height of the navel. Below the arms, in front, leaves and triangles alternate in the same band; as on the bottom, a central diamond and four leaves are included in the same, larger lozenge. Both arms seem to be enfolded or covered by motifs of elegant, wavy leaves, extending from the shoulders to the end of the sleeves below which, at the waist, emerge two main, large chevrons that echo the main geometric theme of the lower body. The whole structure suggests at different levels, and with different combinations, a fundamental opposition between the natural, wavy aspect of the leaf patterns with the static geometry of the larger chevrons.

Given the noticeable hardness of rock crystal and quartz, this sculpture, in technical terms, is the most demanding and ambitious of the sculptures we present. The use of corundum as an abrasive in this stage of dressing the blocks, as well as drilling and carving the rest of the patterns, is highly probable.

Seated statuette with body originally made of three superimposed parts (the lowermost missing) and no arms (Type 3b) in green chlorite or chloritoschist, rich in mica, the head of fine white limestone, badly preserved; and a shallow headdress in a similar but darker stone (Figure 130)

Lower surviving body part: H 5.58 cm, W (at the base) 12.81 x 12.13 cm. Chest: H 6.90, W (at the base) 6.13 x 5.61 cm. Head: H 3.09 cm, W (at the base) 2.35 x 2.09. Headdress: H 3.24 cm, W 2.11 cm, Th 11.46 cm. Weights: lower part of the body 1768 g, upper part 524 g, head 13.68 g, headdress 9.47 g. Well preserved, with minor localized damage to the body. The two surviving parts of the body come from the same original statuette; the lower piece has a large (about 2.24 cm wide) transversal slot similar to that designed for the insertion in the statuette of Figures 120-1, but carved in the opposite direction. The head and the wig have probably been assembled from two other different statuettes. Thus the assemblage illustrated reflects only an antiquarian association and the circumstances of the acquisition.

The head, worn and very damaged, is made of a soft, fine-grained white limestone. The facial features are erased and hardly recognizable. Ears, as in many other cases, were probably in low relief. A short, cone-like neck joins the head to a semicircular base with a flat lower surface. The headdress is long and shallow, and fits poorly with the rounded top of the limestone head; on the rear, like a veil, it bears an inverted V-like motif, and it is crowned by a rectangular top with small protrusions.

The body was made of two – or more probably three – superimposed parts of decreasing size. These parts are described as parallelepipeds with rounded corners; in the lower one, the lap is suggested by a more marked frontal slope. In both the surviving

130. Private collection, c. 2200–1800 BC

body parts, the flaming *mèches* were carefully carved with thin incised line on the blocks' flat surfaces, as in the statuette of Figure 88. They are flame-like features pointing downwards, that start at the girdle and the lap, well planned on the respective volumes, and carefully incised, filling them with multiple concentric wavy lines. On the shoulders and on the corners of the lower block, such flame-like *mèches* are substituted by leaf-like designs. Quite similar statuettes were found in the

settlement and in the graveyard of Gonur.[229] Furthermore, in both parts the residual space between the *mèches* and the base of the pieces was filled with parallel oblique lines. The chest fits precisely on the lower piece through a shallow quadrangular cavity. The upper socket is oval and relatively deep.

Seated elongated statuette made of three parts (lower legs, lap, chest) and other applied features (Type 3c). The three body parts are made of the same homogeneous, dark green chlorite; the head, in white limestone (which does not belong to the same statuette) (Figure 131)

H of the lower part (the legs) 11.33 cm, W (at the base) 7.35 x 2.80 cm. Lap: H 9.05 x 8.87 cm, Th 4.15 cm. Chest: H 7.03 cm, W (at the base) 8.57 x 3.50 cm. Head: H 3.36 cm, W (at the base) 2.27 x 1.79 cm. Weights: legs 502 g, middle section (lap) 755 g, torso/chest 534 g, head 10.53 g.

The head does not belong, but, at least in terms of size, the fit is reasonable; it has a slightly sloping occipital area; the sub-triangular face has no eyes, just a simple triangular nose (damaged), above a thin, linear serrated mouth. The crescents of the ears, in high relief, surround holes made with a tiny drill point and later enlarged by carving. The neck is cylindrical, with concave sides, above a semicircular base with a flat lower surface.

The three parts of this statuette are covered by a continuous *kaunakes* robe-mantle of lozenge-like *mèches*, the *mèches* internally filled with concentric angular motifs. The distribution of the *mèches* is carefully planned and carved so that they develop without breaks from one assembled part to the lower one. Lap and legs form a mortise-and-tenon joint, while the chest fits in the rear of the lap. On the inner surface of the mortise, corresponding to the right knee, there is a flat, round patch of an extraneous whitish material that might have been part of the mortar or adhesive used to fix one part to the other. The back of the legs, and the bottom of the lap are plain. The décolleté is a plain, polished girdle with a raised edge, curved on the rear, and V-shaped in front. The well-formed socket is

131. Private collection, *c.* 2100–1900 BC

oval. A statuette with a similarly built body was auctioned at Paris in June 2003; another, particularly beautiful and with a different joint at the knees, was auctioned also at Paris in December 2007.[230]

Seated elongated statuette made of three parts (legs, lap, chest) endowed with rectangular mortise and tenon joins, and other applied features (Type 3c), without arms. The three body parts and the wig are made of the same dark green chlorite; the head is in white crystalline limestone, the feet in a kind of banded alabaster-like translucent stone (Figure 132–3)

H of the lower part (the legs) 10.32 cm, W (at the base) 5,04 cm. Lap: W 8,02 cm, L 7,52 cm. Chest: 5,41 cm, W (at the base) 6,50 cm. Head: H 2,95 cm, W (at the base) 2,51 cm. Weights: legs 414.5 g, middle section (lap) 580.2 g, torso 312.9 g, head 13.6 g, wig 18.2 g.

All parts of this exceptional image, different from the previous sculpture, are certainly original; but a closer look demonstrates that the 'princess' was modified, to an unknown extent, in ancient times. This is revealed by some damage in the edge of the lower part (just above the sockets for the feet), distinguished by a darker smooth patina and by a rough and defective re-carving of the lozenges of the dress. A spot of the same darker patina, that slightly deepened the oval neck socket, shows that even the statuette's fine head might have been replaced in ancient times. This statuette ultimately tells us that these images might have been used and expediently modified for a long time even during their former life in the Bronze age.

The slender, elegant body proportions are matched by the fine features of the head and wig. The head has a flat, horizontal top; the face is visually engaged by wide, staring almond-like eyes, above a serrated mouth with protruding lips. The ears are placed in an unusually high position. The neck is cylindrical, with concave sides, above a semicircular base with a convex lower surface that fits its modified socket perfectly. The wig, moreover,

132. Private collection, c. 2100–1900 BC

is quite elaborate. It has two frontal crescent-like features, the lowermost being (almost certainly) a crown with a central floreal pattern. Two hair bands depart from the front to close the vertical hairdo at the rear. The feet are well sculpted with realistic, sinuous contours.

The continuous *kaunakes* robe-mantle bears the recurrent lozenge-like *mèches* filled with concentric angular motifs that develop without gaps from one assembled part to the lower one. The décolleté is a threefold concentric girdle with a well-carved radial pattern of triangles. The facial details of this statuette, as well as its lozenges, closely resemble the monolithic standing sculptures presented for the first time in this book. The radial pattern of the décolleté is quite similar to that worn by the standing female figure on the famous 'Persepolis' silver vessel (see Potts 2008) and reinforces the impression that these stylistic features might go back to the 21st century BC.

133

Large head with elongated face and naturalistic traits in fine white limestone (Figure 134)

H 5.66 cm, W (at the base) 3.55 x 3.24 cm. Weight: 68.2 g. This small sculpture retains traces of a yellowish brown sediment (10YR 5/4).

The n eck is long and cylindrical. The upper part of the head is slightly flattened: on top, the surface is worn by the prolonged contact with a headdress, now lost. The base of the head is oval, slightly convex. The head is finely carved; when observed from the front, the facial contour is elongated and resembles a figure of eight, narrowed in the centre at the height of the cheekbones. The nose is a narrow triangle, strongly curved in profile, with marked lower nostrils made with a thin drill point. The upper part of the face is dominated by the excessively large lateral eyes, with thick eyelids and bulging scleras. Below, the eyes are downplayed by the inflated cheeks and protruding mouth, linked to the base of the nose by a strong philtrum and labionasal sulcus. The ears are fashioned as round auricles in relief, ending into hemispherical bulging dots that (unnaturally) stand for the earlobes. The central cavity of both ears was made by drilling. For the naturalistic style and the elongated facial traits, this head is comparable with that of another composite image (Figure 78) and should be considered one of the oldest here presented.

134. Private collection, c. 2300–2200 BC

Head in Neo-Sumerian (?) style, in fine-grained pinkish limestone or saccharoid marble, with fine brownish veins (Figure 135)

H 5.74 cm, W (at the base) 3.88 x 3.02 cm. Weight: 64.2 g. A remarkable small masterpiece of Bactrian art, this head is distinguished by the wide forehead and oval contour of the face, on a long, cylindrical neck with concave sides. The base is sub-rectangular, with rounded edges, and a convex lower surface. Damaged in recent times by a flaking impact on the right side of the base.

The top is round and its surface is slightly worn by the contact with the lost headdress. The eyes are frontal and proportioned to the other facial features; eyelids and palpebral fissures are carved unusually finely and with greater care than normal. Two wide orbital arches converge at the bridge of a thin, short nose, almost straight in profile and emphasized with wide nostrils and deeply incised alae. The details of the mouth and lips are rendered with extraordinary anatomical attention, marking the philtrum, cupid's bow and mentolabial sulcus, as well as the lateral commissures of the lips. Even the 'laughter lines' or labiomental sulci are carefully rendered through a soft modelling of the facial volumes. The ears are large and prominent; the auricles are large crescents in high relief, with little or no evidence of the earlobes; the interior is rendered with two drilled cavities, one on the upper part that stands for the triangular fossa of the antihelix, the lower one, deeper and more visible, for the lower part of the concha.

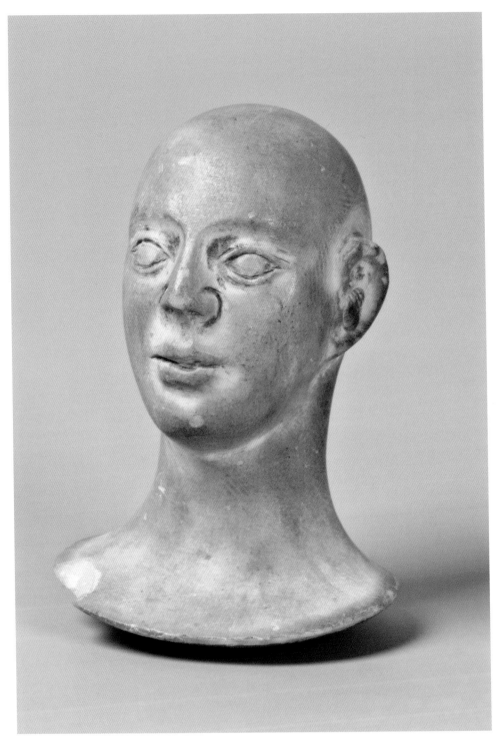

135. Private collection, c. 2100–2000 BC

136. Private collection, *c.* 2200–1800 BC

Head in a yellowish-white calcite, with fine, parallel red-brownish veins (Figure 136)

H 5.12 cm; W (at the base) 2.88 x 2.53 cm; Weight: 64.2 g.

The darker veins run vertically, along plains parallel to that of the face. This head has been intensively reused as a light hammerstone, damaging the upper part of the face, the region of the temples, the occipital area, and (to a lesser extent) the lower face of the base. This latter is oval, almost flat, and supports a short neck with a tapering contour; hese areas are now covered, to a large extent and with variable intensity, with a diffuse pattern of pecking impacts. The impression is that the head was used as a launched (indirect?) percussion tool in a well-controlled craft technique, possibly in a lapidary or jewellery workshop. Dating such phase of reuse is impossible. In spite of the damages, the face was oval, elongated, with schematic features (almond-like frontal eyes, large trapezoidal nose without nostrils, wide mouth with scarcely defined lips and commissures bent downwards). The ears look like spirals in relief, whose inner cavities are substituted by bulging hemispherical dots.

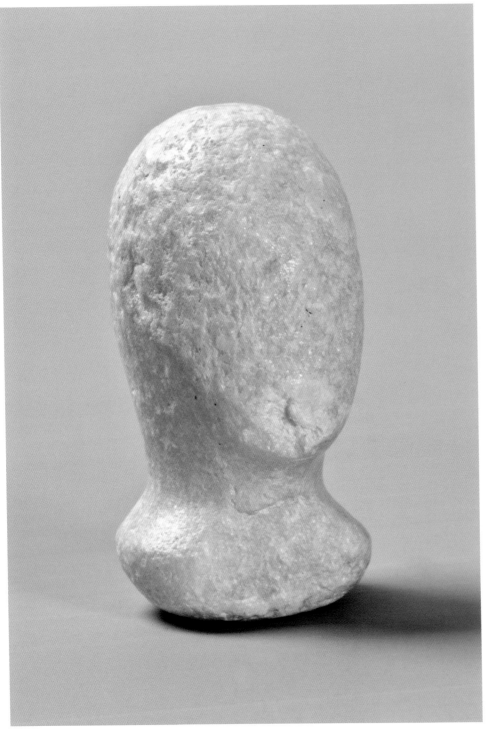

Fragmentary head in yellowish-white calcite (Figure 137)

H 4.63 cm; base Diam 4.64 cm. Weight: 41.8 g.

Very similar to the previous specimen (Figure 136) in terms of general residual form, base material and conditions of reuse, this head is more intensively worn out: the pecked surfaces have completely cancelled the face, the sides and the back, and the edges of the base, reduced by consumption to an oval form with blunt edges. Below the chin, there is a large impact fracture, showing that the natural banding of the rock followed the same orientation described for Figure 136. The only anatomical elements still visible are the crescents in relief of the auricles. For the sketchiness of the facial features, these final statuette heads can be compared with a head published by Ligabue and Rossi Osmida.[231]

137. Private collection, c. 2200–1800 BC

Head in white saccharoid limestone (Figure 138)

H 3.75 cm; base Diam 2.19 x 1.86 cm. Weight: 21.8 g.

This head is asymmetrically worn, more intensively on the right side, where details of the eyes, lips and ear are abraded. The forehead, on the same side, is also worn or even pecked, and it cannot be excluded that, like other heads in the collection, this piece was occasionally used as a light hammerstone. The face has the form of an inverted egg, elongated, with naturalistic features. The nose, without nostrils, is a wide triangle, soft and rounded when see from the sides. The mouth had well defined lips protruding on a well fashioned chin. The ears are two wide crescents in relief, with thicker lobes; the interior is marked by two superimposed drilled cavities (the upper ones for the triangular fossa of the antihelix, and the lower ones, deeper and more visible, for the lower concha). Both holes within the right auricle seem to have been made with two drilling steps, resulting in joined, slightly larger holes.

138. Aron collection, London, *c.* 2200–2000 BC

139. Private collection, *c.* 2300–2000 BC

Finely carved headdress in dark green chlorite with a tiara (Figure 139)

H 2.42 cm, W 2.53 cm, max Th *c.*0.5 cm. Weight: 10.5 g.

On the interior there are traces of two different carving tools in copper or bronze, one similar to a burin, another leaving sequences of fine parallel lines on the surface. The flat top is covered by realistic, spiral-like tufts that fall down on the back. The tiara that crowned the forehead is the same encountered in other two images (Figures 138, 140), with multiple festoon-like lines in front and a fine beaded rim on top. This type of hairdo and/or crown was linked to highly naturalistic heads and possibly belonged to the earliest specimens of the 'princesses'.

Finely carved headdress in dark green chlorite with a tiara (Figure 140)

H 2.42 cm, W 2.53 cm, max Th *c*.0.5 cm.
Weight: 12.2 g.

This is a fine artwork. On the interior there are traces of a thin carving tool in copper or bronze. The top is flat; the hair is animated by realistic, spiral-like forms that fall down on the back in eight distinct tufts. The front is covered by the same kind of tiara as the statuette in Figures 83, 93, 104–6, incised with multiple lines in front and bearing on top a double beaded rim, perhaps a crown.

140. Private collection, *c.* 2300–2000 BC

A cap or headdress in light green chlorite with darker mottling, with a thick braid-like feature (Figure 141)

H 1.54 cm, W 3.42 cm, max Th (on rear) c.1.09 cm. Weight: 19.8 g.

This type of headdress, not otherwise encountered in this collection, seems to represent a kind of round cap encircled by a braid of cloth or leather (the hypothesis that it represents human hair is unlikely). The two braids seem to be tied in the front (where they become thicker) with a knot. A Type 3a princess published by Freeman, without eyes, and with the socket of a lateral protruding foot, seems have the same hairdo, but carved in much finer detail.[232]

141. Private collection, c. 2300–2200 BC

A headdress in light green micaceous chlorite distinguished by an upper cap bearing a large flower-shaped pattern, and a lower part with vertical parallel lines (Figure 142)

H 3.60 cm, W 2.35 cm, max Th (on rear) 0.82 cm. Weight: 13.6 g.

The archaeological significance of this wig goes well beyond its apparent formal simplicity. In fact, its front and sides were doubtless extensively and somewhat grossly ground or filed in ancient times, almost certainly for readapting the piece to a second statuette. This is another important piece of evidence that also in the protohistoric past some parts of the composite statuettes could have been recycled and shifted from one sculpture to another. The interior bears the marks left by a flat copper/bronze chisel, *c.*5 mm wide.

142. Private collection, *c.* 2000–1800 BC

Fan-shaped headdress in dark green chlorite with white bands (Figure 143)

143a. Private collection, c. 2000–1800 BC (?)

143b

H 4.28 cm, W 3.55 cm, max Th 2.60 cm (from the front to the back). Weight 22.7 g.
This large fan-like headdress, formally identical to that of Figures 90–1 has a trapeze-like form. The fan, that bears linear concentric frames both in front and on the rear, is fixed vertically on a protruding occipital area with an elaborate headdress. This latter shows a head covered with a sequence of parallel vertical braids, skilfully rendered in a curved perspective, and fixed on the back by other thicker crossed braids. The comparison with the statuette of Figure 90 and other available examples suggests that the original figurine would have been monolithic, stretched, and had a head with highly schematic facial features.

Monolithic stretched body of a statuette without arms; the head is missing (Figure 144)

Body: L 11.56 cm; W 10.12 cm; Th 5.02 cm.
Weight: 446 g.

Unbroken. Although formally belonging to Type 1b, this sculpture is set apart from the others by its quite unusual base material (bitumen, probably modelled after heating, in plastic state). The body resembles a small 'brick' with rounded edges, trapezoidal in contour (the side proximal to the socket being narrower than the opposite one). The upper recess or socket is sub-rectangular, with a slightly raised edge and a peripheral groove. The modelling process is revealed by sequences of irregular, arch-shaped blunt spatula-like traces on the rear and possibly on the left side. Although the process of sculpting may have left some fine parallel striations on the surface, none is ascribable to cutting; consequently, a reduction technology is ruled out.

While the rear, front and lower surfaces are plain, the upper one and the sides bear an intricate design of stripes, triangles and a single central lozenge traced on the material in plastic state, and filled with sequences of parallel lines.

A central, axial plain band links this stretched body with those of the statuettes of Figures 90-2 and 94; while two symmetrical hatched bands starting at the socket and reaching the lower corners of the sides replicate, from a cognitive viewpoint, the construction of the decoration sculpted on the sculpture in rose quartz (Figure 129). Because of these structural analogies, we are inclined to consider this piece authentic.

144. Private collection, *c.* 2000–1800 BC (?)

Stylistic evolution of the Bactrian princesses: a preliminary hypothesis

So far, the composite statuettes have been classified following a rudimentary subdivision based on the structure and joints of their body.

However, because *'elles ont été dispersées progressivement en assez grand nombre, avec une séduisante diversité'* ('they have been scattered around over time in sufficiently large numbers, with a beguiling diversity'),[233] it is necessary to describe their variations in greater detail, and to discuss their possible changes over the course of time.

In this section, we will further classify/subdivide the robe-mantles into four different styles, respectively named (in a tentative effort) as 'Languettes', 'Wavy tufts', 'Lozenges', 'Graffito' and 'Flames' styles. A further stylistic component, the reinterpretation of the original tufts or flocks of the *kaunakes* robe into leaves and other vegetal features, will describe the gradual transformation of the original Mesopotamian template into something completely different, that in my view might confirm the final interpretation of the 'princesses' as female divinities of fertility, already proposed by several authors.

The '*Languettes*' style

Among the female composite statuettes so far presented, a small group is distinguished by robes having regular rows of *languettes* bearing inner concentric lines, similar to parallel, vertical ones. These *languettes*, incised flat, or more realistically carved in low relief, with round or pointed ends, are probably a rather faithful version of the *kaunakes* tufts of the Mesopotamian tradition. The chlorite statuettes of the '*Languettes*' style share very careful sculpting with a naturalistic, soft rendering of facial features, and in some (later?) specimens the distinctive, elaborated tiara-like headdresses, and the asymmetric shoulder garment we have encountered and described in detail in one of the Louvre images and in two other new statuettes (Figures 78–80, 102, 104–6). Moreover, *languettes* on the robe seem to be linked to faces with bulging eyes and round, fleshy cheeks. Thus a stylistic feature probably derived from the west (the local version of the *kaunakes* pattern) is combined with a totally non-Sumerian trait (the distinctive naturalistic, fleshy rendering of the face).

The most meaningful match between this group of sculptures and the west is with the palaces of the final Early Dynastic period, such as Mari[234] or with the wooden and stone components of the panels of Royal Palace G at Ebla.[235] It is well known that the similarity of the 'Bactrian princesses' with the court art of Ebla includes the general concept, and some of the base materials, of the composite polychrome statuettes found in fragments in the ruins of the same palace, as well as specific details of the fine braided turbans or headdresses made of chlorite and other stones found in good numbers in the same contexts.[236]

Other comparisons with Ebla involve a sitting female figurine with a robed body in chlorite found in the south-western wing of the Administrative Quarter of Royal Palace G. It is stylistically different, but the choice of the stones is the same as that of the Oxus specimens.[237] There are also less compelling, but still meaningful analogies with other examples of the contemporary Syrian statuary. A larger headless Paleosyrian statue of a seated personage at the Cleveland Museum, formally distinguished by its 'solid and heavy ... connecting tissue' might have been conceived in a comparable way, given the position of the hands stretched on the lap and the thick fringe at the base of the robe, to some of our Oxus chlorite specimens. Mazzoni dates it between the Ur III dynasty and the Isin-Larsa periods.[238]

On the whole, the statuettes of the '*Languettes*' style were probably among the earliest to be crafted in the Oxus area, and the closest to their original western inspiration. The similarities with Syria might not be unequivocally due to direct contacts with the upper valley of the Euphrates, but rather to independent local reinterpretations of a shared, prestigious southern source. In terms of chronology, the end of the Early Dynastic III and the early Akkadian periods seems certain, and we should not be too far off in placing the beginning of the production of these fine images in the first half of the twenty-third century BC, or around 2250 BC. Their appearance in a phase of strong militaristic pressure, and probably of intense contacts between Mesopotamia and the eastern polities, might not be coincidental.

Even if positing that the formal evolution of the 'princesses' started from the simplest forms (the fundamental posture of the images and the *mèches* of the robe) might be judged too simplistic, I find it difficult to think otherwise.

Two green chlorite headdresses originally belonging to 'Bactrian princesses' (Figures 145–6)

Left: max Diam 3.4 cm, H 1.9 cm. Right, max Diam 2.5 cm, H 1.4 cm.

The first one recalls, in the braid-like hairdo that surrounded the head, the 'turbans' of the composite statuettes found in Royal Palace G at Ebla; the second, on the right, resembles the tiaras worn by some of the statuettes with garments in the '*Languettes*' style.

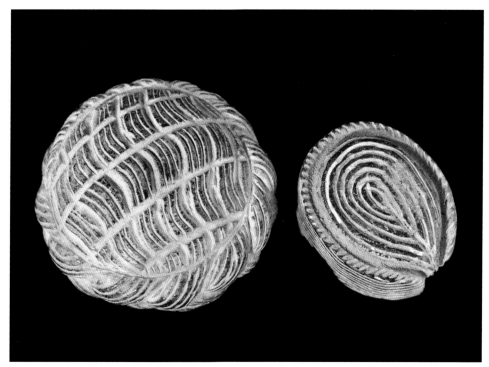

145. Private collection, *c.* 2300–2200 BC

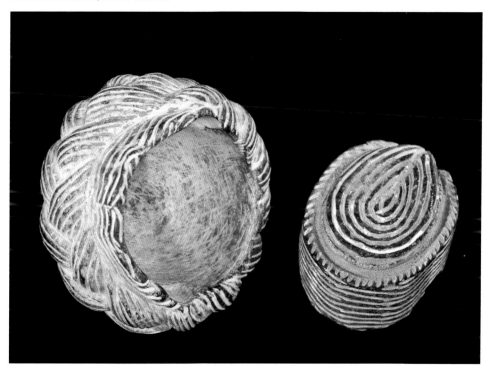

146

The 'Wavy tufts', 'Lozenges', 'Graffito' and 'Flames' styles

The second certain element for the dating of the formal evolution of the 'princesses' is the widely discussed cross-cultural connection of the statuettes to the famous Persepolis vessel.[239] This valuable evidence testifies to the permanence of the robed images and many crucial stylistic features (standing and sitting position, headdress, *kaunakes* tufts radiating from the neck girdle, arms emerging from the robes and others) to the twenty-first century BC, a time span for which the partial contemporaneity of Ur-Nammu and Puzur-Inshushinak (through the use of the Linear Elamite writing) seems to be ascertained. The links, as discussed by Potts, extend to the famous pin-seal, to the related seals of Gonur, as well as to sitting robed ladies that appear in the Anshanite cylinder seals. Indeed, as discussed above, there is no doubt that this system of analogies should be ascribed to a period of strong and enduring influence of the Oxus polities (Tukrish?) into the 'Elamite' sphere.[240] As the classical Anshanite seals, whose images clearly represent the same female robed characters, date to the Sukkalmahs period, that is to the twentieth to nineteenth centuries BC, we are dealing with a time span of not less than four centuries.[241]

Keeping in mind the well-known, serious uncertainties in Mesopotamian chronology, and that the use of the Linear Elamite inscriptions[242] does not necessarily strictly coincide *only* with the kingdom of Puzur-Inshushinak, we can preliminarily accept such a minimum time span – *c*.2250 to 1900/1850 BC – for the production of the standing and sitting 'Bactrian princesses' in their four main stylistic variants so far described, namely the 'Wavy tufts', 'Lozenges', 'Graffito' and 'Flames' styles. Finally, many of the statuettes presented in this book cannot be framed in these categories and we necessarily have to hypothesize that several areas of production (many of which may be still totally unknown) were active for long periods.

The 'Wavy tufts' style might be an early original variation of Mesopotamian prototypes, or a slightly later evolution of the '*Languettes*' style. It is characterized by an incipient break of the regular alignment of the robe tufts, now rendered more dynamically with radiating pointed flocks in low relief, internally marked with concentric lines. Sitting statuettes composed of two pieces (Type 3b), such as Figures 123–5, are good examples of this style. Generally, the same robe features also appear on some of the most beautiful Oxus composite sculptures, made of two superimposed body parts (torso and gown) with applied limestone limbs, the feet sometimes unnaturally protruding bent from

the side.[243] The quite naturalistic facial features of the beautiful statuette of Figure 123 suggests that some of these statuettes might belong to an early period in the time span. It is important to stress that the Persepolis vessel undoubtedly represents exactly this class of composite sculptures: in the sitting figure, indeed, torso and gown are neatly separated by a continuous line, and the feet, although fashioned in a naturalistic way, emerge conventionally from the edge of the gown exactly as in some of the statuettes described above. In the Persepolis vase, moreover, this figure appears side by side with a standing statuette – of type 2 – that is rather to be ascribed to the 'Lozenges' style. The focus of the production of this stylistic variation might be preliminarily identified in the twenty-second and twenty-first centuries BC. The exceptional limestone head of Figure 135 probably belonged to a composite statuette of this style. An example of Amiet's '*humanisme dans le style agadéen mais surtout néo-sumérien*' ('humanism in the Akkadian, but above all Neo-Sumerian style') shared by the art of outer Elam,[244] this small sculpture probably testifies to the permanence of episodic, but direct contacts between the Oxus centres of power and the court of Lagash at the times of Gudea's rule.

The 'Lozenges' style occurs, with variations, more frequently. It is distinguished by a generally flatter relief and by the redundant, conventional rendering of the *kaunakes* tufts in form of standardized lozenges carefully carved with thick, fine concentric patterns. Besides the standing Type 2 statuettes (Figures 112–19) this style is recognizable in specimens from the necropolis of Gonur[245] as well as in many of the surveyed statuettes of different forms surveyed in this book (Types 1a, 1c, 3a and 3c; Figures 81, 95, 98, 100, 126, 132). The faces seem to have lost part of the soft, naturalistic features of the previous styles, assuming more impersonal, conventional features. As it may represent a formal evolution of the 'Wavy tufts' style, one would be tempted to date this style from the twenty-first century BC onwards. In this case, the deviation from the Mesopotamian forms might be explained by decreasing contacts with the west after the political crisis of the late Akkadian period.

The 'Graffito' style is evidently a later development of the 'Lozenges' style. The statuettes thus decorated, as a rule, are monolithic; the sloping lap is scarcely distinguished from the torso, the surface is strongly polished, and the tufts of the *kaunakes* are badly and hurriedly scratched as wide, irregular lozenges, with a sharp pointed tool. Composite figurines of this style seem to have very conventional staring faces with round contours and less pronounced eyes and lips; the chlorite head-dresses, too, are round, simplified turbans.

Good examples of this reoccurring, and somewhat cheap, style include the Louvre specimen, another statuette at the Metropolitan, the body of the statuette presented in this book as Figure 111, a complete statuette found in grave 2900 at Gonur[246] and statuettes from Ligabue's collection published by the owner and Salvatori.[247] Another fine specimen, that looks somewhat transitional between the 'Lozenges' and 'Graffito' styles, confirming the link between simplified tufts and very conventional facial traits, was exhibited in London in 2013.[248] The heads with wigs recovered at Adji Kui, too, belong to this specific style.[249]

In such a simplified hypothesis of stylistic evolution, the 'Wavy tufts', 'Lozenges' and 'Graffito' styles might represent a single, prolonged line of evolution, ending with the 'Graffito' style between the twenty-first and the nineteenth centuries BC. However, needless to say, it is just a conjecture: given the present incomplete state of knowledge there is no certainty that these styles precisely followed and excluded each other over the course of time.[250]

The 'Flames' style is less defined and more formally elaborated. In this style, tufts and/or lozenges radiate from the girdles, cover the shoulders or are variously combined with wavy pointed tongue-like features, or with similar descending symmetric elements with complex curved contours. In both cases, such features may be filled with regular concentric designs, while in some other images plain flames alternated with heavily incised ones. The 'Flames' style looks like a complex elaboration of the 'Languettes' one, through a radical change of the original meaning due to a different set of ideas, that occurred independently from the gradual changes of the 'Languettes' – 'Wavy tufts' – 'Lozenges' – 'Graffito' sequence.

This heterogeneous but highly creative style is represented in a fragmentary statuette found in grave 1022 of the Gonur necropolis;[251] chronologically, therefore, it could preliminarily be considered an independent parallel evolution that took place between the twenty-second and the twenty-first centuries BC, when the influence of the Mesopotamian models, with episodic exceptions, was fading away, and totally new templates could develop freely in southern Central Asia.

The addition of vegetal elements – completely absent from Mesopotamian repertories – to the robe-mantles, and in general to the decoration of the statuettes, further complicates this tentative, uncertain picture. Leaves may have appeared first as flat incised patterns on the shoulders or robes of variants of the 'Lozenges' style (Figure 81 in this book), initially suggested by lozenge-shaped features and intermediate spaces where midribs seem to generate rows of veins.[252] Such leaf designs seem to have

a stronger impact on the 'Flames' style, creating other complex patterns with new and unexpected semantic implications. In some of the statuettes presented in this book (Figures 85 and 129), large leaves acquire quite naturalistic forms, in high relief, and eventually dominate the figuration, creating fascinating and even bizarre figures unlike any others so far known.[253] In one of the composite statuettes presented here for the first time (Figures 126–8), as mentioned above, two contrasting vegetal icons – the ear of wheat and the tree – are tightly carved side by side and alternating, in a complete substitution of the robe *mèches*. The entirely conceptual coupling of ears and trees is also found in an enigmatic object at Gonur, a decayed (cultic?) object. In this case, as already stated, the conclusion that the image represents a deity of fertility, perhaps linked to the idea of a mountain, is difficult to ignore.

Ladies with stretched bodies: an epilogue?

While for the classic 'Bactrian princesses' we have the limited, but certain, archaeological evidence of the context of the discoveries at Gonur, Togolok and Adji Kui (see Table 2), the statuettes with stretched bodies remain a mystery. So far, none has been found in a regular excavation, but many continue to surface on the antiques market. The most obvious explanation is that they were recovered in illegal excavations in regions not yet identified by archaeologists, and out of the control of the presently active archaeological authorities of the Central Asian states. Many of these statuettes (our Type 1b) have quite peculiar bisected symmetrical bodies and designs of wavy flows described above; and in almost every case, the upper and lower surfaces of the stretched bodies are carved in the same fashion and with the same patterns, showing that these statuettes were conceived without a base – as originally suggested by Agnès Benoit, as if they were freely flowing in water.

In the collections that I have examined, the heads whose association with their bodies seems plausible have angular features, flat faces with quite conventional and impersonal traits, and are crowned by tall, wide headdresses resembling fan-like adornments applied on the hair. The socket for the insertion of the neck is often shallow, and the heads rise on the extremity of the stretched bodies in a totally unnatural and somehow unsettling fashion.

It seems impossible to place them in the context of the hypothetical chronological sequence outlined so far. Following the double criteria of an increasing standardization and simplification of the facial features, and of a growing distance from the supposed original western models, we should consider them as a comparatively late production.

Perhaps we should consider the appearance of these strange statuettes in the same way as those covered with leaves: the sign of the fully developed identification of a character, perhaps supernatural, with her own, distinctive qualities and attributes – a goddess of running water. So far it has perhaps not been sufficiently stressed quite how radical the shift in these images was from the common iconographic standards of the near Eastern and Central Asian traditions of the third millennium BC: can you imagine a Mesopotamian statue without a base, rocking on a convex surface?[254]

Moreover, in this last case, iconography on other media does not provide any help. Enrico Ascalone has brought to my attention the series of sketchy female images in profile, with a small torso emerging from long simplified platform-like bodies, that appear on late third-millennium seals of south-eastern Iran.[255] However, these images are not particularly late, and still indicate the torso. The source, meanings and chronology of these images therefore remain open questions.

X

On the tracks of a
'man-dragon': the *balafrés*

According to the most informed scholarship, the 'princesses' should be seen as a counterpart, if not an open and deadly enemy, of the scarred personages we know from a series of statuettes which have appeared on the antiques market in the last 50 or 60 years. These intriguing anthropomorphic statuettes, in French *balafrés* or German *Narbenmänner*,[256] have been more and more frequently interpreted in quite a negative fashion, as images of dangerous demons in which are mixed and hybridized two contrasting natures, man and snake or dragon; however at the end of this book we will try to put forward a possible quite different version.

The bizarre history of these statuettes may start with the story of the discovery in the field of a farmer at Faza, in a rural area some 75 km south-east of Shiraz in the province of Fars in Iran, of six of these statuettes (or perhaps five, as one was very distinct from the others),[257] and their subsequent gradual dispersal to museums and private collections (since Nagel's 1968 article).

Then again, some of them have made their way around auctions on both sides of the Atlantic, adding uncertainty to mystery. As a matter of fact, information of the discovery of the original six stone statuettes should be considered quite unreliable.[258] The statement that they were found together in Fars, a well-known source of important archaeological artefacts, could well have been dictated by the need to offer the buyers a reputable and plausible archaeological provenance, at a time when nobody had ever heard of urban civilizations and artistic centres in northern Afghanistan. In the following years, other statuettes reproducing the same characteristics surfaced in the antiques market,[259] or changed hands in public or private transactions. Several of these statuettes are so similar that compiling a list of them can sometimes turn into quite a puzzling task (see Table 3).

Balafré (No. 1) in chlorite and limestone (Figure 147)

H 11.7 cm, W 5 cm.

One of the six ascribed to the reported discovery at Faza. Made in three parts (torso, skirt, legs) like the other similar statuettes illustrated in this book, this well-known *balafré* is distinguished a slightly more superficial carving of the skin's scales, by small holes visible on the front and at the base of the hair, on rear, whose function is unknown. Another minor difference is that here the end of the hair is a round extremity, whereas in the other examples the tail is pointed.

Agnès Benoit states, on the basis of PIXE analysis carried out by Anne Bouquillon at C2RMF, that 'the head was circled by a band of meteoritic iron'.[260] None of the other statuettes of the same type studied for this book showed remains or stains of an applied iron fillet. The cavity under the arm seems to have hosted an inserted pot, possibly made with another contrasting material.

147. Louvre, Paris, *c.* 2300–1800 BC

Balafré (No. 3) in chlorite and limestone (Figure 148)

H 10.1 cm.

Another of the group that was found by chance at Faza in Fars.[261] The figurine, made in the usual three pieces, reportedly retains applied decorations in gold and iron (the available pictures might suggest the presence of gold residues around the head and in the grooves of the kilt, but there is no detailed information). In this statuette, differently from what we see in the Louvre specimen, the scales widen under the throat to represent a unnatural reptilian 'beard'. Also, the head is distinctively flatter than that of the other statuettes published for the first time in this volume.

148. Metropolitan Museum, New York, *c.* 2300–1800 BC

Table 3. A list of the known *balafrés*, five of which (11–15) are published here for the first time[263]

No.	First notice	Notes	History, other locations	Present location
1 (Fig. 147)	Belonging to the group reportedly found at Faza	Assembled in three parts, missing shoes; face damaged. It reportedly had an iron fillet	Immediately bought by the Louvre	Musée du Louvre, AO21104[262]
2	Belonging to the group reportedly found at Faza	Assembled in four parts, no shoes; cylindrical hat with concave profile; kilt made with 11 superimposed discs	Ex Mohseh Foroughi collection, Tehran	Unknown
3 (Fig. 148)	Belonging to the group reportedly found at Faza	Assembled in three parts, missing shoes; gold foil on head and/or kilt?	Ex Azizbeghlou collection, Tehran	Purchased in 2009 by the Metropolitan Museum of Art, New York, no. 2010.166 (Benefit Fund and Friends of Inanna Gifts; gift of Mr. and Mrs. Horiuchi, 2010)[262]
4	Belonging to the group reportedly found at Faza	Only a torso. It had a hat, now lost, applied hands and beaded eyelids	Ex Mohseh Foroughi collection, Tehran	Museum für Vor- und Frühgeschichte, Staatliche Museen Berlin
5	Belonging to the group reportedly found at Faza	Only a torso. The pot is vertical. The hat is missing	Ex Mohseh Foroughi collection, Tehran; auctioned at Christie's (June 2000), then at Sotheby's (December 2010)	Private collection?
6	Belonging to the group reportedly found at Faza	No scar, no pot, no reptilian skin, and with penis. With hat?	Ex Mohseh Foroughi collection, Tehran	Private collection?
7	Origin unknown	Possibly made of a single piece (?), with elaborate shoes	Exhibited at the Metropolitan Museum of Art, New York. Auctioned at Sotheby's, June 1999	Private collection?
8	Origin unknown		Auctioned at Sotheby's, June 1999	Private collection?
9	Origin unknown	The only *balafré* so far known that retains two white stone shoes	On exhibit at the Galerie Kevorkian, Paris, September 2010 (and exhibited by the same gallery at the 2010 Biennale des Antiquaires, Paris)	Private collection?
10	Origin unknown	Assembled in three parts, missing shoes. The reptilian skin is in higher relief	On exhibit at Drouot, Paris, November 2011. Later at La Galerie Dayan, Paris; than at the Convention and Exhibition Centre, Wanchai, Hong Kong, October 2014	Private collection?
11 (Figs. 149–52)	Origin unknown	Large, made in single piece (?), intensively reworked, and heavily restored. Pot protruding on the back	Acquired at Pescheteau-Badin, Paris, in March 2013	Aron collection, London
12 (Figs. 153–58)	Origin unknown	Assembled in three parts, missing shoes, quite similar to the Louvre specimen (No. 1)	In circulation at least from 1970	Aron collection, London
13 (Figs. 159–62)	Origin unknown	Assembled in three parts, missing shoes; the kilt is made of a reddish marble	No previous information	Private collection
14 (Figs. 163–66)	Origin unknown (reportedly from a mound near Mazar-i Sharif, Afghanistan)	Assembled in three parts, missing shoes; kilt with yellow stains	No previous information	Private collection
15 (Figs. 167–70)	Origin unknown	Assembled in three parts, but the legs end in two shoes	No information	Private collection
16	Origin unknown (reportedly from Bactria)	Assembled in three parts, missing shoes. Unusual deep mortises and long tenons with quadrangular section. Gold foil on the incisions of the kilt?	Exhibited at David Aaron Ancient Arts in 2013; in an unnamed private collection since 1968	Private collection?

Given these conditions, nobody knows for sure where and in what kind of context the statuettes were found, how they should be dated, and which character, hero, supernatural being or myth they actually represent. So far, even the ascription of the *balafrés* to the cultural or religious milieu of the Oxus Civilization is more an academic tradition than an established fact (even if some hints, such as the style of the headdress, do suggest that at least some of these composite figures might have been placed in graves of ancient Margiana and Bactria: see below). A preliminary consideration of their features may help to frame their variations in meaningful patterns (see Table 4).

In this table, the *balafrés* are ordered according to their most relevant formal features. A source of uncertainty, in the proposed ordering, is that in the case of the statuettes that we know from a single appearance in a gallery or auction catalogue, there is always the possibility that some of the pictures were horizontally rotated, thus altering our data.

Some preliminary comments: first, No. 6 has been removed from the list as an intruder, because the only feature he shares with the other 15 statuettes is a bulky body (also the emphasized inlaid penis sets him apart from the rest). Second, with two exceptions (Nos 2 and 8) the scar is always on the right cheek. Third, when a single eye is preserved (seven cases) it is always on the right (in Nos 2–7 and 16 both eye sockets are empty, while No. 5, anomalous from several points of view, has remains of both inlaid eyes).

Thus ordered, the *balafrés* can be easily classified into three different types.

Type 1 (Nos 2, 4 and 5) have or had a hat applied with a mortise-and-tenon joint; the pot is under the left arm, and the beard is rendered in different ways.

Table 4. The *balafrés* classified by their features

No.	Head	Eyes	Scar (s)	Beard	Pot	Hands	Feet/shoes
2	hat	absent	L	vertical lines	L	both with holes?	applied, absent
4	hat	absent	R	scales	L	applied, absent	?
5	hat	absent	R, inlaid and L	circlets	L	plain (one nd)	?
11	nd	R, L	R	scales	R	L with hole	?
9	flat	R	R	scales	R	L with hole	applied, present
16	flat	absent	R, inlaid	scales	L	R, with hole	applied, absent
3	flat	absent	R	scales	R	plain	applied, absent
7	flat	absent	R, inlaid	scales	R	plain	part of the legs
8	flat	R	L	scales	R	plain (?)	applied, absent
15	dome	R	R	scales	R	plain	part of the legs
1	dome	R	R	zigzag bands	L	plain	applied, absent
10	dome	R	R	zigzag bands	L	plain	applied, absent
12	dome	R	R	zigzag bands	L	plain	applied, absent
13	dome	R	R	zigzag bands	L	plain	applied, absent
14	dome	R	R	zigzag bands	L	plain	applied, absent

Table 5. Speculative interpretations of the *balafrés*

Source	Interpretation
Parrot 1963	*'Facies brutal'*; a legendary hero familiar with animals, as for example Enkidu of the Gilgamesh epics
Ghirshman 1963	The same, with the body completely covered with hair
Seidl 1966	Drummer
Nagel 1968	Wounded prisoner in a row of captured enemies, forced to beat the drum for the praise and glory of the conquerors
Parrot 1963, Spycket 1981	A historical hero wounded in an important battle, celebrated by his people for some generations, then forgotten
Francfort 1992	Anthropomorphic avatar of a dragon
Francfort 1994	Scarred face devil, a destructive, negative man-dragon hybrid (seen as covered with reptilian scales). Inversion of stones (chlorite vs limestone) with 'Bactrian princesses'…
Francfort 1994 (same article)	…with reference to the defeat of a dragon by a hero, and liberation of seasonal waters as part of a Eurasian mythology of natural cycles
Amiet 1998	Monstrous giant with a beastly expression, akin to Humbaba of the Gilgamesh epics
Pittman (quoted in Freeman 2013)	Chief administrator (because of the girdle of incised lines ending in round depressions around the skirt, interpreted by Pittman as round stamp seals hanging from the belt)?
Benzel 2010	Monstrous male figure, a decommissioned being whose power was no longer operational, ritually muted and 'killed'
Benoit 2012	An ophidian demon wounded, subdued and silenced through a plug on the lips by the Great Goddess of the Oxus Civilization
David Aaron Ancient Arts 2013 (No. 21)	Exuding masculinity and strength, a terrifying apparition of a man-beast-reptile

Type 2 (Nos 3, 7, 8, 9 and 16) have no hat, and the top of the head, with the hair divided in two, is flat. The pot is mostly held under the right arm, and the beard is covered or made of the same scales of the skin.

Type 3 (Nos 1, 10, 12, 13, 14 and 15), finally, is distinguished by a prominent, dome-shaped head. The vessel, with one exception, is kept under the left arm, and the beard is invariably rendered with bands of alternating zigzag segments.

No. 11 is not ascribed to a type because of its anomalous features and its significant secondary variations. In Types 1 and 2, but not in Type 3, the hands may have cylindrical holes for holding lost objects. The shoes are part of the legs in only two cases. Type 3 seems more standardized than the other two. How far these three types represent morphological changes over time, or contemporary variations made and circulating in different regions, at present cannot be ascertained.

Ultimately, who or what do the *balafrés* represent? Not surprisingly, the interpretations so far proposed have widely diverged and radically changed in time. Previous speculations are listed and summarized in the in Table 5 above.

Large, damaged *balafré* (No. 11) in bluish chlorite (Figures 149–52)

H (residual, the lower legs are fractured and partial) 22.80 cm, max W (at the shoulder) 12.65 cm, Th 6.32 cm (at the kilt). Weight 2026 g. The statue has been abundantly fractured and reassembled, one or more substantial gaps having been filled with a fine-grained dark grey cement with small shiny inclusions (probably a modern abrasive powder). The reconstructed areas, in front, are those of the upper chest and shoulders, left wrist, and a band just below the belt on the waist. On the opposite side, the same filling covers large part of the back and the upper region of the kilt. A layer of brown, translucent glue still visible on a large fracture of the left leg reveals that another fragment, recomposed in the past, is now lost.

This statuette must have been intensively used as a craft tool (probably as an anvil) in an unknown craft process, apparently with— no respect for its original symbolic and/ or ritual meanings: the upper surface of the head shows dot-like impacts from light hammering; the occipital area and the nape are ground with linear abrasion marks (Figure 150); the right side of the head, with the ear region, was carved with deep, parallel burin tracks (Figure 151); the face and beard, again, were flattened and partially cancelled by light hammering; the same punctiform impacts are probably visible on both hands, on the fracture surface of the right leg and in front of the damaged kilt. Finally, the linear interface that runs at mid height, below the belt, seems to have been cut with a metal saw. It seems that when the statuette was found, it lay shattered and even sawn in different pieces – as if it was a workman's tool carelessly handled while working on other materials and other objects.

The statue originally showed a robust bearded man, with a massive oval head,

149. Aron collection, London, *c.* 2300–1800 BC

apparently sunk into the shoulders without any hint of a neck. In the front, two deep parallel grooves suggest the representation of a simple fillet, in the same position as the meteoric iron one (?) reportedly applied on the Louvre *balafré* (No. 1, Figure 147) and in other specimens of the same type. The upper region of the chest is lost, but what is left of the right pectoral suggests impressive, bulging muscles. The reptilian scales are substituted by a fine hatchwork covering the legs, arms and the rear of the head. Before the damage produced through its recycling in some sort of craft activity, the dome of the head was covered by a cross-like hair pattern.

In spite of its unknown original context, its badly damaged state, and the extensive modifications due to its reuse (and final contemporary restoration with extraneous materials) this sculpture is of outstanding interest: many of its features, in fact, are uncommon or unique:

1. The sculpture is twice the standard size of the other statuettes of the same series, making it the largest *balafré* so far known in the archaeological record of ancient Central Asia.

2. The image was probably made out of a single chlorite block, and not by assembling parts of different stones (unless a joint is hidden under the cement used by the last restorer).

3. Although doubtless a *balafré*, it is not certain – because of the bad preservation of the face – whether the personage was scarred like the others or not. Even a quite careful inspection of what remains of the facial features does not solve the question.

150

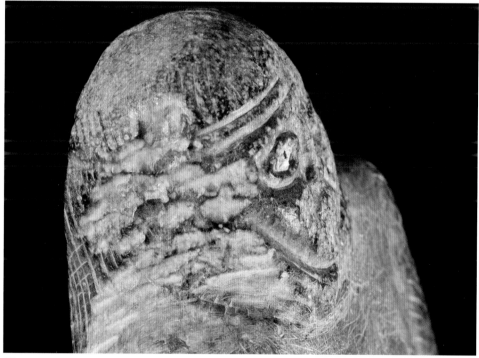

151

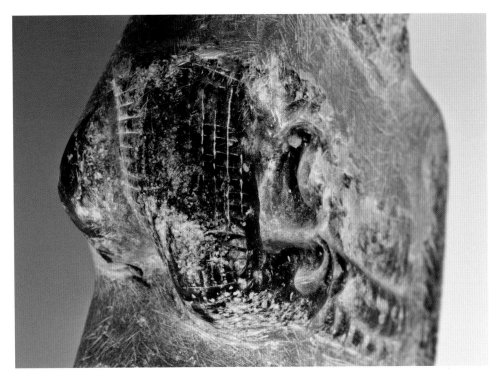

152

4. It is the only statuette where the pouring pot under the armpit is visible also on the rear, with its round body protruding (Figure 152). This form closely reproduces the standard water-jar still in common use in contemporary South Asia.

5. This is the only known case in which the reptilian scale pattern extends to the rear of the kilt, where, as a rule, one finds a sequence of vertical incised lines ending in cup marks. On the left side of the kilt the lines cross in an oblique pattern, while on the right flank they are orthogonal.

6. Only in this statuette is the belt decorated with holes made by drilling. The terminal cup marks on the front of the kilt and even those featuring on the belt seem to have been made by multiple drilling stages, rather than in a single episode. The larger drilled surface partially preserved on the edge of the same kilt, on the right, might have been left at a second time, during the phases of reuse for craft, by using the image as a support for drilling another material, rather than the statuette itself.

7. Differently from other *balafrés* described below, this statuette had a hole in the clutched left hand, that probably originally held an object or weapon.

8. Finally, this larger *balafré* is the only one that retains evidence of both eyes (in the others, the left eye is always missing). In the socket of the right eye, below residues of the white substance inlaid as the sclera, are clearly visible patches of the original glue, a translucent yellowish resin.

Balafré (No. 12) in chlorite and calcite, made of three parts (head and torso, kilt, legs) assembled with mortise-and-tenon joints (Figures 153–8)

H (from the tenon to the head) 6.61 cm, max W (at the shoulder) 6.28 cm, H of the kilt 4.52 cm, max Th of the kilt 4.01 cm, H of the legs 5.93 cm. Total max H of the recomposed statuette 16.10 cm. Weights: torso and head 191 g, kilt 113 g, legs 93 g. Unbroken, in perfect condition. An inlaid eye in white marble or calcite is set in the right eye socket. The upper and lower parts are made of the same dark green, compact chlorite, without visible inclusions. The kilt is made of an alabaster-quality calcite, cream in colour (very pale brown, 10YR 8/3) with a pinkish hue. The skin is rendered with a continuous pattern of round/hexagonal cells, extending all over the body but not the face, ears and beard.

A little masterpiece of ancient Near Eastern and Central Asian sculpture, this *balafré* was carved in the finest detail. The hair is fashioned on the dome-like top in a cross-like pattern; and on the rear (a unique case in the series of the *balafrés* so far known) the same hair converges from the sides to the middle, resulting in a well-formed V-shaped tuft hanging down. The fillet that, like in other statuettes of the same type, holds the hair is also thin and carefully fashioned.

While the ears are geometrically simplified as two concentric crescents in relief, the beard starts beside the eyes as a vertical band, to widen suddenly at the height of the shoulders. It is a wide, thick crescent, with an angular edge, entirely covered with an unbroken sequence of zigzag designs or chevrons set in five concentric rows. The nose is a sharp triangle from the front, straight when seen from the side; the nostrils are two cavities visible only from below.

153. Aron collection, London, *c.* 2300–1800 BC

The eyes, under wide orbital arches, are outlined by thin, well-carved eyelids in relief; the inlay of the right eye (0.68 x 0.31 cm) seems to be made of marble or calcite rather than of shell, as they are frequently assumed to be in other statuettes. There is no trace of a pupil. The protruding lips are tightened, the labionasal sulcus perfectly carved, while the commissures, bent downwards, give to the figure a sad, if not suffering expression. The muscles of the arms and the pectorals without nipples, rounded and bulging, even if not very realistic, convey an image of held, suspended strength. The right arm hangs down; from the wrist, emphasized by the edge of the reptilian skin, emerges a stretched hand with fingers suggested by four parallel incised lines. The left arm holds a circular concave object identifiable with a pot, whose volume is entirely encompassed within the figure's muscular masses. The hand that holds the pot's rim is bent upwards and rendered with the same conventions as in the previous example, four lines representing the five fingers.

The torso ends just below the pectorals with a flat surface, with a cylindrical tenon in the centre (max Diam 1 cm, L 0.43 cm). The tenon perfectly fits in a corresponding mortise (max Diam 1.25, depth 0.49 cm) on the upper surface of the second part of the statuette, a banded calcite or 'alabaster' kilt. This latter bulge on the rear suggests the volume of the backside; on the left side, the sculptor carved a recess for hosting the left wrist.

The kilt, made of a cream-coloured stone with a pinkish shadow (Munsell very pale brown, 10YR 8/3, with inner bands pale brown, 10YR 6/3) has an upper horizontal groove as a belt, from which run, in front only, eight vertical lines ending in round drilled dots (Diam 2.40 mm). Inspecting these features with an optical microscope, we found them filled with silty clay, and could not detect traces of colour or of any other applied or inlaid material.

154

155

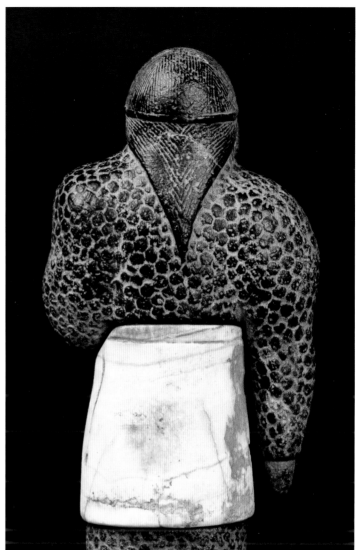

156

The lower surface of the kilt hosts a large round mortise (max Diam 3.25 cm, depth 0.17 cm), made with a large tubular drill. On the inner edge of the mortise there is a faint trace of a translucent dark substance of unknown origin. The third part, the legs, fits here through a large, flat tenon (max Diam 3.77 cm, H 0.24 cm). Comparing the diameters of the mortise below the kilt, and the tenon on the top of the legs, we can conclude that the copper bit of the tubular drill was fashioned to a size of *c*.1.50 mm thickness.

The rear of the legs suggests the buttocks and perfectly matches with the curvature of the kilt. The surface is entirely covered by the same round/hexagonal scales as the torso. The lower surface of the legs is plain where the limbs had to fit into two shoes, probably in white limestone, now lost. As far as the feet are concerned, we may only repeat what originally stated by André Parrot for the Louvre specimen:

Les pieds font donc défaut mais on peut indiquer qu'ils étaient certainement rapportés, car le bas des jambes est creux. On les avait probablement taillés dans une pierre différente, peut-être identique à celle du vêtement. [The feet, therefore, are missing, but there are definite signs that they used to be applied, as the base of the legs is hollow. They were probably carved in a different stone, perhaps the same as that of the kilt.][264]

The closest comparisons to be made are, in fact, with the Louvre *balafré* (No. 1).[265] The main differences are the reported applied iron fillet, the rendering of the pupil, and the position of the left hand of the French specimen, that is more realistically rendered as protruding from the body mass, with well carved and natural-looking fingers.

157

158

Balafré (No. 13) in chlorite and red metamorphosed limestone, made of three parts (head and torso, kilt, legs) assembled with mortise-and-tenon joints (Figures 159–62)

H (from the tenon to the head) 7.75 cm, max W (at the shoulder) 7.72 cm, H of the kilt 4.56 cm; max Th of the kilt 5.00 cm, H of the legs 7.08 cm. Weights: torso, 301 g; kilt, 211 g; legs, 160 g. With a total height of more than 18.30 cm, this statuette is one of the tallest recorded so far. The inlaid eye in shell, with a central drilled pupil (empty) is well preserved. Torso and legs are made of the same dark green, compact chlorite, very similar to that of the previous statuette. The kilt, by contrast, is made of a red metamorphosed limestone or marble (dull reddish brown, 5YR 4/3) with microscopic, lighter fossil inclusions. This statuette is in fairly good condition. The skin, showing the usual round to hexagonal cells, as in the previous example and in the Louvre *balafré*, covers the body but not the hands, the ears or the beard. The statuette has been thoroughly cleaned, and the uniform polish suggests that it might have been handled and circulated for a long time. Traces of the usual reddish sediments are visible in the deepest part of the face and inside the vessel, held under the left arm. The head, dome-shaped, is covered by hair fashioned in cross-like pattern; as in the following statuettes of the same type, the hair falls on the back in parallel, thin lines (in contrast to the converging pattern of the hairdo of the previous statuette, Figure 156) and forms a long V-shaped tuft. The fillet is a continuous, thin band in relief.

The ears are two symmetrical semicircular projections, marked by two concentric crescents in relief. The beard is very similar to that of the previous *balafré* (No. 12), being covered with chevrons set in concentric rows, but this one looks somewhat flatter. The nose

159. Private collection, *c.* 2300–1800 BC

is elongated and more rounded, with deep nostrils; while the lips and their perforations are quite similar and suggest the same worried or suffering expression. The eyes are carved in much greater depth, below wide orbital arches that join straightly to the inner edge of the beard. The scar runs from the cheekbone to the bridge of the nose.

The muscles of the arms and the pectorals, without nipples as in the previous example, are more emphasized. The right arm, in the identical position to that of the previous *balafré*, hangs down; the hand emerges from the wrist in the same posture, but the palm is sculpted as a flat plane. The pot under the left arm is rendered with the same form, with short parallel lines representing the fingers.

The tenon, under the torso, is square, measuring 1.97 x 1.87 cm and projecting 0.55 cm. It fits in a rectangular mortise on the kilt (1.68 x 2.31 cm, depth 0.69 cm). The recess for hosting the left hand was carved after fashioning the kilt. The latter has an upper belt in relief on top, with vertical lines ending, like in the other cases, in drilled cavities (Diam *c*.5 mm), 17 in total. At least one of the holes has a central raised circle, suggesting that the tip of the drill was internally concave. On the lower surface of the kilt there is another rectangular concave mortise (2.55 x 1.80 cm) that hosts the tenon (2.31 x 1.68 cm) of the third part, the legs. This *balafré* is larger, heavier and slightly coarser, in terms of carving, than the previous one, but this impression is balanced by the bulky volumes and the higher relief of the muscles, that emphasize the 'brutal' nature of the personage so frequently stressed by other interpreters. Although there are numerous subtle differences in morphological and technical detail, the proportions and general look of this statuette link it closely to the previous one and to the Louvre specimen, suggesting a common origin within the same craft community.

160

161

162

Balafré (No. 14) in chlorite and pinkish-white veined marble, made of three parts (head and torso, kilt, legs) assembled with mortise-and-tenon joints (Figures 163–6)

Total H 17.00 cm. H (from the tenon to the head) 6.85 cm, max W (at the shoulder) 7.12 cm, H of the kilt 4.53 cm, max Th of the kilt 5.03 cm, H of the legs 6.02 cm. Weights: torso 278.6 g, kilt 160.7 g; legs 123.2 g.

This *balafré* has a well-preserved right inlaid eye made of shell. The torso and legs are made of the same fine, compact dark green-to-black chlorite with large micaceous inclusions. The kilt is made of a pinkish-white veined marble (light brownish grey, 7.5YR 8/2) with wide stress fractures. This statuette, uniformly worn like the others, is in fairly good condition, except for limited damage on the left buttock and on the legs. It retains traces of the usual reddish sediments; a red substance is also visible inside the pot. However, some cracks, the holes and the grooves of the kilt also retain traces of a strong yellow pigment (?) of unknown origin. The skin, like in the other three specimens, is carved in the form of round to hexagonal scales that cover the entire body, but not the hands, the beard or the neck. The head is shaped in a low dome, the hair in the usual cross-like pattern; the top was slightly damaged by a repeated, light hammering, as if the torso of the figurine had been expediently used as a hammer.

On the rear, a long V-shaped tuft is covered by fine parallel vertical lines. The fillet, like in the previous cases, is a continuous thin band in relief. The ears are prominent both from a frontal and a lateral view, and are deeply carved in form of two concentric arches. The beard, extended to the base of the fillet, is a massive crescent covered with thick alternating zigzag lines. The strong nose, with deep nostrils, has a marked triangular contour.

163. Private collection, *c.* 2300–1800 BC

164

165

The well-fashioned, prominent lips are pierced by two fine cone-like holes, certainly made with a thin drill-head. The scar runs from the cheek to the top of the forehead. The general rendering and details of the pectoral muscles, arms, hands and the pot under the left arm are quite similar to the other *balafrés*.

The tenon projecting from the torso is square (1.97 x 1.87 cm, projecting 0.55 cm). It fits in a rectangular mortise on the kilt (2.10 x 1.68 cm, depth 0.56 cm). The concave recess where the extended right hand fits was carved after the kilt. From the belt, in relief, hang 15 vertical incised lines ending in drilled cavities (Diam *c*.3.1–3.8 mm). Below the kilt there is another rectangular concave mortise (2.01 x 1.87 cm, depth 0.67 cm), that fitted the tenon (1.97 x 1.80 x 0.60 cm) of the legs. There are limited traces of abrasion on the lower surface of the legs, where the shoes were applied. This statuette too, in spite of minor differences, is very similar to the Louvre specimen and to the other two previously illustrated (Nos 12 and 13) and should be ascribed to the same workshops and craft tradition.

166

Large *balafré* (No. 15) in chlorite and white limestone, made of three parts (head and torso, kilt, legs with feet and shoes) assembled with mortise-and-tenon joints (Figures 167–70)

H (from the tenon to the head) 8.66 cm, max W (at the shoulder) 8.39 cm, H of the kilt 5.82 cm, max Th of the kilt 6.08 cm, H of the legs 7.39 cm. Total max H of the reassembled statuette *c*.20.4 cm. Weights: torso and head 439.7 g, kilt 300.1 g, legs 240.4 g.

This fifth *balafré* statuette, like the previous one, has an inlaid eye in shell set in the right eye socket. It diverges from the previous three examples because of the bigger size, as well as the different rendering of the beard, facial features and ears. Moreover, this statuette retains its feet, carved together with the leg section as a single block. Torso and legs are carved in dark green-to-black massive chlorite with large micaceous inclusions, while the kilt is made with a light yellowish orange (7.5YR 8/4) homogeneous limestone. The figurine retains traces of a dull yellowish brown sediment (10YR 5/3) in some cavities that also set this statuette apart from the others, supporting the idea of a different provenance.

The reptilian skin, rendered with large round/hexagonal cells, is extended to the lower contour of the face, where it merges with a bulging beard. The head, dome-shaped, is covered as usual by a carefully carved, fine pattern in a St Andrew's cross-like pattern; on the rear, the hair falls, like in the other statuettes, in a long V-shaped tuft covered with thin vertical incisions. The fillet, a thin band in relief, covers this tuft and the temples, but (exceptionally) stops in the front, leaving it plain. The face, almost sunk in above the scales of the beard is a deeply carved oval. The eyebrows are two pronounced arches that join above a short nose, without nostrils, and cover the well-carved eyes with neat eyelids.

167. Private collection, *c.* 2300–1800 BC

168

169

The lips are soft and full, and as usual host two thin and deeply drilled holes. The scar stops after the bridge of the nose, leaving part of the front intact. On the whole, the facial features of this last *balafré* are more naturalistic than in the other cases so far described. The ears are also different: still semicircular projections, with carved concentric crescents, they project laterally, being visible only from the front. The head seems almost imperceptibly turned right, thus emphasizing a certain naturalness of the sculpture. The pot is kept under the right arm, and the five fingers are clearly recognizable. The scales fully envelop the muscular mass of the torso, the arms and pectorals, leaving, like in the other images of the same character, a marked edge at the wrist.

The kilt is massive, moderately worn, with the exception of a limited area under the left extended arm: this might lead us to suppose that, at least in this case, something was inserted between the hand and the side of the kilt. It has a sequence of 20 vertical lines and terminal dots (Diam 3.3–3.7 mm), the most numerous so far encountered. The tenon projecting from the torso is square (1.74 x 19.1 cm, depth 0.66 cm) and fits in a rectangular mortise on the kilt (2.12 x 1.77 cm, depth 0.56 cm). The tenon of the legs (2.50 x 2.58 x 0.65 cm) is also square and fits on the lower surface of the kilt in a deep mortise (2.79 x 2.62 x 0.86 cm). This latter retains some coarse traces left by a flat chisel.

Finally, in this statuette the legs were carved together with the feet. These latter bear 'loafers'-like shoes, with a midrib (perhaps indicating a sewn joint) on top, upturned points, and a raised extremity on the heel, apparently superimposed on the reptilian scales of the rear of the calf. These shoes are apparently identical to those worn by a *balafré* (No. 7) temporarily hosted at the Metropolitan Museum, New York.[266]

170

A controversial reputation

Since the story of the casual find of a hoard of similar statuettes near Faza in Fars reported by the antique dealers is almost certainly a hoax (see n. 242), the actual provenance of the *balafrés* remains an enigma. While a few 'Bactrian princesses' or their parts have been found in more or less controlled excavations in Margiana, both in a settlement and in graves, no *balafré*, or similar image, has ever been discovered in an official dig. That they come, at least in great part, from plundered graves is quite likely, because only if they had been stored in hoards, or deposited in grave pits with other furnishings, would the assembled parts have been found and collected together (albeit almost always losing their applied shoes).

The only possible hint of the original provenance of one or two *balafrés* from cemeteries of middle Bronze Age Margiana are two miniature stone shoes found in graves at Gonur,[267] empty as if intended to host the lower leg of a statuette, and more or less compatible in size with the statuettes in question.[268] Even if the form of the shoe from Grave 1268 at Gonur is quite different from the footwear visible on the two comparable specimens, it is quite possible that two *balafrés* of Gonur, like Cinderella at midnight, lost their applied shoes while being taken somewhere else.

At present, however, at least in strict archaeological terms, the attribution of such statuettes to eastern Iran, Bactria and/or Margiana is still an academic construction based on little reliable evidence. Personally, I believe that they actually come from one of these regions, and that they were contemporary and somehow linked to the 'Bactrian princesses'; and it is for this reason they occupy an important place in this book. The association between *balafrés* and the 'princesses' was proposed in 1994 by Henri-Paul Francfort, based on the structuralistic opposition or inversion between the types of rock that form the different parts of these little sculptures, to which Francfort and his archaeological school has subsequently given much credit. After all, the varieties of chlorite and limestone used in the making of the two series (chlorites for the bodies of the *balafrés* and headdresses and robes of the 'princesses'; varieties of limestone for the kilt of the former and the heads, forearms and feet of the female images) are apparently rather similar, and might well have been extracted from similar and/or contiguous geological formations and mining areas.

A third and last link between the two sculptural series is the unmistakable similarity observable between the rendering of the hair on some of the 'Bactrian princesses' and the hair fashion of some of the *balafrés*. Seen from above, some chlorite head-dresses and the dome-shaped head of the Type 3 *balafrés* look

almost identical (Figures 153, 161, 163, 167), bearing the same cross-like patterns, and with even the tool marks looking closely comparable. But is this enough to postulate an origin from the same craft workshops?

In the first publication of the now world-famous Guennol Lioness (see below), Edith Porada wrote that 'The most striking feature of this sculpture is the impression of monumental power which it conveys. When seen in the original, the figure seems to fill the entire field of vision.'[269] James Osborne stresses that this quality is at odds with the small size of the Lioness: no more than 8.5 cm in height.[270] The same may be said of the composite *balafrés* illustrated in these pages. Our imagination is immediately struck not only by their frontality,[271] bulky complexion, and aura of physical power, but also by their recurrent postures and grave expressions, apparently undisturbed by the deep facial scar and by the sinister implications of the reptilian scales that envelop almost entirely their human form. Out of the 15 *balafrés* so far inventoried (discounting No. 6), only two, Nos 7 and 16, have the deep facial scar still inlaid with a white material, stone or shell;[272] but the evidence does not necessarily imply that the scars of the other statuettes were not filled in the same way.

Also, as a certain number of the other *balafrés* published so far, along with those illustrated in this book, have, almost as a rule, only a single eye preserved in its socket, as we have seen on the right side, while the opposite is empty, one might wonder about the damage sustained by the statuettes. Is the loss of a single eye coincidence? This intriguing evidence will be commented upon and possibly interpreted below.

Whatever ancient myths or ritual duties they might have personified, one feels beyond the expression of the *balafrés* a world of suffering, violence and (possibly) endurance, that has few links (besides a debatable composite materiality) with other artefacts or, at least at first, with known literary sources or traditions. Scholars have had a hard time in the attempt of making sense of them. André Parrot, soon after the reported but unlikely discovery of the hoard near Shiraz, discarded the idea of a deity, but considered among the possible identifications '*un personnage vivant dans la compagnie des animaux et proche d'eux, à bien des égards, tel l'Enkidu de la légende*' ('a figure living in the company of animals and close to them, in many ways like Enkidu in the legend [of Gilgamesh]') – if the skin pattern actually represents hair – or alternatively '*la représentation d'un héros, célèbre par son ardeur au combat dont son corps aurait gardé la marque, insigne de sa vaillance et de son intrépidité*' ('the representation of a hero, glorious for his ardour in battle, of which his body bears the marks, famed for his valour and bravery'): at any rate, a legendary character. The scar on the face, although unexplained, might have been the result of a magic sympathetic ritual.[273]

Almost twenty years later, Agnès Spycket described the figure as an aged man with a massive frame, his head sunk in his shoulders, pectorals in relief and scales on his body but not on his face and hands, thus suggesting hair rather than a reptilian skin. She suggested that the statuettes portrayed a forgotten historical figure, a hero that had defended the local population from an external attack, thus receiving his highly visible scar. This hero would have been the subject of a local cult lasting a few generations, a circumstance that would account for the morphological and stylistic variations observed in the group of objects.[274] A very influential factor in the general interpretation of this personage and the series of images has been the comprehensive study of the Oxus iconography by Henri-Paul Francfort, which aimed to reconstruct, on structuralistic grounds and in a holistic perspective, some aspects of Bronze Age religious beliefs.[275] Francfort seems to have entirely accepted the Oxus provenance of the statuettes; giving them the label of 'scar-faced devils',[276] he proposed to link them to a wide and heterogeneous class of images on stone and metal seals representing monstrous, predatory anthropomorphic dragons. In fact, he proposed that 'The ophidian character of the monster is expressed by the scaled snake skin. The beard is a transposition of the beards of the lion and snake dragons.'[277] The 'ophidian man-monster hybrid' theory was later fully accepted by Michael Witzel, who agrees with the French scholar, apparently equating the balafrés with men-dragons in an anthropomorphic manifestation peculiar to the middle Bronze Age Central Asian Oxus or BMAC civilization.[278]

Francfort also assumed that the Louvre's specimen originally had a couple of metallic horns in front, and two wings on the back (because of little holes in which he reports traces of corroded metal). Such a transformation would have made the statuettes more comparable to the dragons portrayed on the seals. This imaginary being would have combined various dangerous aspects (lion, scorpion, snake; wings, horns and mane-beard; being terrestrial, heavenly and chthonian); but the character, in Francfort's view, would have been overpowered and dominated like a tamed beast by the great fertility goddess. The scar was considered a sign of his evil nature.[279] Note that 'metal wings' and 'horns' are purely conjectural, and there is no sign of similar attachments in the other known statuettes of the same type.[280] The mortise-cavity on the back of the Louvre balafré, in fact, is simply filled by a post-depositional deposit of carbonates.[281]

The linkage with the 'goddess' and its composite chlorite and calcite images found in Margiana is quite indirect, being limited to the inversion of the assembled base materials, as repeated in several papers by Francfort and Benoit, while the female statuettes have chlorite bodies and limbs in limestone, the balafrés have a skirt or short kilt in calcareous rocks, and the body in chlorite.

At this point the discussion takes an unexpected turn, because an identical skirt, but made in chlorite, is worn by an impressive 'Composite stone sculpture of a lioness demon' recently published in the catalogue of the Al-Sabah Collection (Figure 171).[282]

This large statuette (more than 25 cm high) is another version of the famous 'Elamite' anthropomorphic lioness (the 'Guennol Lioness', that was formerly on loan at the Brooklyn Museum of Art, and recently sold to a private collector for an unbelievable, unrealistic amount of money). The volumes of the al-Sabah statuette, judging from the pictures, are less naturalistic and more conventionally stylized in deeply incised lines and sturdy geometries, but the similarity is beyond discussion. The curator of the collection provided unexplained but convincing technical details that, from my point of view, fully support the authenticity of the sculpture (for example, the presence of stains of corroded copper in the holes that should have originally fixed applied feet or paws at the extremity of the lower limbs; they were probably joined with copper/bronze wire or nails). Here, furthermore, we face a major chronological problem, because Edith Porada's attribution of the Guennol Lioness to the late fourth millennium BC, based on the apparently strong similarity of the statuette with images on cylinder seals and seal impressions dating to late Uruk times has been, so far, universally accepted.[283] While Porada's stylistic attribution is only based on formal traits, the analogies between the balafrés and the al-Sabah lioness in Kuwait involve at the same time the form and the subject, the threefold assembly of torso, kilt and legs, and the structural 'inversion' of the base materials already noted by Francfort. Thus, if iconography depends upon a shared rational method, the Kuwait lioness is closely linked to the balafrés. In this new light, and if – as everybody seems to agree – the balafrés were made in the second half of the third millennium BC, both the al-Sabah and the Guennol lionesses should of necessity be dated to the same period. And the Guennol Lioness, most probably, should be removed from the inventories of the Mesopotamian late Uruk art and considered – almost a paradox – among the Oxus masterpieces!

The lioness-demon of the al-Sabah collection has the legs and torso made of a white stone (reportedly in magnesite) while the hand joined at the chest and the skirt are made of chlorite. The system of mortises and tenons for assembling torso, kilt and legs of the statuette, described by the curator,[284] matches exactly that of the first of the 'new' balafrés of this book. With the exception

171. Composite statuette of a lioness, from the al-Sabah collection. The kilt is identical to those of the *balafrés*.

of the hands, the inversion of materials has a precise symmetrical match with our *balafrés*, and, despite the absence of any information on the original contexts, the two lionesses and the *balafrés* should be considered chronologically linked.

If this is true, the widely popularized 'kinship' of *balafrés* with 'Bactrian princesses' would be weakened, and, in contrast, the reptilian human figures would acquire a new, stronger and even more mysterious affinity with the supernatural humanized feline. But to what extent, given the current state of knowledge, may the two series of small sculptures be seriously ascribed to the cultural or mythological *milieu* of the Oxus Civilization?

In 1988, Pierre Amiet commented on the 'beastly expression' and the scale- or hair-covered body of the 'monstrous giant', comparing it to some iconography of the Mesopotamian Humbaba: the scar would represent the fall of the personage, perhaps a semi-divine being, and his 'sentence to death'.[285]

Francfort's and Amiet's views were further elaborated by Agnès Benoit as follows:

'Scarfaces' are anthropomorphic dragon-snakes belonging to the mythology of central Asia, where they incarnated the hostile forces of the underworld. Their power was controlled not by killing them but by reducing them to silence by a slash across the right cheek. Thus dominated, they could become benevolent.[286]

Of such benevolence, however, there is no evidence. Another complicated view of this powerful sculpted image is reported in the commentary on the 'monstrous male figure', another well-known statuette of the same type, at the Metropolitan Museum of Art in New York (our *balafré* No. 3):

In the world of the ancient Near East, images and beings that combined human and animal qualities were thought to possess supernatural powers. This small yet potent figure, with its human face and serpentine-scaled body, probably represents such a creature, enlivened and charged with magical efficacy whether propitious or demonic. The monstrous figure's most enigmatic and distinctive features are the prominent scar across its face and the two holes pierced into its upper and lower lips. The scar may indicate that the figure was defaced, and the holes suggest that the lips may have been sealed, literally. Taken together, the scar and the sealed lips imply

that the figure portrays a decommissioned being whose power is no longer operational. Having served its purpose, it may have been ritually muted and 'killed'.[287]

Perhaps 'muted', but certainly not killed, given the indisputable impression of untamed energy and brutal vigour conveyed by all the statuettes so far reviewed.

The *balafré* of the Louvre collection (No. 1, Figure 147) has long hair falling in parallel lines to the base of the neck, a kind of corroded iron wire circling the occipital area (and originally the front), a deep scar on the right side of the face, crossing it from the root of the nose to the base of the cheek, down to the edge of the beard. The cavity under the left arm must have held a pot in the canonical position, later lost. The beard is rendered with a continuous series of zigzag fine incisions or *chevrons*. The sharply protruding lips, without moustaches, bear on both the nasolabial and mentolabial sulci two tiny deep holes, the lower one still partially filled with a white material of uncertain origin. Benoit, quoting Roman Ghirshman,[288] proposes that the two holes held some kind of brace, the purpose of which would have been to silence the personage for good.

The same author, reporting non-destructive tests carried out by Anne Bouquillon of C2RMF, writes that the head was encircled by a fillet of meteoric iron, and that the eye and the lips were encrusted with a calcium-rich white material, possibly shell.[289] None of the other statuettes, published or not, seems to have had the same attachment, nor show any hole for the attachment of metallic appliqués.

One of the Foroughi specimens (our *balafré* No. 2) was first described in the Italian catalogue of a 1963 exhibition as follows:

Statuette of a bearded man with a shaved lip. Bust and legs in black stone, rendered with snake scales. The body is formed by various disks in black and red stones, with gold encrustations. The eyes are in mica, inlaid. All elements are joined by a central stem. Iran. Elamite period. IIIrd Millennium BC. Height 11.5 cm, Width 5.5 cm. Unpublished. Tehran, Foroughi Collection (Ente Manifestazioni Milanesi 1963).[290]

Certainly, mica, transparent and rather brittle, is quite unlikely to be the rock used as an inlay material for the eyes. The original description, moreover, does not comment on the tall cylinder-like hat in white stone, the pot under the left armpit, nor on the holes that, in the clutched hands, show that the personage originally held two objects, possibly weapons, now lost. Of the *balafrés* here listed in Table 3, besides this latter, only that at the Metropolitan Museum (No. 3, Figure 148), the larger statuette in bluish chlorite of the Aron Collection in London (No. 11, Figure 149) and No. 16, formerly at David Aaron Ancient Arts gallery, have similar holes in one of the hands. Given their divergence from the more standardized model of the Louvre statuette (No. 1) and of those of Type 3, one is tempted to propose that the *balafrés* with 'something' (a weapon?) in their hands were archetypal to the later representations of the same character, and possibly closer to the original semantic implications and ideological function of these statuettes.

Holly Pittman's peculiar interpretation of the personage as the bearer of multiple round stamp seals hanging from the belt is original and possibly intriguing (particularly after Goldstein's observation of traces of copper in the round dots at the lower edge of the skirt) but so far has not found general support, and is on the whole unlikely.

In summary, the discovery of the identity of the *balafré* is a matter of much ongoing speculation and continuous study. As a conclusion to this book, I will propose my own attempt at interpretation, different from what has so far been advanced, but somewhat along the lines of an original intuition of Henri-Paul Francfort.

Rehabilitation of a scarred cosmic hero

Indrasya nu viryani pra vocam
yani cakara prathamani vajri
ahann ahim anu apas tatarda
pra vaksana abhinat parvatanam

I shall proclaim now the heroic deeds of Indra,
the first ones which the club-wielder performed
he slew the serpent, he made a breach for the waters
he split open the bellies of the mountains[291]

From the foregoing review I believe that we can abandon without much regret the idea of a semi-bestial or wild over-powering character somewhat akin to characters like Enkidu and Humbaba of Mesopotamian mythology, because the skin that covers his body is evidently reptilian. Second, we should neatly reject the old interpretation of a wounded prisoner beating a drum (as still proposed in the showcase reconstruction at Berlin[292]), for the simple fact that *balafrés* Nos 5 and 11, and by extension all the others, clearly hold vessels (even if in theory one cannot exclude the possibility that pots themselves were used as drums; but why is there no membrane?).

Spycket's idea of a historical military leader wounded in battle and remembered for some generations by his community or nation, too, finds scant supporting background in the little we know of the statuary of the ancient Near East and Central Asia (no king, priest or ruler was represented in such iconic, standardized forms and carefully chosen materials – not even Gudea in the twenty-first century BC). I am also confident that we should exclude the possibility that the statuettes had wings and horns made of applied metallic parts. I did not examine in person the damaged Louvre specimen that has peculiar cavities on the front and rear interpreted as holes for such applied parts (also the gold foil cover on the Metropolitan specimen remains an anomaly). While I cannot explain these features of the Louvre statuette, none of the other published specimens, nor those that are here illustrated for the first time, have similar cavities in front or in the back. The absence of wings, as a consequence, hinders the possible similarity of the *balafrés* to other characters of Oxus iconography. The *balafrés*, in other words, stand somehow on their own, and have little to do with the iconography on stamp seals. Evidently the narratives or cultual practices in which the statuettes belonged, or the ideas they conveyed, did not permeate the sphere of usage of the seals.

In the end, the imaginative (and inherently post-processual) idea that the character is an evil, brutal demoniac being, half man and half dragon, wounded, defeated and silenced with a mouth clamp (of which there is no evidence whatsoever in the whole repertory of ancient Near Eastern art) by the great goddess of southern Central Asia can be deemed as unsustainable as it is unlikely. I cannot demonstrate whether the holes on the lips of the *balafrés* were actually meant for the insertion of piercing plugs, but as a rule the lip holes show no residues,[293] chemical contacts or traces of wear that would suggest a metal clamp. Another and compelling argument is that such composite figurines could be preserved in their parts (although almost in every case the shoes were lost) like the 'Bactrian princesses' only if deposited in the quiet of graves later plundered by illegal excavators; and – setting aside black magic – who would have placed an openly malevolent, destructive demon such as that described by Amiet, Francfort and Benoit in the grave of a family member?

Ultimately, the statuettes require more convincing explanations. We are looking for a myth, or class of myths, that can account at the same time for a muscular male character covered with a reptilian skin, with a wound on the face and in the act of pouring a liquid from a vessel. It is the opinion of the present writer that a possible thread for solving the riddle of the *balafrés* may have been already provided by a marginal observation of Francfort,[294] when he mentioned the possibility that his destructive, negative man-dragon hybrid was somehow part of a narrative dealing with the defeat of a dragon by a hero, and liberation of seasonal waters as part of an archaic Eurasian mythology of natural cycles.

I believe that the narrative and the characters were there, but with shifted identities and roles: the *balafré*, *contra* Francfort and Witzel,[295] was actually the dragon-slayer and suffering hero, and not the scale-covered felon. And in this light the solution might be ready at hand – the much-discussed Indo-European poetics of the same subject,[296] in what could be its early Indo-Iranian (in Witzel's sense[297]) iconographic expression. A famous article by Benveniste and Renou[298] has long since established the substantial coincidence between the Avestic (old Iranian) and Rgvedic versions of the dragon-slaying myth, to be ascribed to a preceding eastern Indo-European ideological and poetic substratum. According to Calvert Watkins, moreover, the motif of the releasing of the celestial waters might be a specific Indo-Iranian myth, hardly represented elsewhere, linked with a very practical constraint of settled life, the fear for periodic droughts in the land-locked arid basins of Middle Asia, or even specific to the northern regions of the Indo-Pakistani subcontinent.[299]

The myth may be studied in the terms of a 'genetic Indo-European comparative literature' and ultimately be summarized in the expression 'hero slays serpent'. In the present context, it can be expediently linked to the versions 'Indra slays Vrtra' contained in the mandalas of the Rgveda, the oldest part of Hindu sacred literary heritage.[300]

My basic assumption, inspired by familiarity with the general nature of the third-millennium iconography of Central Asia and by its structuralistic interpretation put forward in previous articles by Francfort and Winkelmann,[301] is that the *balafrés* are synoptical icons, that recapitulate by means of unequivocal attributes various steps of the same narrative. In such a light, the *balafrés* might have been images of a supernatural hero somehow ancestral, in an early or Proto-Indo-Iranian cultural milieu, to the Vedic Indra.[302] In a fight with a celestial dragon, he would have been severely wounded on the face and swallowed by the monster, before re-emerging from the mouth with a trick, eventually overpowering and killing his opponent, and finally pouring the salvific waters on earth. I will briefly discuss, in this perspective, first the literary identity of the main Rgvedic characters (Indra and Vrtra), then respectively, for the statuettes, the questions of the reptilian skin, the scar on the face, and finally the pot under the *balafré*'s arm.[303]

As a matter of fact:

Among all Indra's deeds celebrated in the Veda, most important are his coercion of the evil spirits of the air, who in Indian belief arrested the rain, so full of blessings for earth and mankind, and gathered them into compact clouds; and his deliverance of the heavenly streams from their power. No department of his activity is made so prominent, no act of his power related so often, in so many various forms, or with so many poetic embellishments; and the god is besought for no other manifestation of mercy with such fervor as for this: all of which is a further indication of his natural position and duties among Vedic divinities. He is above all the god of battle – of battle in the first instance against the demoniac rain-stealers, then further against all other demons and witches; and he finally becomes the ideal of a pugnacious unconquerable hero and warrior … The arch-demon among the rain-stealers is Vrtra, whose name is a plain enough indication of his nature [accepting] the common derivation from vr 'cover, wrap, hem in, hinder, restrain'.[304]

It is possible that during the fight with the hero, Vrtra 'the Enveloper' (and its postulated early Indo-Iranian ancestor) swallowed him entirely. According to Alexander Lubotsky, the original meaning of the Vedic root *vr-* would be 'to cover': a meaning recognizable in the terms *varman* for 'armour', *varna* for 'colour', *vavri* for 'covering, vesture'.[305] The cognitive implications of all these terms – a kind of peel, tightly stretched onto the bodily parts of the personage – would fit particularly well with the representation of the *balafré*. That the scales are not his skin, but those of the snake while it envelops the body of his enemy, is made clear by the detail of the wrists of all statuettes, where the same unnatural skin was purposefully carved as a thicker superimposed coat, that covered everything but the hands and the face of the hero. If the skin was that of the portrayed character, the scales would have naturally covered also the face and the hands.

Moreover, while in some *balafrés* the reptilian coat stops at the base of the head, in others (particularly in Type 2) it merges with the beard. Where the ophidian scales inflate around the hero's mouth the suggestion of the ingestion by a snake becomes stronger, as if only the face, at one time, emerged from the reptile's mouth. In this light, the name Vrtra, besides the commonly quoted metaphoric values of 'resistance, obstruction'[306] might have conveyed the more immediate and visually powerful image of a gigantic snake that opened its mouth and slowly coated and ingested its opponent, while horribly inflating its throat.[307] The detail of a furniture inlay excavated by Viktor Sarianidi in one of the rich graves of Gonur shows how this template was embedded in the cognitive background of the craftsmen of ancient Margiana (Figure 172).

The reptilian skin of the *balafrés*, according to this interpretation, would efficiently summarize this key episode of the narrative – the swallowed hero – stressing at the same time his state of great 'physical' pain. Together with the facial scar, this condition and this episode fully explain the grave, suffering expression of the statuettes, so far systematically misunderstood by other interpreters as a brutal and sinister feature.

That the hero was actually engulfed by the jaws of a reptilian monster during the clash is further supported by two independent lines of evidence: a series of much later passages of the *Mahabharata*, and by a protohistoric stone statuette from an unknown location, at present held in an oriental collection on the island of San Lazzaro degli Armeni, Venice. This figurine (figure 173) has been published and thoroughly discussed by Daniele Morandi Bonacossi, whose study is my main source in the following discussion.[308]

Although most scholars would place major effort in composing a unitary narrative tissue for the *Mahabharata* ('the Great Epic of India, a compendium of over 100,000 verses ten times as long as the *Iliad* and the *Odyssey* combined'[309]) within the time-range of two powerful 'imperial' powers, the Maurya and the Kushan dynasties, *c.*500 BC to 500 AD, or 300 BC to 300 AD, the compilation of the *Mahabharata* is notoriously the fruit of a constant re-elaboration of an enormous number of mythemes that was carried on for thousands of years, in the contexts of sometimes very different ideological constructions. In such conditions, it is almost impossible to specify a precise chronological horizon for a single scenario or narrative, because 'a passage actually composed in the twelfth century AD, may represent a surprisingly accurate preservation of a myth handed down since the twelfth century BC – or a completely original retelling of the same myth.'[310]

On the other hand, it is clear that the cryptic, highly fragmented nature of many mythological allusions in the Rgveda is also due to the fact that the poets took for granted that the untold details of the narratives were sufficiently clear to the religious audience of the hymns; and that, in this framework, much later commentaries in the epics or in later traditions might *hypothetically* help reconstructing original archaic plots.

Thus Wendy Doniger O'Flaherty has collected passages of the *Mahabharata*, composed in a much later Vishnuite sectarian milieu, that cleary describe the swallowing of Indra by Vrtra; the mighty god is first devoured, then rescued by the other divinities, who create *ad hoc* the goddess Jrmbhika ('The Yawner').[311] It is a yawn that compels Vrtra to open its mouth, from which Indra re-emerges to continue the confrontation. It is therefore possible (if not

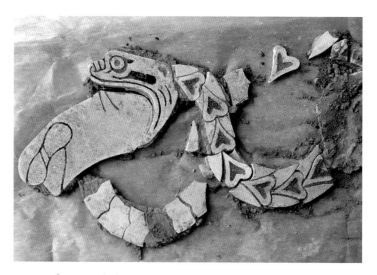

172. Part of a mosaic inlaid in a piece of furniture or panels in a grave of the Gonur necropolis, *c.*2400–1900 BC: a snake dilating its jaws to swallow its large prey

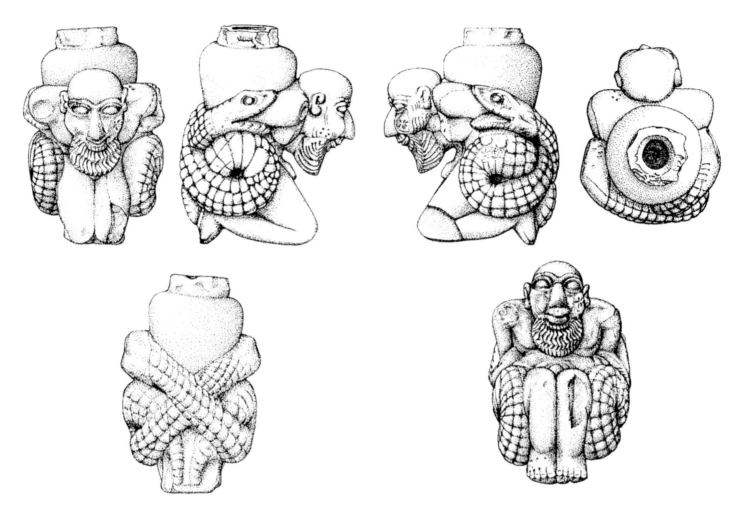

173. A *balafré* in an andesitic rock in the course of being swallowed by two snakes.
S. Lazzaro degli Armeni, Venice, *c.* 2300–1800 BC

demonstrated) that the theme of the swallowing by the dragon was also part of archaic versions of this poetic-religious narrative.

A piece of evidence that in my opinion could provide a resolution is the stone statuette mentioned above. Kept in the the collection of San Lazzaro degli Armeni, Venice, it measures *c.*8.4 x 5.4 cm and it is made of a fine variety of andesite (Figure 173).[312] Unfortunately, there is no reliable information on the provenance of the artefact; Morandi Bonacossi writes that it could possibly have come from the central-western Iranian Plateau or from Khuzestan. It has been defined as an '*homme aux serpents*': the man is bald, but with a large beard, rendered with rows of alternating oblique strokes, exactly as observed on the beards of some of the *balafrés*. He is crouching below a heavy narrow-mouthed jar supported on his back, evidently meant for a liquid. His arms look bent backwards, in the position of prisoners in shackles, but both are being devoured, almost up to the the shoulders, by two large snakes that coil along his sides, with their powerful spirals crossing over on his back.

Not only does this *homme aux serpents* have the same beard as the *balafrés*, holds a vessel and is devoured alive by reptiles; but also, while both cheeks have inlaid rosettes (a quite uncommon feature in Mesopotamian and Central Asian human figures), on the left one run three parallel winding scars. The character of this unique image was doubtless a *balafré* sharing the three basic attributes of the model: bodily parts covered by reptilian scales, the scar on the face and the vessel. The statuette clearly shows the hero in the process of being swallowed[313] (in this case by two powerful reptiles) and seems to demonstrate that in the original narrative the facial wound was inflicted by the reptile to the hero before his ingestion.[314]

Furthermore, on one side of a round stamp seal reportedly 'from Bactria', there figures a man swallowed up to the waist by a gigantic snake (Figure 174), that demonstrates a similar mythological theme in circulation.[315] The opposite face shows a scene most probably belonging to the narratives of 'vulture/eagle devouring the young snakes' so prominent in the iconography of the Halil Rud civilization.[316]

Following the track of the second attribute, the scar on the face, we may approach a problematic passage of Mandala IV of the Rgveda. This book belongs to the so-called six Family Books, Mandalas II–VII, that are unanimously considered the oldest layer of the Rgveda; and in terms of chronological sequence, it is placed in an intermediate position.[317]

In this light, and considering the traditionally accepted dates for the oral composition of Rgveda, perhaps we are not too far from the truth if we place this Mandala closer to the mid second millennium BC than to its end – and therefore close enough to the times of the earliest written evidence in Syria of the theonym Indra.[318]

Hymn 18 of Mandala IV, quite famous, is one of the main sources for the myth of Indra and Vrtra. When compared to the other 57 hymns of the book, Hymn 18 is considered (in Perry's words) 'certainly very ancient'.[319] The same author emphasized its 'fragmentary and heterogeneous character' and the lack of clear connections among several verses of the composition, so that it cannot be interpreted as a coherent narrative. Like many others, might have been a residual collection of archaic fragmentary poetry from different original sources, taking the form of cryptic mythological allusions, now quite hard to follow.

A crucial passage of Mandala IV, Hymn 18 is verse 9, part of a unusual dialogue between the unborn Indra and his obscure mother. The translation is apparently problematic, but both in Griffith's 1896 and Watkins' 2005 version, the sense is the same:

Not on my account, o generous one, did Vyaṁsa smite off your two jaws, having wounded you; then, though wounded, you smashed in the head of the Dāsa with your weapon.[320]

174. A double-faced stamp seal from Bactria or Margiana: a serpent swallowing a human figure, and an eagle fighting snakes. Private collection, *c.* 2300–1800 BC

The verse, leaving aside the precise meaning of the strange expression 'two jaws', seems to suggest that Indra, in a moment of his fight with the monster, was badly wounded on the face, and his mouth was cut off. The match with the iconography is admittedly partial (the cut on the face of the *balafrés* canonically starts from the root of the nose and stops, enlarged, at the join of the mouth); but on the whole (if the translation of this verse is correct[321]) the apparent coincidence is hard to ignore.

Finally, the pot. All *balafrés*, with the exception of the partial torso (No. 5), whose container is a cylinder-like open bowl kept with the mouth upwards,[322] hold the pot horizontally, the mouth emerging from the armpit. *Balafré* No. 5, as above discussed, demonstrates for certain that the container was meant as a narrow-mouthed vessel of the type still commonly used in wider regions of Central and South Asia for carrying water. The gesture clearly suggests that the liquid fell from the mouth of the vessel downwards. I believe that the gesture, in the synoptic, all-embracing logic of this pregnant icon, refers to the final release of the cosmic waters after the killing of the dragon-Vrtra, and their pouring from the sky to earth.[323] Because, as stated by Perry, 'In the Veda "water" and all corresponding terms, such as stream, river, torrent, ocean, etc., are used indiscriminately of the water upon the earth, and of the aqueous vapor in the sky or the rain in the air',[324] the vessel from which the hero pours might well be an analogue to the cave or hidden shelter where the monster had constrained the penned up waters (whether the allusion was to the theft of rain-bearing clouds, or rather to the caps of the Hindu Kush peaks encapsulated by snow and ice, as suggested by Falk and Witzel).[325]

In conclusion, I would like to mention a last iconographic detail that has so far escaped attention. When the new statuettes from private collections published here for the first time are considered together with those previously known, it becomes clear that, with few exceptions, the *balafrés* were actually imagined as having only one eye, that is as single-eyed heroes. We have to admit that this important feature would not have been realized if collectors had not rescued the statuettes from the vortex of the antiques market and given the present writer the chance to study them as a whole group.

This new and somehow surprising detail would place 'our hero' in the range of other outstanding characters (gods and/ or tricksters) of Indo-European mythologies, like Odin in Scandinavian and Lug in Irish myths, or the abundantly quoted stereotyped heroes recognized by George Dumézil in the traditional versions of Rome's legendary history.[326]

While testing the idea and the implications of such a hypothesis is far beyond my scientific capabilities and the scope of this book, it is worth noting that in Dumézil's perspective the single-eyed or single-handed heroes are characters that, in defending their kin, undergo mutilation and sacrifice parts of their bodies, thus obtaining supernatural wisdom or new magic powers as sorcerers.[327] One wonders if, on the same lines, by losing an eye, the *balafré* had acquired some supernatural powers required to overcome the rain-stealing monster.

Can we thus rehabilitate for good the icon, the image and the historical meaning of *balafrés*? Ultimately, I feel that when the Oxus people (if the *balafrés*, as is likely, came actually from this part of the ancient world) placed the statuettes in a grave they did this with a pious attitude – offering to the dead not only an image of strength and salvation from the darkness of the grave (the belly of the monster), but also of perennially renewed fertility.

How far the proposed interpretation is reliable will be a matter of opinion. In defence of my views, I stress that the structuralist reconstructions by Francfort of the main religious mythemes of the Oxus Civilization can be further implemented and partially modified.[328]

Francfort's theory of the maleficent 'scale-covered felon', as a peculiarly Central Asian human transformation of the rain-stealing monster, seems to have encountered, so far, general favour: not only because of the great prestige of the French scholar, but also because he had the great merit of positing the question for the first time in holistic and rational terms of correspondences, associations, and structural oppositions. However, the evidence on which he builds is strictly limited to a subjective interpretation of the iconography; supported by an invalid argument (the idea that the statuettes might have horns and wings in the form of applied metal parts), it did not explain in narrative terms two of the crucial attributes of the *balafrés*, since even if the reptilian skin might have been a result of bodily hybridization between man and dragon, the scar and the pot were not accounted for.

In contrast, the view here proposed – that the *balafré* represented an early Indo-Iranian ancestor of the Ṛgvedic Indra as dragon-slayer, by means of a synoptic visual narrative – might find support in other sculptures and artworks of the same period as well as in later (?) literary religious texts of the Hindu tradition, while also possibly accounting for all three iconographic components mentioned. What I cannot explain are the holes on the lips; I believe that they may have suggested or even contained lip-plugs, but besides the hypothesis of an exotic allusion or a purposeful archaism, at present there is no progress with regard to this detail.

Notes

1. Sarianidi 1977.

2. Sarianidi 1990, 1993, 1998.

3. Hiebert 1993, 1994a and b; Hiebert and Moore 1993; Gubaev, Koshelenko and Tosi 1998; Salvatori 1993; Salvatori and Tosi 2008; Rouse and Cerasetti 2014; Boroffka 2014.

4. Boucharlat et al. 2005; Bendezu-Sarmiento and Lhuillier 2011; Lecomte 2011, 2013; Lecomte et al. 2002.

5. Bendezu-Sarmiento and Mustafakulov 2013.

6. Avanessova and Lyonnet 1995.

7. Kaniuth et al. 2007, 2010.

8. Lombardo et al. 2014.

9. P'jankova et al. 2009.

10. Kaniuth et al. 2006.

11. Salvatori 2008a and b.

12. Limited excavations at the site had been conducted from 1981 to 1983: Hiebert 1994a: 29.

13. Salvatori 1993, 1994a, 1994b, 1995a.

14. Sarianidi 2007.

15. Pottier 1984; Ligabue and Salvatori 1988; Sarianidi 1998; Francfort 2003.

16. Simpson 2012: 10–11.

17. Ghirshman 1963.

18. Pottier 1984: 11.

19. See e.g. Benoit 2010.

20. When, together with the invaluable help of Gianluca Bonora, we attempted to count the 'Bactrian princesses' in public and private collections (authentic and fake) or appearing on the internet, the preliminary estimate came close to 150 specimens.

21. Andrianov 1969; see also Vercellin 1988: 28.

22. Gentelle 1989.

23. Bushmakin 2007; Beattie 1989.

24. Simpson 2012: 15–19.

25. Good 2010.

26. For the archaeological evidence of domestication and hybridization of camels in Central Asia in the third millennium BC see Potts 2008, footnote 48. Bones of possibly domesticated camels dating to the late fourth–early third millennium BC seem to have been found in the Neolithic-Chalcolithic site of Ayakagytma, in Uzbekistan, but given the difficulty of distinguishing domesticated bone forms from wild ones this information needs to be confirmed (G. L. Bonora, personal communication).

27. Thornton 2013: 182.

28. Ibid. 195.

29. Dalton 2007.

30. Pottier 1984: 7.

31. Ligabue and Salvatori 1988.

32. Hiebert and Lamberg-Karlovsky 1992; Hiebert 1994a; Lamberg-Karlovsky 2003, 2007.

33. Sarianidi and Dubova 2013: 120.

34. In this book, the chronology of the cultural-chronological partitions is that commonly defined, in Mesopotamian terms, as 'Middle chronology'. However, the dates here adopted are also affected by the recognition that the different dating of the 'Low chronology', that consistently shift downwards (by as much as a century) some of the most important events of Mesopotamian history of the early second millennium BC, sometimes fits better the archaeological scenarios of the eastern regions.

35. The short reconstruction that follows is based upon J. Shaffer's (1992) original periodization of the pattern of social evolution in the Indo-Pakistani subcontinent in terms of four consecutive eras (Early Food Producing Regionalization, Integration, Localization). Even if the historical forms of socio-political organization are completely different, the four steps are generally recognizable and have turned out quite useful also for framing the evolutionary trajectories of southern Central Asia in a meaningful pattern. To this basic description was applied the body of information given in Kohl 1984, still one of the most useful summaries on the prehistory and protohistory of the region, and the main results of the last three decades of archaeological investigations by Soviet, post-Soviet and Italian scholars.

36. Harris 2010.

37. Bonora and Vidale 2013.

38. Jarrige 2007, 2008.

39. Vidale 2015.

40. Dupree et al. 1071; Tosi and Wardak 1972; Maxwell-Hyslop 1982; Jarrige 2007.

41. As above, and see also Sarianidi 1986b and Jarrige 2008; for the later dating see Olijdam 2000.

42. See as examples Fullol vessel 7, in silver, in Dupree et al. 1971; Tosi and Wardak 1972: Figs 5b, 10; Morello 2015a: cat. 39; Fullol vessel 8, in silver, in Dupree et al. 1971; Tosi and Wardak 1972: 5a, 11, 12; Morello 2015a: cat. 63; the weight in copper or bronze in form of a bull at the Miho Museum, in Arnold 1995: n. 9; or the dish at the

Louvre in Amiet 1988: Figure 4a. See also the androcephalic bulls on the silver vessel of the Reza Abbasi Museum in Tehran, whose frontal part is covered with parallel bands of alternating oblique dashes, crossed by rows of inscribed circles: Morello 2015a: cat. 91.

43. Tosi and Wardak 1972: 16, Figure 2a, 15–16; Morello 2015a: cat. 42; Jarrige 2007: 101, 103.

44. Gian Luca Bonora has commented in a personal communication that: 'One should not forget the discovery of painted late Chalcolithic sherds and a female figurine of Geoksyurian type in the Kelleli area of the Murghab delta, as well as of grey ware vessels of the late Namazga IV period (or early Namazga V) in the Kelleli 1 site. Also, some Namazga IV painted sherds were found in the bottom of a trench dug in Gonur North.'

45. Personal communication from Sandro Salvatori.

46. Moorey 2005.

47. Steinkeller 2014.

48. Potts 2008 (Šimaški); Francfort and Tramblay 2010 (Marhaši).

49. Sarianidi 2007, 118–119; Ligabue and Rossi Osmida 2007: 162, Fig. 10.

50. Rossi-Osmida 2002: 99–100.

51. Francfort 1992: 197.

52. For this footwear see also Amiet 1979.

53. Kirtcho 2009.

54. Kohl 2007: 210.

55. Sarianidi and Dubova 2013: 132.

56. Measurements from Morello 2015; Amiet 2005; Amiet 2007a: Fig. 17.

57. Sarianidi 1998: 44.

58. Lawergren 2003; Amiet 1986: p. 164, pp. 196–197, p. 315, n 167; 1972: 427–428.

59. Amiet 1972; 1986: 164, 196–197, 315, no. 167.

60. See the discussion in Lawergren 2003; various hypotheses are reviewed in Ligabue and Rossi Osmida 2007: 173–174.

61. As argued in Steinkeller 2014.

62. Ligabue and Salvatori 1988: Fig. 44.

63. Sotheby's 1992: Fig. 6.

64. Previously published in Ligabue and Salvatori 1988: Fig. 101; Sarianidi 1998: Figure 25, 1–3; Sarianidi 2005: 281.

65. Khinaman: Curtis 1988: 102, Fig. 2, 1b; Shahdad: Hakemi 1972: Pl. 20a; 1997: 693 Qa. 1.

66. Steinkeller 2014: 699.

67. Potts 2008.

68. Amiet 1966: 243, n. 176.

69. Ibid.; Amiet 1994: 92, no. 56.

70. See Amiet 1991; Francfort 2005: Fig. 14; Pittman 1984: Figure 6; Amiet 1988: Figure 4a

71. Hakemi 1997: 645–648; Ligabue and Salvatori 1988: 147 (Shahdad); Madjidzadeh 2003: 153 (Halil Rud); Amiet 1988: Fig. 4 (Louvre).

72. Kovtun 2012.

73. Cf. Rossi Osmida 2002: 118–119.

74. Several examples are given in Ligabue and Salvatori 1988.

75. Francfort 2009.

76. Bendezu-Sarmiento et al. 2013

77. Ligabue and Rossi Osmida 2007: 262–269.

78. Pittman 1984: 42–46; Amiet 1988: Fig. 11; Ligabue and Salvatori 1988: Figs 80–83, 107.

79. Pittman 1984: 42.

80. Benoit 2010: for a preliminary discussion on a chlorite receptacle found on the surface of Shahdad, see Vidale et. al. 2012.

81. See for example the specimens in Ligabue and Salvatori 1988: Fig. 80; Rossi Osmida 2002: 203–207; Ligabue and Rossi-Osmida 2007: 269.

82. Cf. Madjidzadeh 2003: 116, 119.

83. Pottier 1984: Fig. 31, 227.

84. Ligabue and Salvatori 1988: 219, Fig. 86; Ligabue and Rossi Osmida 2007: 286.

85. Woolley 1934: Pl. 174 a.

86. See for example Ligabue and Salvatori 1988: Fig. 7a; and Pottier 1984: n. 191.

87. Masson 1988: 63–80.

88. Pottier 1984: 6–7.

89. For the following we are indebted to Sarianidi 2007.

90. Ibid: 40.

91. Amiet 2007b: Fig. 1a–1b.

92. Sarianidi 2007: 42.

93. Sarianidi 2002, 2007, 2008a; Salvatori 2010.

94. N. Dubova, personal communication; Sarianidi and Dubova 2013: 52, 94.

95. Salvatori 2010.

96. Sarianidi 1998: 71.

97. Ibid.

98. Madjidzadeh 2003.

99. Personal communication from Mohammad Heidary.

100. Rossi Osmida 2002: 38.

101. Hiebert and Lamberg-Karlovsky 1992.

102. Salvatori 1995.

103. See, among others, Kaniuth 2010: 6–9.

104. Franke 2010.

105. Sarianidi 1998: Fig. 27, 5.

106. During Caspers 1993–5; Vidale 2004; Laursen 2010.

107. Bushmakin 2007: Figs 1, 4.

108. Ligabue and Salvatori 1988: Figs 60–61; see Sarianidi 2008b: 1618, 3,4.

109. Sarianidi 1998: Fig. 27, 4; Sarianidi and Dubova 2013: 167.

110. Spycket 1981: 141.

111. Ardeleanu-Jansen 1984.

112. Sarianidi 2008a.

113. Cortesi et al. 2008: 28.

114. Sarianidi 1998.

115. See Steinkeller 2014: n. 23, and Kohl 2007, 221.

116. Lyonnet 2005.

117. Hiebert 1994b; Ligabue and Salvatori 1988.

118. Francfort 2007: 111.

119. Salvatori 2010.

120. This expression here and in other sections of the book is used with caution, in the absence of proper analyses; actually, the seals are commonly made with arsenical copper, or with copper and lead mixtures.

121. Sarianidi 1986a; 1998: 52–53. According to Sandro Salvatori (personal communication): the finds from Togolok 21 (late Bronze age) was an open air

activity area, with several columns abandoned while being reused as raw materials for making other objects (Page 81, note 9 of Sarianidi 2002). The reuse of the columns in the same period is confirmed by a supposed cenotaph at Ulug Depe (with two miniature columns), found in a house of the late Middle Bronze Age (and therefore dug in a later moment) together with some children' graves: 'One of the houses in the dwelling area dating to the end of the Middle Bronze Age presented an unusual case, associating seven individual child burials with a cenotaph: several grinding stones and stone columns, of a type usually related to funerary practices, had been deliberately positioned so as to look like a prone human figure.' (Bendezu-Sarmiento 2012).

122. Cf. Madjidzadeh 2003: 144–146.

123. See among others, Lamberg-Karlovsky 2003, 2007 and 2013.

124. Actually, some Andronovo potsherds were inventoried both in the upper levels of Gonur North and Gonur South, but without links with the middle or late Bronze Age occupations (S. Salvatori, personal communication).

125. Lamberg-Karlovsky 2007: 92.

126. Sarianidi 2007: 72; Benoit 2010: 12, Fig. 12.

127. Sarianidi 1998: Fig. 11, 3.

128. Sarianidi 2007: 71. See also Sarianidi and Dubova 2013: 145.

129. Rossi Osmida 2002: 136, Type 3.

130. Santoni 1984: Fig. 8.1.3; Jarrige 1987a: Fig. 77; Jarrige et al. 1995: Figs 7.27, b and c; see also the *Coupe profonde à pied* in Amiet 1977b: 95, Fig. 4.

131. Rostovzeff 1920.

132. Morello 2015a: cat. 19, p. 147.

133. Francfort 2005: Fig. 6 a–d (Private collection).

134. Ibid: Fig. 7a–i (Private collection).

135. Ibid: Fig. 22 (Metropolitan Museum, New York).

136. Ibid: Fig. 25a–b (Louvre).

137. Ibid: Fig. 26a–c (Miho Museum).

138. Sarianidi 1998: 52.

139. Steinkeller 2014: Fig. 9.

140. Francfort 2003: Fig. 13; 2005, Figure 7, a–i.

141. Vidale 2015; Aruz 2003: cat. 243; see for comparison the statuette of a male personage reportedly 'from South-eastern Iran' auctioned in Boisgirard & Associés 2003: 47, cat. 112; Freeman 2013: 30, 45, inv. no. LNS 1564 M, cat.

10. While there is little doubt that the long vertical braid was a distinctive male hair style of ancient Marhaši (Vidale 2015: n. 7), we cannot exclude that in some cases it was also adopted by the Oxus people. In fact, looking to the most enigmatic scene represented in the *gobelet à la bataille* in silver, the lower panel (Francfort 2005: Fig. 7 e–f) shows two crouching male personages with two different headdresses: one, on the left, with the long braid falling on shoulder, seems to embrace another man, whose hair conforms to the most common Oxus fashion. While Amiet thinks of a cremation (a ritual very rare, if not totally absent, in the Oxus Civilization), Francfort (2005: 26, 39–40) proposes that the artist conceptually represented a grave as seen in section; what is considered by Amiet as bursting flames, for Francfort is the rendering of branches and leaves of the grave's chamber walls. As the position of the crouching/embraced man on the right is the conventional posture of the prisoner, we would rather agree with Amiet, and wonder whether the man on the right was tied, rather than embraced in support, before being burnt in a pyre, or a kind of wooden cage. In this light, we would be dealing with another execution. The implications of the actions of the man with the braid in this case might be quite peculiar – if he was a southern enemy, as the braid might suggest, the vessel would fix the memory of his cruelty. But this is just another possible, conjectural view of what remains a quite mysterious image.

142. Aruz 2003: 330–332, cat. 227.

143. Francfort 2005: Fig. 7,b; Kohl 2007, Fig. 5.17.

144. Francfort (2003, 2005) recognized in the art of the silver 'Bactrian' vessels a male-centred iconographic system in which characters were organized in a threefold hierarchy: nude adolescents, bearded commoners, adults in *kaunakes* in dominion roles. I think that this observation perfectly grasps the essence of the visual messages.

145. Bergé & Associés 2015: 74–75, no. 83.

146. Ligabue and Salvatori 1988: Fig. 99; Francfort 2007: 114; see also a second axe with a similar subject in Pittman 1984: Fig. 7.

147. Kohl 2007: Fig. 3.28, 115–119.

148. Edens 1995.

149. Reade 2001.

150. Amiet 1977a: Pl. 367.

151. With a portable XRF system X-Met 8000 Oxford Instruments, tube rating 4W, 50 Kv 80 µA.

152. Freeman 2013: 205.

153. Rossi Osmida 2002: 91, Grave 500 (intact); 87, Grave 1996 (plundered). See also other

specimens found at Adji Kui, Rossi Osmida 2011: 151. Note that the excavations of Adji Kui and the standards of the dig publication have met considerable criticism: see Salvatori 2007.

154. Freeman 2013: 52–53, Inv. No. LNS 1408 M a-b.

155. Ligabue and Salvatori 1988: Fig. 99.

156. Cf. Rossi Osmida 2002: 87, 91, 112–113.

157. Sarianidi and Dubova 2013: 36, 52–53.

158. Sarianidi 1998: 74–75.

159. Illustrated in Ligabue and Rossi Osmida 2007: 170, Figs. 23 and 25.

160. Illustrated in Pottier 1984 (e.g. Pl. XVIII,117–119, 121, 122); and Ligabue and Salvatori 1988: Figs. 80, 84.

161. Ligabue and Rossi Osmida 2007: 289, second from right; and the following Figure for the ibex. Private collection.

162. Sarianidi 1998: 143–148.

163. Sarianidi and Dubova 2013: 21–25.

164. Francfort 1992.

165. Sarianidi and Dubova 2013: 158.

166. Metropolitan Museum, New York, No. 1982.5; Ligabue and Salvatori 1988: 231, Fig. 100.

167. Sarianidi and Dubova 2013: 166.

168. Francfort 2002: 35; see also Francfort 1992.

169. Lamberg-Karlovsky 2007.

170. See Bonora et al. 2014.

171. Sarianidi 1998: Fig. 41.

172. Potts 2008.

173. As demonstrated by the Indo-Aryan words spoken by the Mitanni aristocracy of the Hurrians: see among others Anthony 2007: 48–52; Mallory 1989: 37–41.

174. Anthony 2007: 374–375.

175. Mallory 1989: 24–65; Anthony 2007: 39–58.

176. Hiebert and Lamberg-Karlovsky 1992; other versions with minor differences discussed in Kohl 2007: 235.

177. Parpola 1997.

178. Witzel 1999: 2006.

179. For Ebla see Fiorentino et al. 2008.

180. Weiss 2015: 46.

181. Kohl 2007: 200, 230–231.

182. Cerasetti 1998.

183. Cattani 2008; S. Salvatori, personal communication.

184. Gankovsky 1985: 17–19.

185. Potts 1998: wider discussion in Salvatori 2009

186. Salvatori 2008a.

187. Kufterin and Dubova 2013.

188. Salvatori 2008b.

189. Jarrige 1985, 1987b; Jarrige and Hassan 1989; Jarrige and Quivron 2008.

190. Another grave that hosted complete or partial composite statuettes in chlorite and other materials is Number 3214; another head comes from the settlement's Area 5, upper layer, in the open space between the second and the third walled enclosures (N. Dubova, personal communication). Therefore, on the whole, the number of these figurines found in Margiana both by professional and illegal excavators must have been rather substantial. The find of unbaked clay statuettes of this type, painted black and with a flat elongated body, from the Gonur settlement (Sarianidi and Dubova 2013: 143; Sarianidis 2008: Figs 55a, b; p. 311) shows that these images were also used by ordinary inhabitants.

191. See also Potts 2008: n. 41.

192. Benoit 2010.

193. In Grave 1300 at Gonur there was reportedly found part of a statuette covered with a *kaunakes* pattern made in gypsum and faience, and covered with gold leaf (Ligabue and Rossi Osmida 2007: 164).

194. Pittman 1984: 51.

195. Amiet 1986: 159; see also Winkelmann 1994, 820–822.

196. Potts 2008: 186.

197. Ibid: 187.

198. Charnier and Bertholot 2013: 39.

199. Benoit 2010: 20.

200. Amiet 2010.

201. Luneau 2008: 147.

202. Artcurial 2014a: 16–17, 10.

203. Sarianidi 2006: no. 79, 217.

204. Of a similar statuette, Amiet observed that 'Le vêtement … s'apparente directement au *kaunakès* mésopotamien, que l'on observe sous sa forme la plus archaïque, avec de grandes languettes allongées, sur les statuettes de même conception, acquises précédemment par M. Foroughi et le Musée du Louvre.' ['The clothing … directly resembles the Mesopotamian *kaunakes* such as can be seen in its most archaic form, with large elongated tufts, on statuettes of the same design earlier acquired by M. Foroughi and the Musée du Louvre.'] (1977b: 103). Amiet explicitly considers such *grandes languettes allongées* an archaic stylema.

205. Rossi Osmida 2002: 68, 104–107; Benoit 2010: Figs 6 and 8; Artcurial 2014b: 18–19, 33.

206. This type of unnatural, stretched body is shared by a large group of chlorite composite figurines in public or private collections. See for example Timeline Auctions 2011, 122, nr. 452, with similar carved patterns and the same flat base; Benoit 2010, 47, Fig. 19; and another statuette auctioned at Paris, in Bergé & Associatés 2015: 73, no. 82, whose head and body did not originally belong together and had been remounted.

207. Benoit 2010: 13.

208. Thierry de Maigret 2014: 9, 37.

209. Amiet 1977b: 103.

210. Ibid.

211. Ibid: Pl. 4.

212. Musée du Louvre, AO 22918; Benoit 2010: 12–13; Fig. 13a–c.

213. See Benoit's detailed comments: 2010: 13–14.

214. Ligabue and Rossi Osmida 2007: 238, lower left.

215. Sarianidi 2008: Fig. 58, p. 314.

216. Musée du Louvre, AO 28056; Benoit 2010: Figs 14–15.

217. Mertens et al. 1992. To the same type of statuette presumably belonged the two heads with a round turban-like headdress found at Adji Kui in Margiana (Rossi Osmida 2008: 176–177), the specimen in Amiet 1977b: Pl. III and the statuettes in Francfort 2003: Figs 1a and 2a. Other specimens of the same kind (chunky body, featureless head without eyes or simplified facial traits, and flat incised *mèches* of the robe-mantle) were sold in London (Sotheby's 2004: 100, 70), more recently in Paris (Castor and Hara 2013: 114, 115; Bergé & Associés 2014: 90–91, 88) and in New York (Christie's 2014: 84, 83).

218. Charnier and Bertholod 2013: 41.

219. Some doubts are raised by the fact that the headdress, although fitting the head reasonably well both in terms of volume and proportions, has two faint, symmetric notches at the height of the ears that do not match perfectly the tip of the auricles. This might have been a minor manufacturing defect, or the headdress has been substituted – it is now impossible to say. However, in this second hypothetical case, the original headdress must have been almost identical to the present one.

220. Sarianidi 1998: Fig. 18, 8.

221. Freeman 2013: 57.

222. Boisgirard & Associés 2006: 169.

223. E.G. Freeman 2013: Inv. LNS 266 S, cat. 21, 57.

224. Potts 2008: Fig. 3.

225. Freeman 2013: Inv. no. LNS 1429 M, cat. 22, 58.

226. Boisgirard-Antonini 2014: 30, 101.

227. Jarrige and Hassan 1989.

228. Potts 1988: 181.

229. Sarianidi 2008: Fig. 56e, p. 312; 57a, p. 313; 57b, p. 313.

230. Boisgirard & Associés 2003: 44–45; Pierre Bergé & Associés 2007: 124, 313.

231. Ligabue and Rossi Osmida 2007: 238, upper right.

232. Freeman 2013: Inv. LNS 266 S, cat. 21, 57.

233. Amiet 2010: 3.

234. Matthiae 1984: Fig. 52; Matthiae et al. 1985: cat. 55, 56, 58, 59, pp. 190–191, 193–194.

235. Matthiae 1979: Figs 3, 8a–b, Pl. 42; Figure 41; see also Matthiae 1984: Figs 39–40; Matthiae et al. 1995: Pl. 44 and others; cat. 36, 71–76, 77–79, 80–85, and pp. 279, 311–313 and 337.

236. Matthiae 1979: Figs 5–7; Fig. 41, pp. 20–21; Matthiae 1984: Figs. 59–64; Matthiae et al. 1995: cat. 63 and 64, 65–67, 70, 89 and 90; pp. 288–289, 300–302, 315.

237. Ibid: cat. 95, pp. 317 and 336.

238. Mazzoni 1980: Figs 17a–d. In another contemporary headless image at the National Archaeological Museum of Damascus mentioned in the same paper (Ibid: Figs 19a–d) the superimposed rows of *kaunakes* tufts are rendered with a thick pattern of stylized alternating triangles, not so different from the 'Lozenges style' so distinctive of the robes a good number of 'princesses' described above.

239. Hinz 1969; Potts 2008.

240. Ibid.

241. Ibid. and Amiet 2007b, 2010.

242. These are in the course of being partially translated by François Desset, Tehran.

243. Cf. Ligabue and Salvatori 1988: pp. 246–247; Sarianidi 2007: Grave 1028, Fig. 55; even the body part in the Quetta hoard belongs in the same group.

244. Amiet 2010: 5.

245. Grave 2655; Sarianidi 2007: Fig. 60.

246. Sarianidi 2002: 140; 2007: Figs 38–39, p. 153; Sarianidi 2008: Fig. 141; Ligabue and Rossi Osmida 2007, Fig. 21.

247. 1988: 240, 243.

248. David Aaron Ancient Arts 2013: no. 22.

249. Ligabue and Rossi Osmida 2007: Fig. 20; Rossi Osmida 2011, 176–180.

250. For example, the 'Languettes' style statuette in the Louvre has a head whose features, apparently, would be more compatible with the 'Graffito' style. However, the face is badly corroded, and there is always the possibility that in this and many other cases the heads were not the original ones, and could have been substituted not only in recent times, but also in the past. In the Persepolis silver vessel, in the strict typological and stylistic terms here proposed, the 'Wavy tuft' style is shared by the sitting image and by the standing lady, but the rendering of the robe of this latter reminds one also of the 'Lozenges' style. The hypothesis of stylistic variation here presented is admittedly only a preliminary working idea, to be, hopefully, tested or even rejected by further stratigraphic evidence.

251. Sarianidi 2007: Fig. 56.

252. See also Sarianidi 2007: Grave 1799, Fig. 54, p. 73.

253. I nearly gave in to the temptation to ascribe such stylistic choice to a 'Peter Pan' style. My friend and colleague Sara Levi, who uses similarly audacious names for prehistoric styles, knows what I mean. Perhaps the presence of leaves on the statuettes also depended on the popularity of *pipal*-like leaves on imported Indus artefacts (Kaniuth 2010: 6–9; Sarianidi 1998: Fig. 17, 9).

254. Among the statuettes presented in this book, one of the Type 1b/stretched body type (Figures 90, 91, 92, 94, 144) has a bulky, flat base, and its carvings are not much different from those seen in the standard sitting types (except for the unusual presence of circles made with tubular copper drills). It looks like a transition from the common sitting to the stretched forms. This is the only statuette here presented whose authenticity, in my opinion, leaves a margin of doubt; but because of its overall formal and stylistic coherence, it has been included in the book.

255. Personal communication: see also Pittman 2001: 237, Figs 10.49 and 10.51; Ascalone 2011: Pl. LX, in particular 4B.5 and 4B.6 and Pl. LXI, 4B.17; and Ascalone 2013.

256. Respectively Benzel 2010; Nagel 1968.

257. Ghirshman 1968.

258. Muscarella 2000.

259. In his article on the Persepolis silver vessel, Potts (1988: 182) remarks, quoting Pottier 1984, that 'Although two typically "Bactrian" statuettes of females wearing the *kaunakes* (then in the Foroughi Collection), published in 1968 by Ghirshman and compared by him with those shown on the Persepolis silver vessel 34, were initially said to have come from Fars, it was later revealed that the dealer who sold the pieces to M. Foroughi had actually said they were "more likely to have come from the north or from Afghanistan".' The Foroughi *balafrés*, most probably, had the same origin too. This places the early lootings of Bactrian and Central Asian Bronze Age cemeteries even before the impact of the conflicts following the Soviet invasion of Afghanistan.

260. Benoit 2013: 344.

261. Ghirshman 1963.

262. The Metropolitan Museum website reports the complex history and the vagaries of this statuette, from the reported discovery at Faza, to the Azizbeghlou collection in Tehran, Iran, from where it was sold before 1963 to another private collector. In 1966, it was exhibited at the Musée Rath in Geneva and according to the catalogue of the exhibition the artwork belonged to a private collection, perhaps that of Charles Gillet. After his death in 1966, the statuette passed to Marion Schuster, Lausanne, Switzerland. When she died, one of her daughters, Mathilde de Goldschmidt Rothschild inherited the *balafré*. In 1989, the work was sold at a Sotheby's auction in London as lot 59. In 1992, the work was again sold by Robin Symes to Bodo Schöps. The latter, in 2004, transferred the ownership to the Exartis Foundation, that in turn gave it to Hiroko Horiuchi who eventually, in 2010, transferred ownership to Noriyoshi Horiuchi 'from whom The Metropolitan Museum of Art acquired the work'. http://www.metmuseum.org/collection/the-collection-online/search/328593?rpp=30&pg=6&gallerynos=403&rndkey=20150530&ft=*&pos=155&imgno=0&tabname=object-information (last accessed 10/2016)

263. For 1–6, see Ghirshman 1963; for 7, Francfort 1994; 8, 9, 10 are unpublished, and only mentioned in the auctions' records; 11, before entering the Aron Collection, was published in Pescheteau-Badin 2013, 30, 155; 16 appeared with excellent pictures in David Aaron Ancient Arts 2013.

264. Parrot 1963: 233.

265. Benoit 2001: Figure 151; Ligabue and Salvatori 1988: Figure 106.

266. Francfort 1994: Fig. 4.

267. One in chlorite from Grave 1268, see Sarianidi 2007: Fig. 228; Sarianidi and Dubova 2013: 156.

268. Nadezhda Dubova, personal communication.

269. Porada 1950: 253.

270. Osborne 2014: 1.

271. The *balafrés* are usually portrayed frontally, less commonly from the side. The drawings of the *balafrés* in Nagel 1968, Pl. XVI, clearly show the asymmetric if not clumsy construction of their composite bodies.

272. David Aaron Ancient Arts 2013: no. 21.

273. Parrot 1963: 236.

274. Spycket 1981: 215–217.

275. Francfort 1992; 1994; 2016.

276. Francfort 1994: 409.

277. Ibid.

278. Witzel 2008.

279. Francfort 1994: 410.

280. It is not clear whether the torso No. 4, now at Berlin, the only whose hands were applied and probably made with another material, had a similar small mortise under the armpit.

281. Benoit 2003a: 484.

282. Inv. No. LNS 339 S; Goldstein 2013: 24–26, 50, cat. 15.

283. Porada 1950.

284. Goldstein 2013: 24–26.

285. Amiet 1988: 177.

286. http://www.louvre.fr/en/oeuvre-notices/composite-statuette-anthropomorphic-dragon-snake (last accessed 10/2016).

287. Metropolitan Museum, accession No. 2010.166; http://www.metmuseum.org/collection/the-collection-online/search/328593?rpp=30&pg=6&gallerynos=403&rndkey=20150530&ft=*&pos=155 (last accessed 10/2016).

288. Ghirshman 1963: 154.

289. Benoit 2003: 344.

290. Author's translation.

291. Mallory 1989: 36. From Rgveda I.32, Cf. Embree 1988: 12–13.

292. I am very grateful to David Meier for this information.

293. The only possible exception might be *balafré* No. 14, which, judging from the published picture, might retain a tiny white inlay in the hole of the lower lip. The same statuette is also one of the two that seem to have retained white inlays in the facial scars, but, belonging to private collections, cannot be properly observed and studied. The metal clamp, at any rate, is excluded.

294. Francfort 1994.

295. Francfort 1992, 1994; Witzel 2004 and 2008.

296. See among others Watkins 2005.

297. Witzel 2001, 2004.

298. Benveniste and Renou 1934.

299. Watkins 2005: 298. Cf. Witzel 2004: 600; Falk 1997; Witzel 2005 and Lyle 2015 expanded the scope of the myth to much wider spheres of cultural interaction and intersections of meanings.

300. Witzel 2004: 299, 301, 303.

301. Francfort 1994; Winkelmann 2003.

302. The possible chronological horizon, assuming (arbitrarily) as a first working hypothesis the likely but undemonstrated contemporaneity of the *balafrés* with the 'Bactrian princesses', might stretch from part of the twenty-third century to the beginning of the second millennium BC. As the cross-like hairdo pattern of some *balafrés* precisely mirrors the rendering of the same feature in 'Bactrian princesses' of the 'Lozenges' style, the third style in our hypothetical sequence, at least some of the statuettes might be preliminarily and loosely dated around 2000 BC. This time threshold, corresponding to a still full urban/palatial phase of ancient Margiana, is framed by Witzel (2004) and others within a context of Indo-Iranian cultural unity. The earliest written evidence for the name of Indra remain the famous and widely discussed Mitanni documents of Syria, dated to the early fourteenth century BC, together with Indo-Aryan names and technical terms referring to horse breeding and training. See Witzel 2004: 588 ff.; Anthony 2007: 48–52; Mallory 1989: 37–41.

303. Please note that I am not a philologist, and that I have no background in Sanskrit and in Vedic literature. What follows is a strong and somehow arbitrary simplification of matters discussed at length over two centuries by eminent scholars, often with uncertain and controversial results, as witnessed by an enormous specialized literature. My sources are entirely secondary: the English translations in Griffith 1896 and Jamieson and Breton 2014, plus a few other articles quoted in the text. I am conscious of the manifold hermeneutic problems involved in the use of the archaic and cryptic religious poetry of the Rgveda, and do not pretend to propose a complete solution to many of the problems here superficially touched. I rather would like to emphasize the need, clearly stated in Witzel 2001, but carefully ignored by many archaeologists, to accompany the interpretation of material culture and iconography of the middle Bronze Age with the most archaic written literary heritage of the subcontinent and Central Asia, whose protohistoric roots are beyond question.

304. Perry 1885: 133, 135.

305. Lubotsky 2000: 315.

306. Watkins 2005: 298.

307. Even more so because the other possible semantic implication of the same root (coiling and spiraling around the victim's body, at least according to Griffith) might be rather implicit in Ahi, another name given to Vrtra by the Rgvedic hymns. In fact, 'Ahi, "Serpent, Dragon" ("Wurm" of German mythology), designates both a demon and a mysterious being ... "the dragon of the depths". In most cases, however, Ahi is the demon, identified with Vrtra ... The root is ah, in the signification "squeeze". The reference is probably to snakes of the constrictor kind' (Perry 1885: 200).

308. Morandi Bonacossi 2003.

309. O'Flaherty 1987: 15.

310. Ibid: 16.

311. Ibid: 76–85, with further reference literature at 320.

312. Morandi Bonacossi 1993, 15–24.

313. Other round seals in copper or stone published in Sarianidi 2008b might refer to the same mytheme, but the reproductions in the quoted books are not detailed enough to justify speculation. However, another exceptional seal, again 'from Bactria' (ibid., 45), shows a muscular bearded hero, quite similar to our *balafrés*, partially enveloped by a big spiralling snake, in what could look like a mountan scenario; in front of the man, there are some wavy incisions that may stand for water. For more and better information one would need to examine, directly and in detail, this important artefact.

314. Morandi Bonacossi ascribes the San Lazzaro statuette (and incidentally also the 'Narbenmänner', i.e. our *balafrés*, 1993: 22) to an archaic Sumerian context of the late Uruk period, on the basis of holistic formal and stylistic analysis, but *contra* Francfort and the other interpreters of the Oxus sculptures I would rather maintain a dating to the second half of the third millennium BC. Also, Morandi Bonacossi interprets the three winding scars on the left cheek as a due to a manufacturing accident, while for me the coincidence with the scars of our images and the regularity of the incisions convincingly point to an intentional carving. His discussion of the San Lazzaro statuette in the collection's catalogue contains an exhaustive set of parallels with other artworks from Mesopotamia or Central Asia depicting men attacked by snakes, variously dated from the late Uruk to the Early Dynastic periods (see also Winkelmann 2003), that might support the hypothesis of the depiction of episodes and/or variations of the 'hero slays serpent' mytheme.

315. Sarianidi 2008b: 10101.1

316. As discussed in Vidale 2015.

317. Witzel 1989; Jamieson and Breton 2014: 10–13.

318. See n. 286.

319. Perry 1885: 128.

320. Watkins 2005: 354; cf. Griffith 1896: 164.

321. Jamieson and Breton (2014: 584), although with strong doubts, propose a quite different reading: 'It was not because of me that the cobra pierced you down, smashed apart his jaws (to swallow you, o bounteous one'. Thus the jaws in this reading would be those of the snake, and not of the wounded hero, and the verse would refer 'to snakes' ability to reconfigure their jaws to swallow large prey'. In this second interpretation, the wound on the hero's face would remain unexplained, while the act of engulfing and swallowing the body of the hero would be further emphasized.

322. This *balafré*, not illustrated in this book, is preserved only as a partial torso. The beard is rendered with circlets, and the *balafré* is anomalous also because on the face he bears a double scar, instead of a single cut.

323. Witzel (2005: 34) and Falk (1997) also link the water pouring gesture in some traditional rituals of the subcontinent to the mythical release of the spring waters by the Vedic hero.

324. Perry 1885: 135.

325. Falk 1997; Witzel 2005: 34.

326. See among others, Dumézil and Strutynski 1980; Scott Littleton 1973; Belier 1991.

327. But see the different interpretations proposed in Kershaw 2000. For the possibility that the one-eye in early Indo-European mythologies was in itself a powerful weapon, as an extreme form of *grimace héroïque*, to paralyze the enemy in war, see Belier 1991: 158-159.

328. Francfort 1994.

Bibliography

Amiet P. 1966. *Élam*. Archée, Auvers-sur-Oise.

— 1972. 'Les Antiquités orientales de la collection David-Weill'. *La revue du Louvre*, 22, 427–428.

— 1977a. *L'Art antique du Moyen-Orient*. Citadelles & Mazenod, Paris.

— 1977b. 'Bactriane Protohistorique'. *Syria* 54, 1–2, 89–121.

— 1978. 'Antiquités de Bactriane'. *La revue du Louvre et des Musées de France* 3, 153–164.

— 1979. 'Iconographie archaïque de l'Iran. Quelques documents nouveaux'. *Syria* 56, 3–4, 333–352.

— 1986. *L'âge des échanges inter-iraniens*. Notes et documents des Musées de France, 11. Editions de la Réunion des musées nationaux, Paris.

— 1988. 'Le Antichità della Battriana e dell'Iran Esterno al Museo del Louvre'. In G. Ligabue and S. Salvatori (eds), *Battriana, una antica civiltà delle oasi dalle sabbie dell'Afghanistan*. Erizzo, Venice, 159–180.

— 1991. 'Une statuette de zébu de Bactriane?' *Arts Asiatiques* 46, 146–147.

— 1994. *La Cité royale de Suse. Catalogue d'exposition, New York, Metropolitan Museum of Art, 17 novembre 1992–7 mars 1993*. Éditions de la Réunion des musées nationaux, Paris.

— 2005. 'Art de cour de Margiane-Bactriane'. *La revue du Louvre et des Musées de France* 55, 2, 29–36.

— 2007a. 'L'âge des échanges inter-iraniens'. In G. Ligabue and G. Rossi Osmida (eds), *Sulla Via delle Oasi: Tesori Dell'Oriente Antico*. Il Punto edizioni, Trebaseleghe, 74–87.

— 2007b. 'Elam et Trans-Elam. À Propos de Sceaux-Cylindres de La Collection du Dr. Serge Rabenou'. *Revue d'assyriologie et d'archéologie orientale* 2007/1, 101, 51–58.

—2010. 'Princesses de Bactriane ou Gracieuses mères trans-élamites?' *Revue d'assyriologie et d'archéologie orientale*, 2010/1, 104, 3–7.

Andrianov B. V. 1969. *Drevinie orositel'nye systemy Priaral'ya*. Nauka, Moscow.

Anthony D. W. 2007. *The Horse, the Wheel and Language: How Bronze-Age Riders from the Eurasian Steppes Shaped the Modern World*. Princeton University Press, Princeton and Oxford.

Ardeleanu-Jansen A. 1984. 'Stone Sculptures from Mohenjo-daro'. In M. Jansen and G. Urban (eds), *Interim Reports 1*. IsMEO/RWTH, Aachen, 139–157.

Arnold D. (ed.) 1995. *Ancient Art from the Shumei Family Collection*. New York.

Artcurial 2014a. *Arts d'Orient et de l'Islam provenant des Collections Xavier Guerrand-Hermès*. [25 March 2014.] Auction catalogue. Briest–Poulain–F. Tajan, Paris.

— 2014b. *Arts d'Orient et de l'Islam. Quatre Collections Privées*. [12 May 2014.] Auction catalogue. Briest–Poulain–F. Tajan, Paris.

Aruz J. (ed.) 2003. *Art of the First Cities: The Third Millennium B.C. from the Mediterranean to the Indus*. The Metropolitan Museum of Art, New York.

Ascalone E. 2011. *Glittica Elamita*. L'Erma di Bretschneider, Rome.

— 2013. 'A New South-Eastern Iranian Glyptic Evidence'. In K. De Graef and J. Tavernier (eds), *Susa and Elam: Archaeological, Philological, Historical and Geographical*

Perspectives. Proceedings of the International Congress Held at Ghent University, December 14–17, 2009. Brill, Leiden and Boston, 3–26.

Avanessova N. and B. Lyonnet 1995. 'Bustan VI, une nécropole de l'âge du Bronze dans l'ancienne Bactriane (Ouzbékistan méridional: témoignage des cultes du feu'). *Arts asiatiques* 50, 31–46.

Beattie H. 1989. *Afghanistan*. http://afghandata. org:8080/xmlui/handle/azu/3069 (accessed 10/2016).

Bekas M. 2014. 'Les dragons de la civilisation de l'Oxus (2500–1700): diversité des formes et unité symbolique'. http://www.academia.edu/12698467/Les_dragons_de_la_civilisation_de_lOxus_2500–1700_diversit_des_formes_et_unit_symbolique (accessed 10/2016).

Belier W. W. 1991. *Decayed Gods: Origin and Development of Georges Dumézil's 'Idéologie Tripartie'*. E. J. Brill, Leiden.

Bendezu-Sarmiento J. 2012. *Ulug Depe a forgotten city in Central Asia*. MAFTUR. Mission Archéologique Franco-Turkmène, MAE, CNRS.

Bendezu-Sarmiento J. and J. Lhuillier 2011. 'Iron Age in Turkmenistan: Ulug-depe in the Kopetdagh piedmont'. *Historical and Cultural Sites of Turkmenistan*. Ashgabat, 239–250.

Bendezu-Sarmiento J., J. Lhuillier and É. Luneau 2013. 'Les différentes formes de richesse dans les sociétés d'Asie Centrale aux Âges du Bronze et du Fer (III–I millénaire av. J.-C.'. In C. Baroin and C. Michel (eds), *Richesse et Sociétés*. René-Ginouvès, Nanterre, 253–263.

Bendezu-Sarmiento J. & S. Mustafakulov 2013. 'Le site proto-urbain de Dzharkutan durant les âges du bronze et du fer. Recherches de la Mission archéologique franco-ouzbèke-Protohistoire'. In J. Bendezu-Sarmiento (ed.), *L'archéologie française en Asie centrale. Nouvelles recherches et enjeux socioculturels*. De Boccard, Paris, 207–236.

Benoit A. 2003a. *Art et Archéologie: les civilisations du Proche-Orient ancien*. École du Louvre, Réunion des musées nationaux, Paris.

— 2003b. 'Statuette féminine'. In O. Bopearachchi, C. Landes and C. Sachs (eds), *De L'Indus a l'Oxus. Archéologie de l'Asie Centrale*. Catalogue de l'Exposition du Musée de Lattes. Imago, Lattes, 36.

— 2004. 'À propos d'un don récent de la Société des Amis du Louvre: les "princesses" de Bactriane'. *La revue du Louvre et des Musées de France* 4, 35–43.

— 2009. 'Some thoughts on the cosmetology of the Near East during the Third Millennium BC.: containers and contents'. In P. M. Kozhin, M. F. Kosarev and N. A. Dubova (eds), *On the Track of Uncovering a Civilization: A Volume in Honor of the 80th-Anniversary of Victor Sarianidi*. Aletheia, St Petersburg, 308–318.

— 2010. *La Princesse de Bactriane*. Collection Solo, Department des Antiquités Orientales, Louvre éditions, Paris.

— 2011. 'The mystery of the Bactrian Princesses, Surprising Clues to an Unknown Civilization'. *Ligabue Magazine* 59, 180–196.

— 2013. 'Standing Male with a Scarred Face'. In J. Aruz (ed.), *Art of the First Cities*, The Metropolitan Museum of Art, New York, cat. 344, 344–345.

Benveniste E. and L. Renou 1934. *Vrtra et Vrthragna. Etude de mythologie indo-iranienne*. Cahiers de la Société Asiatique 3. Imprimerie Nationale, Paris.

Benzel K. 2010. 'Monstrous Male Figure'. *The Metropolitan Museum of Art Bulletin, Fall 2010: Recent Acquisitions: A Selection 2008–2010*, 4.

Bergé P. & Associés 2007. *Vente Archéologie*. [1 December 2007.] Auction catalogue. Drouot-Richelieu, Paris.

— 2014. *Archéologie*. [21 May 2014.] Auction catalogue. Drouot-Richelieu, Paris.

— 2015. *Archéologie*. [Paris, 30 May 2015.] Auction catalogue. Paris and Brussels.

Boisgirard & Associés 2003. *Collection Bouvier. Textiles d'Egypte A Divers Arts D'Orient*. [26 June 2003.] Auction catalogue. Drouot, Paris. 2003.

— 2006. *Arts D'Orient*. [16 December 2006.] Auction catalogue. Drouot, Paris.

Boisgirard-Antonini 2014. *Archéologie – Arts D'Orient*. [18 June 2014.] Auction catalogue. Druot, Paris.

Bonora G. and M. Vidale 2013. 'The Middle Chalcolithic in southern Turkmenistan and the Archaeological Rcord of Ilgynly Depe'. In C. A. Petrie (ed.), *Ancient Iran and its Neighbours: Local Developments and Long-Range Interactions in the Fourth Millenium BC*. Oxbow Books, Oxford and Oakville, Connecticut, 145–170.

Bonora G. L., M. Vidale, M. Mariottini and G. Guida 2014. 'On the Use of Tokens and Seals along the Kopet Dagh Piedmont, Turkmenistan (*ca*. 6000–3000 BCE)'. *Paléorient* 40, 1, 55–71.

Boroffka, N. 2014. 'Gonur-Depe. Eine bronzezeitliche Königsstadt in Mittelasien'. *Mitteilungen der Berliner Gesellschaft für Anthropologie, Ethnologie und Urgeschichte* 35, 15–24.

Boucharlat, R., H.-P. Francfort and O. Lecomte 2005. 'The Citadel of Ulug Depe and the Iron Age Archaeological Sequence in Southern Central Asia'. *Iranica Antiqua* 40, 479–514.

Bushmakin A. G. 2007. 'Minerals and Metals of Bactria and Margiana'. In G. Ligabue and G. Rossi Osmida (eds), *Sulla Via delle Oasi: Tesori Dell'Oriente Antico*. Il Punto edizioni, Trebaseleghe, 178–189.

Castor A. and L. Hara 2013. *Tableaux, Mobilier et Objets d'Art*. [9 December 2013.] Auction catalogue. Drouot, Paris.

Cattani M. 2008. 'The Final Phase of the Bronze Age and the "Andronovo Question" in Margiana'. In S. Salvatori and M. Tosi (eds), *The Archaeological Map of the Murghab Delta II. The Bronze Age and Early Iron Age in the Margiana Lowlands: Facts and Methodological Proposal for a Redefinition of the Research Strategies*. BAR International Series 1806, Oxford, 133–151.

Cerasetti B. 1998. 'Preliminary Report on Ornamental Elements of "Incised Coarse Ware"'. In A. Guabaev, G. Koshelenko and M. Tosi (eds), *The Archaeological Map of the Murghab Delta: Preliminary Reports 1990–95*. IsIAO, Rome, 67–74.

Charnier J.-F. and A. Berthelot 2013. 'The Birth of the Figure'. In L. Descars (ed.) *Louvre Abu Dhabi: Birth of a Museum*. Skira Flammarion, Paris, 38–42.

Christie's 2014. *Antiquities. New York, Thursday 11 December 2014*. Auction catalogue. New York.

Cortesi E., M. Tosi, A. Lazzari. and M. Vidale 2008. 'Cultural Relationships beyond the Iranian Plateau: The Helmand Civilization, Baluchistan and the Indus Valley in the 3rd Millennium BCE'. *Paléorient* 34, 2, 5–35.

Curtis J. 1998. 'A Reconsideration of the Cemetery at Khinaman, South-East Iran'. *Iranica Antiqua* 23, 97–128.

Dalton R. 2007. 'Pieces of the Puzzle'. *Nature*, 450, 13, 940–941.

David Aaron Ancient Arts 2013. *Important Works from the Near East, October 2013*. Catalogue. London.

Dumézil G. and U. Strutynski 1980. *Camillus: A Study of Indo-European Religion as Roman History*. University of California Press, Berkeley, Los Angeles and London.

Dupree L., P. Gouin and N. Omer 1971. 'The Khosh Tapa Hoard from North Afghanistan'. *Archaeology* 24, 28–34.

During Caspers E. C. L. 1993–5. 'The Meluhhan Heritage: Indianesque Stamps and Cylinders Seals, and their Relevance for the Acculturation Processes of the Harappan Abroad'. *Persica*, XV, 7–27.

Edens C. 1995. 'Transcaucasia at the End of the Early Bronze Age'. *Bulletin of the American Schools of Oriental Research* 299/300, 53–64.

Embree A. T. 1988. *Sources of Indian Tradition. Volume I: From the Beginning to 1800*. Second Edition. Columbia University Press, New York.

Ente Manifestazioni Milanesi (ed.) 1963. *7000 Anni d'Arte Iranica*. Bramante Editrice, Milan.

Falk H. 1997. 'The Purpose of Rgvedic Ritual'. In M. Witzel (ed.), *Inside the Texts, Beyond the Texts: New Approaches to the Study of the Vedas*. Harvard Oriental Series, Opera Minora, Cambridge, Massachusetts, 67–88.

Fiorentino G., V. Caracuta, L. Calcagnile, M. D'Elia, P. Matthiae, F. Mavelli and G. Quarta 2008. 'Third Millennium B.C. Climate Change in Syria Highlighted by Carbon Stable Isotope Analysis of 14C-AMS Dated Plant Remains from Ebla'. *Palaeogeography, Palaeoclimatology, Palaeoecology* 266, 51–58.

Francfort H.-P 1992. 'Dungeons and Dragons: Reflections on the System of Iconography in Protohistoric Bactria and Margiana'. In G. Possehl (ed.), *South Asian Archaeology Studies*, Oxford and IBH Publishing Co. Put. Ltd, New Delhi, Bombay and Calcutta, 179–208.

— 1994. 'The Central Asian Dimension of the Symbolic System in Bactria and Margiana'. *Antiquity* 68, 406–418.

— 1998. Les sceaux de l'Oxus: diversité de formes et variabilité de fonctions. *Ancient Civilizations from Scythia to Siberia* 5, 1, 59–71.

— 2002. 'Archéologie de l'Asie intérieure de l'âge du bronze à l'âge du fer'.

École pratique des hautes études. Section des sciences historiques et philologiques. Livret-Annuaire 16, 2000–01, 34–37.

— 2003. 'La Civilisation de l'Asie Centrale à l'âge du bronze à l'âge du fer'. In O. Bopearachchi, C. Landes and C. Sachs (eds), *De l'Indus à l'Oxus, Archéologie de l'Asie Centrale. Catalogue de l'Exposition*. Imago, Musée de Lattes, Lattes, 29–59.

— 2005. 'Observations sur la toreutique de la civilisation de l'Oxus'. In O. Bopearachchi and M.-F. Boussac (eds), *Afghanistan. Ancien carrefour entre l'Est et l'Ouest* (Indicopleustoi 3). Brepols, Turnhout, 21–63.

— 2007. 'L'art de la Civilisation de l'Oxus'. In G. Ligabue and G. Rossi Osmida (eds), *Sulla Via delle Oasi: Tesori Dell'Oriente Antico*. Il Punto edizioni, Trebaseleghe, 102–127.

— 2009. 'Le vin en Asie centrale à la Protohistoire, du IIIe millénaire aux Achéménides'. *Cahier des thèmes transversaux ArScAn (vol. IX 2007–2008 Thème IX : Le vin en Asie centrale à la Protohistoire du IIIe millénaire aux Achéménides*. UMR 7041 – Archéologies et Sciences de l'Antiquité, Nanterre, 393–404.

— 2010. 'Bird, Snakes, and Deities in the Oxus Civilization: An Essay Dedicated to Professor Viktor I. Sarianidi on a Cylinder Seal from Gonur Depe'. In N. Miklukho-Maklay (ed.), *On the Track of Uncovering a Civilization: A Volume in Honor of the 80th-Anniversary of Viktor Sarianidi*. Aletheia, St Petersburg, 67–85.

Francfort H.-P. and X. Tremblay 2010. 'Marhaši et la civilisation de l'Oxus'. *Iranica Antiqua* 45, 51–224.

Franke U. 2010. 'From the Oxus to the Indus: Two Compartmented Seals from Mohenjo-daro Pakistan'. In A. Parpola, B. M. Pande and P. Koskikallio (eds), *Corpus of Indus Seals and Inscriptions, 3.1: Supplement to Mohenjo-daro and Harappa*. Suomalainen Tiedeakademia, Helsinki, xvii-xliii.

Freeman D. (ed.) 2013. *Splendors of the Ancient East: Antiquities from The al-Sabah Collection*. Thames and Hudson, London.

Frenez D. and M. Vidale 2012. 'Harappan Chimaeras as "Symbolic Hypertexts". Some Thoughts on Plato, Chimaera and the Indus Civilization'. *South Asian Studies* 28, 2, 107–130.

Gankovsky Yu. V. (ed.) 1985. *History of Afghanistan*. Progress Publishers, Moscow.

Gentelle P. 1989. *Prospections archéologiques en Bactriane orientale (1974–1978). Données paléogéographiques et fondements de l'irrigation*, (Mémoires de la mission archéologique française en Asie Centrale 1). Éditions Recherche sur les civilisations, Paris.

Ghirshman R. 1963. 'Notes iraniennes XII. Statuettes élamites archaïques du Fars (Iran)'. *Artibus Asiae*, 26, 151–160.

— 1968. 'Notes iraniennes XVI. Deux statues élamites du plateau iranien'. *Artibus Asiae* 30, 237–48.

Goldstein S. 2013. 'Lioness Demon or Monster'. In D. Freeman (ed.), *Splendors of the Ancient East: Antiquities from The al-Sabah Collection*. Thames and Hudson, London, 24–26.

Good I. 2010. 'When East Met West: Interpretative Problems in Assessing Eurasian Contact and Exchange in Antiquity'. *Archäologische Mitteilungen aus Iran und Turan* 42, 23–46.

Griffith R. T. H. 1896. *The Hymns of the Rigveda*. Kotagiri, Nilgiri.

Gubaev, A., G. Koshelenko and M. Tosi (eds), 1998. *The Archaeological Map of the Murghab*

Delta: Preliminary Reports 1990–95. IsIAO, Roma.

Hakemi A. 1972. *Catalogue de l'exposition Lut Xabis (Shahdad)*. Tehran.

— 1997. *Shahdad: Archaeological Excavations of a Bronze Age Center in Iran*. IsIAO, Rome.

Harris D.R. 2010. *Origins of Agriculture in Western Central Asia: An Environmental-Archaeological Study*. University of Pennsylvania Press, Philadelphia.

Hiebert, F.T. 1993. 'Excavations of Domestic Quarters from Gonur Depe (North: Excavations of Spring 1989'. *IASCCA Information Bulletin* 19, 78–95).

— 1994a. *Origins of the Bronze Age Oasis Civilization in Central Asia*. American School of Prehistoric Research Bulletin 42, Cambridge, Massachusetts.

— 1994b. 'Production Evidence for the Origins of the Oxus Civilization'. *Antiquity* 68, 259, 372–387.

Hiebert F. T. and C. C. Lamberg-Karlovsky 1992. 'Central Asia and the Indo-Iranian Borderlands'. *Iran* 30, 1–15.

Hiebert, F.T. and K. Moore 1993. 'New Stratigraphic Excavations at Gonur Depe (North'. *IASCCA Information Bulletin* 19, 96–108).

Hinz W. 1969. *Altiranische Funde und Forschungen*. W. De Gruyter, Berlin.

Jamieson S. W. and J. P. Breton (trans. 2014. *The Rigveda: The Earliest Religious Poetry of India*. Oxford University Press, Oxford and New York.

Jarrige J.-F. 1985. 'Les relations entre l'Asie central méridional, le Baluchistan et la vallée de l'Indus à la fin du 3e et au début du 2e millénaire'. In J.-C. Gardin (ed.), *L'Archéologie de la Bactriane ancienne*. Paris, 105–118.

— 1987a. 'Der Kulturkomplex von Mehrgarh Periode VIII und Sibri. Der « Schatz » von Quetta'. In *Vergessene Städte am Indus*, Verlag Philipp von Zabern, Mainz am Rhein, 102–111.

— 1987b. 'A Prehistoric Elite Burial in Quetta'. *Newsletter of Baluchistan Studies* 4, 3–12.

— 2007. 'Il tesoro di Fullol'. In P. Cambon, *Afghanistan. I Tesori Ritrovati. Collezioni del Museo nazionale di Kabul*. Umberto Allemandi & C., Turin [etc.], 25–32.

— 2008. 'The Treasure of Tepe Fullol'. In F. Hiebert and P. Cambon (eds). *Afghanistan: Hidden Treasures from the National Museum, Kabul*. National Gallery of Art, National Geographic Society, Washington, DC, 67–79.

Jarrige J.-F. and M. U. Hassan 1989. 'Funerary Complexes in Baluchistan at the End of the Third Millennium in the Light of Recent Discoveries at Mehrgarh and Quetta'. In K. Frifelt and P. Sørensen (eds), *South Asian Archaeology 1985*. Curzon/Riverdale: London and Riverdale, 150–166.

Jarrige J.F. and G. Quivron 2008. 'The Indus Valley and the Indo-Iranian Borderlands at the End of the 3rd and the Beginning of the 2nd Millennium B.C.' In E. M. Raven (ed.), *South Asian Archaeology 1999*, Groningen, 61–83.

Kaniuth K. 2010. 'Long Distance Imports in the Bronze Age of Southern Central Asia: Recent Finds and their Implications for Chronology and Trade'. *Archäologische Mitteilungen aus Iran und Turan* 42, 3–22.

Kaniuth, K., M. Gruber and A. Kurmangaliev 2010. 'Tilla Bulak 2009 – Vorbericht zur dritten Kampagne'. *Archäologische Mitteilungen aus Iran und Turan* 42, 129–164.

Kaniuth, K., M. Teufer and J. Iljasov 2007. Tilla Bulak 2007 – Vorbericht zur ersten Kampagne. *Archäologische Mitteilungen aus Iran und Turan* 38, 81–102.

Kaniuth, K., M. Teufer and N. M. Vinogradova 2006. 'Neue bronzezeitliche Funde aus Südwest-Tadžikistan'. *Archäologische Mitteilungen aus Iran und Turan* 39, 31–47.

Keddie G. 1989. *Symbolism and Context: The History of the Labret and Cultural Diffusion on the Pacific Rim*. Paper presented at The Circum-Pacific Prehistory Conference, Seattle. Accessed 10/2016 from http://royalbcmuseum. bc.ca/staffprofiles/files/2013/09/LABRET-PAPER-1989-Grant-Keddie.pdf.

Kershaw K. 2000. 'The One-Eyed God: Odin and the (Indo-Germanic Männerbünde'. *Journal of Indo-European Studies*, Monograph No. 36, Institute for the Study of Man, Washington DC.

Khaniki R. A. L. 2003. 'Neyshabur, a Link among Mesopotamia, Indus Valley, Bactria and Iran (of Bronze Age)'. *Nâme-ye Pažuhešgâh-e Mirâs-e Farhangi Quarterly* 1/1 (2003), 36–46 (in Farsi).

Kirtcho L. B. 2009. 'The Earliest Wheeled Transport in Southwestern Central Asia: New Finds from Altyn-Depe'. *Archaeology, Ethnology & Anthropology of Eurasia* 37/1, 25–33.

Kohl P.L. (ed.). 1981. *The Bronze Age Civilization of Central Asia: Recent Soviet Discoveries*. M. E. Sharpe, Armonk, New York.

— 1984. *Central Asia: Palaeolithic Beginnings to the Iron Age – L'Asie Centrale des Origines a l'Age du Fer*. Synthèse no. 14. Éditions Recherche sur les civilisations, Paris.

— 2007. *The Making of Bronze Age Eurasia*. Cambridge University Press, New York.

Kohl P. L. and M.-H. Pottier 1990–1992. '"Central Asian" materials from Baluchistan and Southeastern Iran at the End of the Third Millennium B.C.: Some Preliminary Observations'. *Persica* 14, 91–102.

Kovtun I. V. 2012. '"Horse-Headed" Staffs and the Cult of the Horse Head in Northwestern Asia in the 2nd Millennium BC'. *Archaeology, Ethnology & Anthropology of Eurasia* 40/4, 95–105.

Kufterin V. and N. Dubova 2013. 'A Preliminary Analysis of Late Bronze Age Human Skeletal Remains from Gonur-depe, Turkmenistan'. *Bioarchaeology of the Near East*, 7:33–46.

Lamberg-Karlovsky C. C. 1996. *Beyond the Tigris and the Euphrates: Bronze Age Civilizations*. Ben-Gurion University of the Negev Press, Jerusalem.

— 2003. 'Civilization, State, or Tribes? Bactria and Margiana in the Bronze Age'. *The Review of Archaeology* 24, 1, 11–19.

— 2007. 'The BMAC. Pivot of the Four Quarters: Temples, Palaces, Factories and Bazaars?' In G. Ligabue and G. Rossi Osmida (eds), *Sulla Via delle Oasi: Tesori Dell'Oriente Antico*. Il Punto edizioni, Trebaseleghe, 88–101.

— 2013. 'The Oxus Civilization'. *Cuadernos Prehistoria y Arqueología Universidad Autónoma de Madrid* 39, 21–63.

Laursen S. T. 2010. 'The Westward Transmission of Indus Valley Sealing Technology: Origin and Development of the "Gulf Type" Seal and Other Administrative Technologies in Early Dilmun, c. 2100–2000 BC'. *Arabian Archaeology and Epigraphy* 21, 96–134.

Lawergren B. 2003. 'Oxus Trumpets, ca. 2200–1800 BCE: Material Overview, Usage, Societal Role, and Catalog'. *Iranica Antiqua* 38, 41–118.

Lecomte O. 2011. 'Ulug-depe: 4000 Years of Evolution between Plain and Desert'. *Historical and Cultural Sites of Turkmenistan*. Ashgabat, 221–238.

— 2013. 'Activités archéologiques françaises au Turkménistan'. In J. Bendezu-Sarmiento (ed.), *L'archéologie Française en Asie centrale. Nouvelles recherches et enjeux socioculturels*. (Cahiers d'Asie centrale 21/22). De Boccard, Paris, 165–190.

Lecomte, O., H.-P. Francfort, R. Boucharlat and M. Mamedow 2002. 'Recherches archéologiques récentes à Ulug Dépé (Turkménistan). *Paléorient* 28, 2, 123–132.

Ligabue G. and G. Rossi Osmida 2007. *Sulla via delle oasi. Tesori dell'Oriente Antico*. Il Punto, Trebaseleghe.

Ligabue G. and S. Salvatori (eds), 1988. *Battriana, una antica civiltà delle oasi dalle sabbie dell'Afghanistan*. Erizzo, Venice.

Lombardo, G., N. Vinogradova, J. Kutimov, M. Teufer and T. Filimonova 2014. 'Excavations of the Burial Ground of Gelot in 2007–2010'. *Bollettino di Archeologia on line* 5, 1–28.

Lubotsky A. 2000. 'The Vedic root vr- "to cover" and its present'. In B. Forssman and R. Plath (eds), *Indoarisch, Iranisch und die Indogermanistik. Arbeitstagung der Indogermanistischen Gesellschaft vom 2. bis 5. Oktober 1997 in Erlangen*. Reichert Verlag, Wiesbaden, 315–325.

Luneau É. 2008. 'Tombes féminines et pratiques funéraires en Asie centrale protohistorique. Quelques réflexions sur le « statut social » des femmes dans la civilisation de l'Oxus'. *Paléorient* 34, 1,131–157.

— 2014. 'Identifier le prestige: elements de controverse à propos de quelques objets singuliers de la civilisation de l'Oxus (Asie Centrale), Âge du Bronze'. In Fr. Hurlet, I. Rivoal and I. Sidéra (eds), *Le prestige. Autour des formes de la différenciation sociale*. Paris, Éditions de Boccard, 147–160.

Lyle E. 2015. 'The Hero Who Releases the Waters and Defeats the Flood Dragon'. *Comparative Mythology*, 1.1, 1–12.

Lyonnet B. 2005. 'Another Possible Interpretation of the Bactro-Margiana Culture (BMAC) of Central Asia: The Tin Trade'. In C. Jarrige and V. Lefèvre (eds), *South Asian Archaeology 2001*. Éditions Recherche sur les civilisations, Paris, 191–200.

Madjidzadeh Y. 2003. *Jiroft: The Earliest Oriental Civilization*. Ministry of Culture and Islamic Guidance, Printing and Publishing Organization, Cultural Heritage Organization, Tehran.

Madjidzadeh Y. and H. Pittman 2008. 'Excavations at Konar Sandal in the Region of Jiroft in the Halil Basin: First Preliminary Report (2002–2008). *Iran* 46, 69–103.

Mallory J. P. 1989. *In Search of the Indo-Europeans: Language, Archaeology and Myth*. Thames and Hudson, London.

Masson V. M. 1988. *Altyn-Depe*. The University Museum, University of Pennsylvania, Philadelphia.

Masson, V. M. and V. I. Sarianidi 1972. *Central Asia: Turkmenia before the Achaemenids*. Thames and Hudson, London.

Matthiae P. 1979. 'Appunti di Iconografia Eblaita, I'. *Studi Eblaiti* I, 2.

— 1984. *I Tesori di Ebla*. Laterza, Rome and Bari.

Matthiae P., S. Mazzoni Archi and G.Scandone Matthiae 1985. *Da Ebla a Damasco. Diecimila Anni di Archeologia in Siria*. Electa, Milan.

Matthiae P., F. Pinnock and G. Scandone Matthiae 1995. *Ebla, Alle Origini della Civiltà Urbana. Trent'anni di Scavi in Siria dell'Università di Roma*. Electa, Milan.

Maxwell-Hyslop K.R. 1982. 'The Khosh Tapa-Fullol Hoard'. *Afghan Studies* 3, 4, 25–38.

Mazzoni S. 1980. 'Una statua paleosiriana del Cleveland Museum'. *Studi Eblaiti* III, 5–8, 79–98.

Meadow R. H. 2002. 'The Chronological and Cultural Signification of a Steatite Wig from Harappa'. *Iranica Antiqua* 37, 191–202.

Mertens, J. R., O. W. Muscarella, C. H. Roerig, M. Hill and E. J. Milleker 1992. 'Ancient Art: Gifts from the Norbert Schimmel Collection'. *The Metropolitan Museum of Art Bulletin* 49, 4 (Spring 1992.

Moorey R. 2005. 'The Eastern Land of Tukrish'. In U. Finkbeiner, R. Dittman and H. Hauptmann (eds), *Beiträge zur Kulturgeschichte Vorderasiens: Festschrift fur Rainer Michael Boehmer*. Verlag Phillip von Zabern in Wissenschaftliche Buchgesellschaft, Mainz, 439–448.

Morandi Bonacossi D. 2003. *Il Vicino Oriente antico nella collezione del monastero armeno di San Lazzaro*. Biblioteca Nazionale Marciana, Collana di Studi 2, Padua.

Morello M. 2015a. 'La produzione vascolare in metallo prezioso nell'Asia Media dell'Età del Bronzo'. Università degli Studi di Napoli 'L'Orientale'. Dipartimento di Asia, Africa e Mediterraneo. Tesi di Dottorato di ricerca in Turchia, Iran e Asia Centrale, XI Ciclo N.S.

— 2015b, 'Human Iconography on Metal Vessels from Bronze Age Central Asia'. In G. Affanni, C. Baccarin, L. Cordera, A. Di Michele and K. Gavagnin (eds), *Broadening Horizons 4. A Conference of Young Researchers Working on the Ancient Near East, Egypt and*

Central Asia. University of Torino, October 2011. British Archaeological Reports International Series 2698, Oxford, Archeopress, 117–126.

Mousavi A. 2012. *Ancient Near Eastern Art at the Los Angeles County Museum of Art*. Los Angeles County Museum of Art, Los Angeles.

Muscarella O. W. 2000. *The Lie Became Great: The Forgery of Ancient Near Eastern Culture*. STYX Publications, Groningen, 132.

Musée d'art et d'histoire de Genève 1966. *Trésors de l'Ancien Iran*. Atar S. A., Genève.

Nagel W. 1968. 'Westmakkanische Rundplastik'. *Berliner Jahrbuch für Vor- und Frühgeschichte*, 8, 104–119.

O'Flaherty W. D. 1975. *Hindu Myths*. Penguin Books, Harmondsworth.

Olijdam E. 2000. 'Additional Evidence of a Late Second Millennium Lapis Lazuli Route: The Fullol Hoard (Afghanistan). In M. Taddei and G. De Marco (eds), *South Asian Archaeology 1997. Proceedings of the Fourteenth International Conference of the European Association of South Asian Archaeologists, Held in the Istituto Italiano per l'Africa e l'Oriente, Palazzo Brancaccio, Rome, 7–14 July 1997*. Istituto Italiano per L'Africa e L'Oriente, Rome, 397–407.

Osborne, J. F. 2014. 'Monuments and Monumentality' in idem (ed.), *Approaching Monumentality in Archaeology*. State University of New York Press, Albany, 1–19.

Parpola A. 1997. 'The Dasas and the Coming of the Aryans'. In M. Witzel (ed.), *Inside the Texts, Beyond the Texts: New Approaches to the Study of the Vedas*. Harvard Oriental Series, Opera Minora 2. Cambridge, Massachusetts, 193–202.

Parrot A. 1963. 'Acquisitions et inédits du Musée du Louvre'. *Syria* 40, 3–4, 229–251.

Perry E. D. 1885. 'Indra in The Rig-Veda'. *Journal of the American Oriental Society* 11, 117–208.

Pescheteau-Badin 2013. *Art Islamique, Archéologie*. [6 March 2013.] Auction catalogue. Paris.

Pittman H. 1984. *Art of the Bronze Age: Southeastern Iran, Western Central Asia, and the Indus Valley*. The Metropolitan Museum of Art, New York.

— 2001. 'Glyptic Art of Period IV'. In C. C. Lamberg-Karlovsky and D. T. Potts (eds), *Excavations at Tepe Yahya, Iran 1967–1975*. Peabody Museum of Archaeology and Ethnology, Harvard University, Cambridge, Massachusetts, 231–268.

P'jankova, L.T., B.A. Litvinskij, B. Bobomulloev, K. Kaniuth and M. Teufer 2009. 'Das bronzezeitliche Gräberfeld von Makonimor, Tadžikistan'. *Archäologische Mitteilungen aus Iran und Turan* 41, 97–140.

Porada, E. 1950. 'A Leonine Figure of the Protoliterate Period of Mesopotamia', *Journal of the American Oriental Society*, vol. 70, 1950, pp. 223–226.

Pottier M.-H. 1984. *Matériel funéraire de la Bactriane méridionale de l'âge du bronze*. Éditions Recherche sur les civilisations, Paris.

Potts D. 2008. 'Puzur-Inshushinak and the Oxus Civilization (BMAC): Reflections on Shimashki and the Geo-Political Landscape of Iran and Central Asia in the Ur III Period'. *Zeitschrift für Assyriologie* 98, 165–194.

Reade J. 1991. *Mesopotamia*. The British Museum Press, London.

— 2001. 'Assyrian King-Lists, the Royal Tombs of Ur, and Indus Origins'. *Journal of Near Eastern Studies* 60, 1–29.

Rodríguez Pérez D. 2015. 'Guardian Snakes and Combat Myths: An Iconographical Approach'. In C. Lang-Auinger and E. Trinkl (eds), *Φιτα και Ζοια. Pflanzen und Tieren auf Groechischen Vasen*. Corpus Vasorum Antiquorum Österreich Beiheft 2, Verlag der Österreichischen Akademie der Wissenschaften, Vienna, 147–154.

Rossi Osmida G. 2002. *Margiana Gonur-depe Necropolis: 10 years of excavations by Ligabue Study and Research Centre*. Il Punto, Trebaseleghe.

— 2008. *Adji Kui Oasis*, vol. 1. Il Punto, Trebaseleghe.

— 2011. *Adji Kui Oasis*, vol. 2. Il Punto, Trebaseleghe.

Rostovzeff M. 1920. 'The Sumerian Treasure of Astrabad'. *Journal of Egyptian Archaeology*, 6, 4–27.

Rouse, L.M. and B. Cerasetti 2014. 'Ojakly: A Late Bronze Age Mobile Pastoralist Site in the Murghab Region, Turkmenistan'. *Journal of Field Archaeology* 39 (1), 32–50.

Salvatori S. 1993. 'The Discovery of the Graveyard of Gonur-depe 1 (Murghab Delta, Turkmenistan): 1992 Campaign Preliminary Report'. *Rivista di Archeologia* XVII, 5–13.

— 1994a. 'Excavations at the Namazga V Late Graveyard of Gonur 1 (Murghab Delta, Turkmenistan). Preliminary Report on the 1993 Field Season'. *Rivista di Archeologia* XVIII, 5–37.

— 1994b. 'A Late 3rd Millennium Graveyard at Gonur-depe 1 (Murghab Delta, Turkmenistan). In A. Parpola and P. Koskikallio (eds), *South Asian Archaeology 1993. Proceedings of the Twelfth International Conference of European Association of South Asian Archaeologists held

in Helsinki University, 5–9 July 1993*. (Annales Academiae Scientiarum Fennicae, Series B, Vol. 271. Helsinki, 657–566.

— 1995a. 'Protohistoric Margiana: On a Recent Contribution'. [Review of *IASSCA Information Bulletin* 19, Moscow 1993.] *Rivista di Archeologia* 19, 38–55.

— 1995b. 'Gonur-Depe 1 (Margiana, Turkmenistan): The Middle Bronze Age Graveyard. Preliminary Report on the 1994 Excavation Campaign). *Rivista di Archeologia* XIX, 5–37.

— 2007. 'About Recent Excavations at a Bronze Age Site in Margiana (Turkmenistan). *Rivista di Archeologia* 31, 11–28.

— 2008a. 'The Margiana Settlement Pattern from the Middle Bronze Age to the Parthian-Sasanian: A Contribution to the Study of Complexity'. In S. Salvatori and M. Tosi (eds), *The Archaeological Map of the Murghab Delta II. The Bronze Age and Early Iron Age in the Margiana Lowlands: Facts and Methodological Proposal for a Redefinition of the Research Strategies*. BAR International Series 1806, Oxford, 57–74.

— 2008b. 'Cultural Variability in the Bronze Age Oxus Civilisation and its Relations with the Surrounding Regions of Central Asia and Iran'. In S.Salvatori and M. Tosi (eds), *The Archaeological Map of the Murghab Delta II. The Bronze Age and Early Iron Age in the Margiana Lowlands: Facts and Methodological Proposal for a Redefinition of the Research Strategies*. BAR International Series 1806, Oxford, 75–98.

— 2010. 'Thinking around Grave 3245 in the "Royal Graveyard" of Gonur (Murghab Delta, Turkmenistan). In P. M. Kozhin, M. F. Kosarev and N. A. Dubova (eds)., *On the Track of Uncovering a Civilization: A Volume in Honor of the 80th-Anniversary of Victor Sarianidi*. Aletheia, St Petersburg, 239–252.

Salvatori S. and M. Tosi (eds) 2008. *The Archaeological Map of the Murghab Delta II. The Bronze Age and Early Iron Age in the Margiana Lowlands: Facts and Methodological Proposal for a Redefinition of the Research Strategies*. BAR International Series 1806, Oxford.

Santoni G. 1984. 'Sibri and the South Cemetery of Mehrgarh: Third Millennium Connections between the Northern Kachi Plain Pakistan and Central Asia'. In B. Allchin (ed.), *South Asian Archaeology 1981*. Cambridge University Press, Cambridge, 52–60.

Sarianidi V.I. 1977. *Drevnie zemledel'zy Afganistana*. Moskva.

— 1986a. 'Le complexe culturel de Togolok 21 en Margiane'. *Arts Asiatiques* 41, 5–21.

— 1986b. *Die Kunst des alten Afghanistan. Architektur, Keramik, Siegel: Kunstwerke aus Stein und Metall*. E. A. Seeman Verlag, Leipzig.

— 1990. *Drevnosti strany Margush*. Ashgabat.

— 1993. 'Excavations at Southern Gonur'. *Iran* 31, 25–37.

— 1998. *Margiana and Protozoroastrism*. Kapon editions, Athens.

— 2002. *Margush: Ancient Oriental Kingdom in the Old Delta of Murghab*. Turkmen Dowlet Habarlar, Ashgabat.

— 2005. *Gonurdepe: City of Kings and Gods*. Miras, Ashgabat.

— 2007. *Necropolis of Gonur*. Kapon editions, Athens.

— 2008a. *Margush, Turkmenistan. Mystery and True of the Great Culture*. Ashgabat.

— 2008b. *Myths of Ancient Bactria and Margiana on its Seals and Amulets*. Pentagraphic Ltd, Moscow.

— [Sarianidis V. I.] 2008. *Zoroastrianism: A New Motherland for an Old Religion*. Kiriakidis Brothers s.a., Athens.

Sarianidi V.I. and N. Dubova 2013. *Gadymy Marginin Genji-Hazynasy – Treasures of Ancient Margiana*. Türkmen döwlet neshiryat gullugy, Ashgabat.

Scott Littleton C. 1973. *The New Comparative Mythology: An Anthropological Assessment of the Theories of George Dumézil*. Revised edition. University of California Press, Berkeley, Los Angeles and London.

Seidl U. 1966. 'Zur Moortgat-Festschrift Djamdat Nasr bis Akkade – Assyrer – Hethiter'. *Berliner Jahrbuch für Vor- und Frühgeschichte 6*. Berlin, 195–202.

Shaffer J. 1992, 'The Indus Valley, Baluchistan, and Helmand Traditions: Neolithic Through Bronze Age'. In R. W. Ehrlich (ed.), *Chronologies in Old World Archaeology*, The University of Chicago Press, Chicago, vol. 1, 441–464.

Simpson St J. 2012. *Afghanistan: A Cultural History*. The British Museum Press, London.

Sotheby's 1992. *Important Antiquities from the Norbert Schimmel Collection*, New York, 16 December 1992. Auction catalogue (vol. 6382). New York.

Sotheby's 2004. *Persian & Islamic Art: The Collection of the Berkeley Trust. London, 12 October 2004*. [Auction catalogue.] London.

Spycket A. 1981. *La Statuaire du Proche-Orient Ancien*. E. J. Brill, Leiden.

Steinkeller P. 1982. 'The Question of Marhashi: A Contribution to the Historical Geography of Iran in the Third Millennium B.C.'. *Zeitschrift für Assyriologie und Vorderasiatische Archäologie* 72, II, 237–264.

— 2006. 'New Light on Marhashi and its Contacts with Makkan and Babylonia'. *Journal of Magan Studies*, 1, 1–17.

— 2008. 'Marhashi and Beyond: The Jiroft Civilization in a Historical Perspective'. Paper presented at Tehran, 5–9 May 2008.

— 2014. 'Marhaši and Beyond: The Jiroft Civilization in a Historical Perspective'. In C. C. Lamberg-Karlovsky and B. Genito (eds), *'My Life is like the Summer Rose'. Maurizio Tosi e l'Archeologia come Modo di Vivere. Papers in honour of Maurizio Tosi for his 70th birthday*. BAR International Series 2690, Archeopress, Oxford, 691–707.

Strommenger E. 1980. '39. Oberkörper eine männlichen Statuette'. In *Kunstbibliothek- Die Meisterwerke aus dem Museum für Vor- und Frühgeschichte Berlin, Staatliche Museen Preußischer Kulturbesitz*, Belser Verlag, Stuttgart and Zürich, 92–93, 124.

Thierry de Maigret 2014. *Arts Precolombiens – Archeologie Arts Asiatiques – Ceramiques*. [13 June 2014.] Auction catalogue. Drouot, Paris.

Thornton, C. 2013. 'The Bronze Age in North-Western Iran'. In D. T. Potts (ed.), *The Oxford Handbook of Ancient Iran*. Oxford University Press, Oxford, 179–202.

Timeline Auctions 2011. *Antiquities. 23 and 24 June 2011*. [Auction catalogue.] London.

Tosi M. and R. Wardak 1972. 'The Fullol Hoard: A New Find from Bronze-Age Afghanistan'. *East and West* 22, 1/2 (March–June 1972), 9–17.

Vercellin G. 1998. 'La Battriana tra Preistoria e Futuro'. In G. Ligabue and S. Salvatori (eds) *Battriana, una antica civiltà delle oasi dalle sabbie dell'Afghanistan*. Erizzo, Venice, 27–39.

Vidale M. 2004. 'Growing in a Foreign World: For a History of the "Meluhha Villages" in Mesopotamia in the 3rd Millennium BC'. In A. Panaino and A. Piras (eds), *Schools of Oriental Studies and the Development of Modern Historiography. Proceedings of the Fourth Annual Symposium of the Assyrian and Babylonian Intellectual Heritage Project. Held in Ravenna, Italy, October 13–17, 2001*. Università di Bologna & IsIAO 2004. Milan, 261–80.

Vidale M. 2010. *A Oriente di Sumer, Archeologia dei primi stati euroasiatici, 4000–2000 a.C.* Carocci, Rome.

— 2015. 'Searching for Mythological Themes on The "Jiroft" Chlorite Artefacts'. *Iranica Antiqua*, 50, 15–58.

Vidale M., O. Craig, F. Desset, G. Guida, P. Bianchetti, G. Sidoti, M. Mariottini and E. Battistella 2012. 'A Chlorite Container Found on the Surface of Shahdad (Kerman, Iran and its Cosmetic Content'. *Iran* 50, 27–44.

Watkins C. 2005. *How to Kill a Dragon: Aspects of Indo-European Poetics*. Oxford University Press, New York and Oxford.

Weiss H. 2015. 'Megadrought, Collapse and Resilience in Late 3rd Millennium BC Mesopotamia'. In H. Meller, H. W. Arz, R. Jung and R. Risch (eds), *2200 BC: Ein Klimasturz als Ursache für den Zerfall der Alten Welt? – 2200 BC: A Climatic Breakdown as the Cause for the Collapse of the Old World?* Landesamt für Denkmalpflege und Archäologie Sachsen-Anhalt, Landesmuseum für Vorgeschichte, Halle (Saale), 35–52.

Winkelmann S. 1993. 'Elam-Beluchistan-Baktrien: Wo Liegen die Vorläuder der Hockerplastiken der Induskultur? Erste Gedanken'. *Iranica Antiqua* 28, 57–96.

— 1994. 'Intercultural Relations between Iran, Central Asia and Northwestern India in the Light of the Squatting Stone Sculptures from Mohenjo-Daro'. In A. Parola and P. Koskikallio (eds), *South Asian Archaeology 1993*, Suomalainen Tiedeakatemia, Helsinki, 815–831.

— 2003. 'Berliner Schlangenbecken, Trichterbecher und Cincinnati-Mann: verkannte Schlüssel-Objekte der altorientalischen Archäologie'. In R. Dittmann, R. C. Eder and B. Jacobs (eds), *Altertumswissenschaften im Dialog. Festschrift für Wolfram Nagel zur Vollendung seines 80. Lebensjahres*. Alter Orient und Altes Testament (AOAT 306, Münster, 567–678.

— 2005. 'Deciphering the Intercultural Style?' In U. Franke-Vogt and H.-J. Weisshaar (eds), *South Asian Archaeology 2003*. Linden Soft Verlag eK, Bonn, 185–197.

— 2013. 'Transformation of Near Eastern Animal Motifs in Murghabo-Bactrian Bronze Age Art'. In A. Peruzzetto, F. Dorna Metzger and L. Dirven (eds), *Animals, Gods and Men from East to West: Papers on Archaeology and History in Honour of Roberta Venco Ricciardi*. BAR International Series 2516, 47–64.

— 2014. '"Trading Religions" from Bronze Age Iran to Bactria'. In P. Wick and V. Rabens (eds), *Religions and Trade: Religious Formation, Transformation and Cross-Cultural Exchange Between East and West*. Brill, Leiden and Boston, 199–232.

Witzel M. 1989. 'Tracing the Vedic Dialects'. In C. Caillat (ed.), *Dialects dans les litteratures indo-aryennes*. Institut de Civilisation Indienne, Paris, 97–264.

— 1999. 'Substrate Languages in Old Indo-Aryan (Rgvedic, Middle and Late Vedic'. *Electronic Journal of Vedic Studies (EJVS)*, 5–1,1–67.

— 2001. 'Autochthonous Aryans? The Evidence from Old Indian and Iranian Texts'. *Electronic Journal of Vedic Studies (EJVS)*, 7–3, 1–115.

— 2004. 'The Rgvedic Religious System and its Central Asian and Hindukush Antecedents'. In A. Griffiths and J. E. M. Houben (eds), *The Vedas: Texts, Language and Ritual. Proceedings of the Third International Vedic Workshop, Leiden 2002*. Egbert Forsten, Groningen, 581–636.

— 2005. 'Vala and Iwato: The Myth of the Hidden Sun in India, Japan and Beyond'. *Electronic Journal of Vedic Studies (EJVS)*, 12–1, 1–69.

— 2006. 'Early Loan Words in Western Central Asia: Indicators of Substrate Populations, Migrations, and Trade Relations'. In W. H. Mair (ed.), *Contact and Exchange in the Ancient World*. University of Hawai'i Press, Honolulu, 158–190.

— 2008, 'Slaying the Dragon across Eurasia'. In J. D. Bengston (ed.), *In Hot Pursuit of Language in Prehistory*. John Benjamins Publishing Company, Amsterdam and Philadelphia, 263–286.

Woolley C. L. 1934. *Ur Excavations, II: The Royal Cemetery*. Trustees of the British Museum & Museum of the University of Pennsylvania, London.

Image credits

Figure 89. Private collection. Photo V. Ricciardi

Figure 90. Private collection. Photo V. Ricciardi

Figure 91. Private collection. Photo V. Ricciardi

Figure 92. Private collection. Photo V. Ricciardi

Figure 93. Private collection. Photo V. Ricciardi

Figure 94. Private collection. Photo V. Ricciardi

Figure 95. Private collection. Photo V. Ricciardi

Figure 96. Private collection. Photo V. Ricciardi

Figure 97. Private collection. Photo V. Ricciardi

Figure 98. Private collection. Photo V. Ricciardi

Figure 99. Private collection. Photo V. Ricciardi

Figure 100. Private collection. Photo V. Ricciardi

Figure 101. Private collection. Photo V. Ricciardi

Figure 102. Private collection. Photo V. Ricciardi

Figure 103. Private collection. Photo V. Ricciardi

Figure 104. Private collection. Photo V. Ricciardi

Figure 105. Private collection. Photo V. Ricciardi

Figure 106. Private collection. Photo V. Ricciardi

Figure 107. M. Vidale

Figure 108. Private collection. Photo V. Ricciardi

Figure 109. Private collection. Photo V. Ricciardi

Figure 110. Private collection. Photo V. Ricciardi

Figure 111. Private collection. Photo V. Ricciardi

Figure 112. Louvre Abu Dhabi, LAD.2011.024

Figure 113. Louvre Abu Dhabi, LAD.2011.024

Figure 114. Private collection. Photo V. Ricciardi

Figure 115. Private collection. Photo V. Ricciardi

Figure 116. Private collection. Photo V. Ricciardi

Figure 117. Private collection. Photo V. Ricciardi

Figure 118. Private collection. Photo V. Ricciardi

Figure 119. Private collection. Photo V. Ricciardi

Figure 120. Private collection. Photo V. Ricciardi

Figure 121. Private collection. Photo V. Ricciardi

Figure 122. Private collection. Photo V. Ricciardi

Figure 123. Private collection. Photo V. Ricciardi

Figure 124. Private collection. Photo V. Ricciardi

Figure 125. Private collection. Photo V. Ricciardi

Figure 126. Private collection. Photo V. Ricciardi

Figure 127. Private collection. Photo V. Ricciardi

Figure 128. Private collection. Photo V. Ricciardi

Figure 129. Private collection. Photo V. Ricciardi

Figure 130. Private collection. Photo V. Ricciardi

Figure 131. Private collection. Photo V. Ricciardi

Figure 132. Private collection. Photo V. Ricciardi

Figure 133. Private collection. Photo V. Ricciardi

Figure 134. Private collection. Photo V. Ricciardi

Figure 135. Private collection. Photo V. Ricciardi

Figure 136. Private collection. Photo V. Ricciardi

Figure 137. Private collection. Photo V. Ricciardi

Figure 138 Private collection. Photo V. Ricciardi

Figure 139. Private collection. Photo V. Ricciardi

Figure 140. Private collection. Photo V. Ricciardi

Figure 141. Private collection. Photo V. Ricciardi

Figure 142. Private collection. Photo V. Ricciardi

Figure 143. Private collection. Photo V. Ricciardi

Figure 144. Private collection. Photo V. Ricciardi

Figure 145. Private collection. Photo V. Ricciardi

Figure 146. Private collection. Photo V. Ricciardi

Figure 147. Louvre, Département des Antiquités Orientales, AO21104

Figure 148. Metropolitan Museum of Arts, New York, 2010.166

Figure 149. Aron Collection, London. Photo V. Ricciardi

Figure 150. Aron Collection, London. Photo V. Ricciardi

Figure 151. Aron Collection, London. Photo V. Ricciardi

Figure 152. Aron Collection, London. Photo V. Ricciardi

Figure 153. Aron Collection, London. Photo V. Ricciardi

Figure 154. Aron Collection, London. Photo V. Ricciardi

Figure 155. Aron Collection, London. Photo V. Ricciardi

Figure 156. Aron Collection, London. Photo V. Ricciardi

Figure 157. Aron Collection, London. Photo V. Ricciardi

Figure 158. Aron Collection, London. Photo V. Ricciardi

Figure 159. Private collection. Photo V. Ricciardi

Figure 160. Private collection. Photo V. Ricciardi

Figure 161. Private collection. Photo V. Ricciardi

Figure 162. Private collection. Photo V. Ricciardi

Figure 163. Private collection. Photo V. Ricciardi

Figure 164. Private collection. Photo V. Ricciardi

Figure 165. Private collection. Photo V. Ricciardi

Figure 166. Private collection. Photo V. Ricciardi

Figure 167. Private collection. Photo V. Ricciardi

Figure 168. Private collection. Photo V. Ricciardi

Figure 169. Private collection. Photo V. Ricciardi

Figure 170. Private collection. Photo V. Ricciardi

Figure 171. al-Sabah Collection, Dar al-Athar al-Islamiyyah, Kuwait.

Figure 172. Photo courtesy of N. Dubova

Figure 173. Archaeological collection of the monastery of San Lazzaro degli Armeni, Venice; by kind permission of Daniele Morandi

Figure 174. from Sarianidi 2008b

Acknowledgements

My earnest hope is that this volume will adequately express that sense of wonder, and that state of continuous enthusiastic learning, which took possession of me while I was studying and documenting the European collections of Bactria-Margianan artefacts and discoveries. Having conduted excavations for several years in the ruinously pillaged graveyard of Mathoutabad (near Jiroft, Kerman, in Iran), which we can now date to the second half of the 3rd millennium BC, I now have a much better idea of the damage that the lootings did – not only there, but also in countless other ancient sites throughout the region. I hope that the extent and quality of the new information, or at least of those new ideas, which this book contains will compensate at least in small part for the multiple ambiguities that regrettably are so intrinsic to, and unavoidable in, the study of artefacts that so often have ended up in private collections. Vital scholarly analysis of the objects themselves of course remains at a very preliminary stage; and so I look forward with enthusiasm to the prospect of further studying – even for many years to come – the technology, materiality and meanings of the new finds which, even if they may sometimes be of ambiguous provenance, are yet so fascinating and so important and which are discussed in this book.

There are many people whom I wish to thank most warmly for their assistance:

Francesca Ghedini (Department of Cultural Heritage, University of Padua), who gave me this unique research opportunity;

Armando Tagliacozzo, the owner of the Aron Collection, London, whose passionate interest in the arts of ancient Bactria and Margiana made this study possible;

Valerio Ricciardi, who, besides being creator of the splendid photographs of the book, was a terrific companion in arms. He not only assisted me with geological identification of the artworks' base materials, but also continuously suggested to me important new insights in relation to a great many objects;

Sandro Salvatori, for forty years of continuous, invaluable teaching and of critical and crucial support for my research; and also for sharing not only his field experience in Turkmenistan but also his precious library;

Nadezhda Dubova, who generously made available an important archive of pictures recording Viktor Sarianidi's excavations at Gonur;

Gianluca Bonora, for furnishing me with his fine pictures on the Kopet Dagh (Turkmen-Khorasan mountain range), correcting the cultural- sequential chronology of Bronze Age Central Asia, and discussing with me at length, and on various occasions, many intriguing archaeological questions;

Gian Pietro Basello, who encouraged me by emphasising the historical importance of the silver goblet depicting a prisoner in shackles (Fig. 55).

Alex Wright, **Daniele Morandi Bonaccossi**, **Andreas Steiner** and **Lucia Mori**, who all seemingly found interesting, and worth discussing, my new ideas about the possible meanings and implications of the *balafrés* as 'dragon slayers'…;

…and last, but certainly not least, the editors of the book, whose dedication and skill has enormously improved my original efforts.

Index

copper/bronze holder 35, *35*, 58
    pots for 39, *39*
craft technologies 58
    metallurgy 9, 18, 22, 58
cremation 80, 204n141
cuneiform 18
cup, silver 11–17, *11–16*
cypress trees 144

D

Darius 3, 4
Dashli 1 ix
Dashli 3 ix, 20
defences *see* fortifications
deserts 3, 95
diet 95
Djarkutan 20
Djeitun culture 9, 9t
dogs
    and burials 26, 42, 76
    hunting with 28
    silver figurines 26, *26*
dragons 58, 80, 81–2, *81*, 191, 196
dress *see* kilts; robe-mantles of Bactrian princesses
Dubova, N. 8
Dumézil, George 199–200
Dupree, L. 17
dwarfs 41

E

eagles, copper or bronze axe with eagle-like
    protome 26, 27–8, *27–8*, 58
Early Food-Producing Era 9, 9t
Ebla 162, 163
Elam 28, 41, 44, 99
    and Linear Elamite 90–1, 100, 164
    see also 'Guennol Lioness'
elites
    burials 6, 9–10, 18
    lifestyles 24–39
'enemy in shackles' motifs 74
execution 71, 73, 74, 80
    see also ritual, killing
eyes
    and the *balafrés* ('scarred men') 199–200
    see also individual *balafrés* ('scarred men')

F

falcon, statuette *xiii*
Faza (Iran) 168, 190
feasting 24, 73, 76
'fire temples' 64
flagons, limestone cubic 39, *39*
'Flames' style 111, 117, 120, 141, 147, 162,
    164, 165
flasks, gold 41, *41*
flower, gold *xiv*
forgeries *xiv*

G

games/gaming 23, 34
Gautama 4
gazelles 31
Ghirshman, Roman 194
goblets, pedestalled silver *xi*, 16, 44, 56, 66–74,
    66–7, 69–72
gods/goddesses *see* religion
Gonur 8
    burials 40, *40*, 42, *42*, 58, 65
    North *viii*, x, 20, *21*, 22, *22*, 58, 65
    South 20, 22, 25, 51, 53, *94*
government 84
'Graffito' style 131, 162, 164–5
griffins 51
    lozenge-shaped in green steatite seal 86, *86*
    rectangular steatite with animal figures
        seal 87, *87*
Griffith, R. T. H. 199
Guennol Lioness 190, 191

H

hammers 28
    copper with birds' heads 30, *30*
headdresses 156, *156*, 157, *157*, 158, *158*, 159, *159*,
    160, *160*, 163, *163*
heads of 'Bactrian princesses'
    with elongated face 151, *151*
    found in Gonur *x*
    fragmentary in yellowish-white calcite 154,
        154
    Neo-Sumerian (?) style 152, *152*
    white saccharoid limestone 155, *155*
    yellowish-white calcite 153, *153*
'hommes aux serpents' 197, 198
horses 32
    and burials 32
    domestication of 91
hunting 25, 26, 27–8, 31

I

ibexes
    copper figurine 79, *79*
    on flat cauldron 30–2, *30–2*
    mace-head with 76, 77–8, *77–8*
Ilgynly Depe 9t, 10, 44
immigrants 6, 18, 95
Indra 195, 196, 197, 199, 200
industry 22
inlay, furniture 197, *197*
Integration Era 8, 9t, 18, 20, 90, 91, 95

J

Jaxartes (Sir Darya) (river) 3
jewellery/jewels 32
    beads 9, 10, 26, 33–4, *33–4*, *34*, 51, 56
    and burials 42
    silver pin 76

K

kaunakes 23
    on the silver goblet 69, *69*, 73
    on silver pin 76
    see also 'Bactrian princesses'
Kelleli 20
khanates 84
kilts 23, 99
    on stamp seal 81, *81*
    see also '*balafrés*' ('scarred men')
Kohl, Philip ix, 95
Kopet Dagh *2–3*, 4, 5
Kosh Tepe 17

L

Lamberg-Karlovsky, C. C. 64
language 91–2
languettes style 103, 104, *104*, 127, 162, 163
lapis lazuli
    pot 39, *39*
    trade in 17
Late Bronze Age *see* Localization Era
Late Regionalisation Era 9t
Lawergren, Bo 25
leaves *see* vegetal elements
leopards 5, 27
    faience/steatite head *xii*
Linear Elamite 90–1, 100, 164
lioness-demon statuettes 190, 191, *192–3*, 194
lips, and the *balafrés* ('scarred men') 194, 196,
    200
'Localization Era' 8, 9t, 84
'Lozenges' style 99, 106, 107, 119, 123, 127, 131,
    132, 135, 136–7, 138, 144, 146, 148, 149, 150,
    61, 162, 164, 165, 204n238
Luneau, Élise 100

M

mace-heads, lead with ibexes in the round 77–8,
    77–8
Mahabharata 197
Margiana *xiv*, 4, 5, 6, 8, 9t, 20, 58, 64, 84
    and the 'Bactrian Princesses' 190, 191
    collapse 95

and serpent imagery 197, *199*
social structure 91
and trade 90
see also Gonur
Marhaši 18, 44, 72
markhors (*Capra falconeri*) 5
Masson, Vadim M. ix
Mazzoni, S. 162
mèches see 'Lozenges' style
Mesolithic 8
Mesopotamia 18
metallurgy 9, 18, 22, 58
Middle Bronze Age *see* Integration Era
Morandi Bonacossi, Daniele 197, 198
Murghab river 8, 18
see also Margiana
'muting' 194
mythology *see* religion

N

Namazga Depe 8, 10, 18
Narbenmänner see balafrés ('scarred men')
necklaces 33, *33*, 58
see also beads
Neolithic 8, 9, 9t 90
Neo-Sumerian (?) style head 152, *152*
nomadic peoples 3, 18, 20, 32, 62, 64, 84

O

O'Flaherty, Wendy Doniger 197
onyx 52
'ophidian man-monster hybrid' theory 191
Osborne, James 190
'Oxus Civilization' (term) 8
Oxus river 3–5

P

palaces
Dashli 3 20
Djarkutan 20
Gonur North 20, *22*
Parrot, André 180, 190
Perry, E. D. 199
Persepolis 4
Persepolis vessel 100, 164, 206n250
Pittman, Holly 99, 195
PIXE analysis 169
plundering of cemeteries xiii–xiv, 95–6, 98
Porada, Edith 190, 191
pottery/pots 10, 18, 44
chlorite 36–7, *36*
lapis lazuli 39, *39*
ovoid limestone 62, *62*
see also *balafrés*
Pottier, M.-H. xiv, 8, 37, 40, 97

Potts, Daniel 28, 95, 99, 100, 164
'Priestess burial' 42
'Priest-King' 56
pyxis, silver 24, *24*, 101

R

Regionalisation Era 8, 9t, 10
religion 64, 80, 82, 100
and the *balafrés* ('scarred men') 190–1, 196–9
Renou, L. 196
Rgveda 74, 91, 196, 197, 199, 200
ritual 10, 34
and the 'Bactrian princesses' 62
burial 32, 40–2, *40–2*, 51, 64, 76
dress *see kaunakes*
gift giving 32
killing 42, 71, 73, 74, 76
processions 72
robe-mantles of Bactrian princesses
'Flames' style 111, 117, 120, 141, 147, 162, 164, 165
'Graffito' style 131, 162, 164–5
'Languettes' style 103, 104, *104*, 127, 162, 163
'Lozenges' style 99, 106, 107, 119, 123, 127, 131, 132, 135, 136–7, 138, 144, 146, 148, 149, 150, 161, 162, 164, 165, 204n238
and vegetal elements 101, 108, *108*, 143–4, *143–4*, 145–6, *145*, 162, 165
'Wavy tufts' style 162, 164, 165

S

Salvatori, Sandro x, 20, 51, 84
Sapalli 20, 22
Sarianidi, Viktor ix–x, 8, 24, 41, 42, 56, 80, 90, 101, 197
scales, reptilian *see* skin, reptilian
scarf/shawl/stole 104, *104*, *126*, 127, *128*
'scarred men' *see balafrés* ('scarred men')
scars
on *balafrés* ('scarred men') statuettes 190–1, 194, 196, 197, 198, 207n314
see also *individual* balafrés *('scarred men')*
statuettes
sceptres *see* staves/sceptres
Scythians 3
seals/sealings 51, 53, 84, 90, 164, 207n313
and *balafrés* 195
copper stamp seal *90*
dwarfs depicted on 41
Gulf-type 51
lozenge-shaped in green steatite 86, *86*
lozenge-shaped with toothed sides 85, *85*
rectangular steatite with animal figures 87, *87*
round in green steatite with winged monster 88, *88*
round steatite with animal carvings 89, *89*
stamp in copper and lead 81–2, *81*
stamp seal with serpents swallowing human figure 198, *199*
serpents *see* snakes
Shah Tepe 6
shoes 23

balafrés statuettes 190, 196
Shulgi, King 30
Šimaški 18, 28, 95
Simpson, St John xiii, 5
Sir Darya *see* Jaxartes
Sir Darya river *see* Jaxartes
skin
reptilian 80, 190, 191, 196, 197, 200
see also *individual* balafrés ('scarred men')
snakes 197, *197*, 198, *198*
see also skin, reptilian
social organization 9, 10, 74, 84, 90–1
and women 100
Sogdiana 3, 5
Soviet Union xiii, 3, 8, 64
and Afghanistan 8
Spycket, Agnès 191, 195
stamp seals *see* seals/sealings
statuettes 41
bovine onyx 52–3, *52–3*
bovine in steatite 54–5, 55
composite of falcon of gold and faience *xiii*
limestone arms 22
personage on a stool 64, 65, *65*
'Priest-King' 56
see also 'Bactrian princesses'; *balafrés* ('scarred men')
staves/sceptres 74, 76
dark grey mica schist 75, *75*
Steinkeller, Piotr 18, 71, 72
stretched bodies, 'Bactrian princess' with
see Type 1b 'Bactrian princesses'
Sumner, W. M. 142
symbolism
axes 28
and Gonur 20
hammers 30
and 'miniature columns' 6, 47, *48–50*, 51

T

Tedjen river 8
Tepe Chalow 6
Tepe Hissar 6, 20
trumpets 25
tiaras 106, *126*, 127, 156, *156*, 157, *157*, 162, 163, *163*
tin, trade 56
Togolok 20, 42
tokens, clay 90
Tosi, M. 17
trade 5, 6, 10, 17, 35, 44, 51, 56, 84
trumpets 25
small silver 25, *25*
Tukrish 18
Tureng Tepe 6
Turkmenistan ix, xiii, 3

V

vases
    banded calcite or travertine 59, *59*
    cylindrical silver 23, *23*
    gold Fullol hoard 17
    sub-cylindrical in banded calcite or
      travertine 60, *60-1*
vegetal elements
    'Bactrian princesses' 101, 162, 165
    seals/sealings 86, 88, 89
Vrtra 196, 197, 199

W

wagons 10
    in burials 42, *42*, 74, 76
war beakers *xi*, 16, 44, 56, 66–74, *66-7*, *69-72*
Wardak, R. 17
water
    and irrigation 4–5, 8, 9
    in mythology 196, 199
    and ritual washing 10, 20
    theme on 'Bactrian princesses' 115, 166
Watkins, Calvert 196, 199
'Wavy tufts' style 162, 164, 165
WD-XRF analysis, silver goblet 74
weights 44, 58
    chloritic breccia 46, *46*
    travertine 45, *45*
Weiss, Harvey 94
Winkelmann, S. 196
Witzel, Michael 191, 196
women, and social organization 34–5, 100
writing 90-1
    cuneiform 18
    Linear Elamite 91, 100, 164

Z

Zoroastrianism ix, 64

Aral Sea

Urgench

Kyzylkum
Desert

UZBEKISTAN

Karakum
Desert

Bukhara

TURKMENISTAN

Turkmenabat

Amu Darya

Kelleli

Gonur Tepe

Adji Kui

Togolok 21

Ashgabat

MARGIANA

Merv

Namazga Depe

Geoksyur

Murghab

Ulug Depe

Tedjen

Altyn Depe

Ilgynly Depe

Tedjen

Monjukli Depe

Nishapur

KHORASAN

ARCHAEOLOGICAL SITES
OF THE OXUS

Archaeological sites — Rivers

Cities and towns

Scale (km)

N

0   50   100   150   200

Herat

Tedjen